Power for Mission

The Africa Assemblies of God Mobilizing the Reach the Nations

Papers from the First
World Missions Congress
Organized by the
World Missions Commission
of the
Africa Assemblies of God Alliance
Held in Conjunction with the
Quadrennial AAGA General Assembly
February 24–March 2, 2013

Brackenhurst Conference Center
Limuru, Kenya

Denzil R. Miller
Editor
Enson Mbilikile Lwesya
Associate Editor

Power for Mission: The Africa Assemblies of God Mobilizing to Reach the Nations. © 2014 AIA Publications/Acts in Africa Initiative. All rights reserved. No part of this book may be reproduced, stored in a retrieval system, or transmitted in any form or by any means— electronic, mechanical, photocopy, recording, or otherwise—without prior written permission of the copyright owner, except brief quotations used in connection with reviews in magazines or newspapers.

Individual copyright notices:

"Power for Mission" © 2014 Denzil R. Miller
"Comparing Apples with Mangoes" © 2014 Enson Mbilikile Lwesya
"Three Pillars for Successful Missions" © 2014 Arto Hämäläinen
"The Nigeria Experience—Part 1" © 2014 Anthony E. Ogba
"The Nigeria Experience—Part 2" © 2014 Paul M. Oganya
"Missionary Care" © 2014 Milward Mwamvani
"Missions Possible" © 2014 Brad Walz
"Resource Mobilization for Africa's Mission" © 2014 Tony Pedrozo
"Apostolic Ambition: By Way of Reminder" © 2014 John L. Easter

Library of Congress Cataloging-in-Publication Data
Miller, Denzil R., editor, 1946—
Lwesya, Enson Mbilikile, associate editor, 1967—

Power for Mission: The Africa Assemblies of God Mobilizing to Reach the Nations. / Denzil R. Miller, Editor and Enson Mbilikile Lwesya, Associate Editor

1. Missions   2. Pentecostal   3. Africa   4. Holy Spirit

ISBN 978-0-9882487-3-1

Printed in the United States of America
© 2014 - AIA Publications, Springfield, MO, USA

Contents

Foreword by *Mitre Djakouti* 5

Acronyms Used in This Book 7

Introduction by *Enson Mbilikile Lwesya* 9

1. Power for Mission: Africa's Decade of Pentecost and
   the New Testament "Strategy of the Spirit"
   Denzil R. Miller 11

2. Comparing Apples with Mangoes: Towards Evaluating
   the AAGA Missions Enterprise
   Enson Mbilikile Lwesya 37

3. Four Pillars for Successful Missions
   Arto Hämäläinen 101

4. The Nigeria Experience—Part 1: The Challenges and
   Joys of Developing a Missions Agency
   Anthony E. Ogba 113

5. The Nigeria Experience—Part 2: The Challenges and
   Joys of Missions Participation
   Paul M. Oganya 123

6. Missionary Care: The African Church's Challenge in
   Its Missions Enterprise
   Milward Mwamvani 141

7. Missions Possible: The Argentine Experience and the
   Africa Missions Movement
   Brad Walz 165

8. Resource Mobilization for Africa's Mission: Lessons
   Learned from Argentina
   Tony Pedrozo 189

9. Apostolic Ambition: By Way of Reminder: Missiological
   Reflections from Romans 15:14-29
   John L. Easter 203

Appendices

    Appendix 1: Africa Assemblies of God Decade of
   Pentecost (2010-2020) Continental Goals 221

    Appendix 2: National Church Decade of Pentecost
   Goals Summary (2010-2020) 223

    Appendix 3: Declaration of Commitment to the
   Worldwide "Decade of Harvest" Through Africa
   Harvest 2000 227

    Appendix 4: Declaration of Commitment – "Decade of
   Harvest" "Harvest Africa – 2000" February 22-26, 1988 –
   Harare, Zimbabwe 229

Contributors 231

Other Decade of Pentecost Publications 233

Foreword

Africa's Church is rising to accept the challenge of missions. In the past centuries, Africa was called a "receiving church" in terms of missionary enterprise. However during the last two decades the situation has changed. Many national Assemblies of God (AG) churches in Africa have started sending their own missionaries to other nations in Africa and beyond. Even though Africa still needs missionaries from the West, the church in Africa is becoming a "sending church."

The General Assembly of the Africa Assemblies of God Alliance (AAGA) held in Nairobi in March 2009 adopted a resolution to launch the "Decade of Pentecost" during 2010-2020. Two objectives of this initiative were to "deploy hundreds of Spirit-filled African missionaries" and to "reach the more than 900 ethnic groups in Africa, and beyond, who have not yet heard the Good News." Africa is definitely rising to meet the missionary challenge!

In spite of multiple socio-economic and political crises, including under-development, poverty, famine, and socio-political conflicts, the church in Africa has unlimited potential for missions. In 2010, the Christian population in Sub-Saharan Africa was estimated at 516,470,000, representing 62.7% of the population and 23.6% of world Christians.[1] In terms of laborers for the missions harvest, this Christian population is certainly a strength. Socially and culturally, African missionaries to African nations can easily adapt to the realities of the receiving cultures. When the Gospel is preached by Africans to Africans, it makes a greater impact since it can no longer be considered a "white man's religion." Theologically, well-trained African missionaries are better able to contextualize the Gospel in different African social and cultural contexts. The church in Africa must rise to accept the missionary challenge.

This book contains the papers presented at the AAGA conference held in Nairobi on February 26-28, 2013. During this conference presenters shared strategies for accomplishing missions. I sincerely appreciate the presenters and participants at this conference, as well as the

Foreword

partnership of the Assemblies of God World Missions (USA).

As president of AAGA I appeal to all AG national and local church leaders to incorporate cross-cultural missions in their visions, programs and activities. It is our hope that every church and every believer in Africa be committed and engaged in missions so that all Africa and all "ethne" (nations) be saved. For this reason, I sincerely recommend this book to every pastor and to every believer. In these pages men with a great hearts for missions in Africa and beyond call us to a new commitment to missions. May our missionary God raise up a great army to take the Gospel back to North Africa and to the rest of the world!

"And this gospel of the kingdom will be preached in the whole world as a testimony to all nations, and then the end will come." (Matt. 24:14)

Rev. Mitre Djakouti
President
Africa Assemblies of God Alliance

---

[1]"Global Christianity: A Report on the Size and Distribution of the World's Christian Population," pewforum.org, http://www.pewforum.org/Christian/ Global-Christianity-exec.aspx (accessed April 19, 2013).

Acronyms Used in This Book

AAGA	Argentina Assemblies of God
AAGA	Africa Assemblies of God Alliance
AFE	Africa Financial Empowerment
AG	Assemblies of God
AGC	Assemblies of God Cameroon
AGWM	Assemblies of God World Missions (U.S.)
AH	Africa's Hope
AIA	Acts in Africa Initiative
AICs-1	Africa Independent Church
AICs-2	African Initiated Church
AICs-3	African Indigenous Church
ATTS	Africa Theological Training Services
CAAGA	Central Africa Assemblies of God Alliance
DOH	Decade of Harvest (1990-2000)
DOP	Decade of Pentecost (2010-2020)
EAAGA	East Africa Assemblies of God Alliance
EHI	Eleventh Hour Institute
MCP	Missions Covenant Price
NMD	Argentina Assemblies of God National Missions Department
RMB	East Africa Regional Missions Board
SAAGA	Southern Africa Assemblies of God Alliance
TTW	Two-thirds World Missionary
UPG	Unreached People Group
WAAGA	West Africa Assemblies of God Alliance
WAAST	West Africa Advanced School of Theology
WMC	Africa Assemblies of God Alliance World Missions Commission

Introduction

Does God have a plan for the nations? I believe that He does, and that the African Church has a key role in fulfilling that plan. God has gracious-ly invited the Church of Africa to join Him in His mission to redeem the nations through Christ. This sentiment is held by Assemblies of God leaders and pastors across the continent.

Today, as never before, the 50 national churches making up the Africa Assemblies of God Alliance (AAGA) are mobilizing to reach the unreached people and places of Africa and the world with the gospel before the soon coming of Christ. The AAGA World Missions Commission (AAGA-WMC) exists to serve the Church in carrying out this mission. The agency was created and mandated by AAGA "to facilitate and encourage the missionary enterprises of our national churches across Africa by every means possible" (WMC Constitution). In light of this high calling, the WMC planned and conducted the first ever World Missions Congress held in Limuru, Kenya, at the Brackenhurst Conference Center on February 24 through March 2, 2013. The congress was held in con-junction with the quadrennial AAGA General Assembly conducted just prior to the gathering. AG leaders gathered from across Africa to prepare themselves to more effectively carry out their missionary mandate.

I want to express my sincere thanks to outgoing AAGA Chairman, Dr. Lazarus Chakwera of Malawi, and to incoming Chairman, Rev. Djikouti Mitre of Togo, for their selfless support for both this congress and the ongoing work of the AAGA-WMC. Special thanks also goes out to the scholars who presented and participants who gathered from throughout Africa and beyond for the congress. This book is a compila-tion of the papers presented at this congress. It was prepared to encourage and help to facilitate Africa's mission to the nations. It is our hope that the book will be widely read and used by Africa scholars and practitioners across the continent.

In Chapter 1, "Power for Mission," Denzil R. Miller reviews the missionary history of the Africa AG since 1990. He then calls for a new surge of Spirit-empowered missions across the continent, recommending a "New Testament Strategy of the Spirit." In Chapter 2, "Comparing Apples with Mangoes," I suggest the possibility that the missions outreach of the African church has been unduly hampered by uncritically following western missions models. I call on the African church to investigate new more scriptural and culturally relevant models for doing missions. In Chapter 3, Arto Hämäläinen discusses "Four Pillars for Successful Mission." He recommends that the African church build its missions work on the four firm foundations of recruiting, training, sending, and partner-ing. In Chapter 4, "The Nigeria Experience—Part 1," Anthony Ogba shares his insights on developing and sustaining an effective national missions agency. Then, in Chapter 5, "The Nigeria Experience—Part 2," Paul M. Oganya shares his perspective on the "Challenges and Joys of Missions Participation." He addresses some of the unique challenges of being an African missionary. In Chapter 6, "Missionary Care," Milward Mwamvani challenges the African church in the areas of missionary care, support, and training. In Chapter 7, "Missions Possible: The Argentine Experience," Brad Walz offers practical advice on how the African church can mobilize for missions. In Chapter 8,"Resource Mobilization for Africa's Mission," Argentine missionary Tony Pedrozo addresses the critical issues of recruiting qualified candidates and financing a national missions program. And finally in Chapter 9, "Apostolic Ambition," John L. Easter, calls on the church in Africa to discover and implement Paul's apostolic strategy of missions revealed in Romans 15:14-29

I commend this work to you with the hope that it will aid you in mobilizing the church in Africa to reach the nations in the power of the Holy Spirit.

Enson Mbilikile Lwesya, D.Min.
Chairman
AAGA World Missions Commission

Power for Mission: Africa's Decade of Pentecost and the New Testament "Strategy of the Spirit"

DENZIL R. MILLER

The Africa Assemblies of God is poised for what could be the greatest evangelistic and missionary advance in the movement's more than 100 year history, since, in the early months of 1907, the first Pentecostal missionaries from the Azusa Street Mission set foot on the shores of West Africa.[1] Across the continent Assemblies of God (AG) churches are committing themselves to more perfectly heed the commission of Jesus to "make disciples of all the *ethnē*" (Matt. 28:19).[2] Realizing that Jesus' coming is near, and sensing the unrelenting compulsion of the Spirit, they are rising up to evangelize the unreached peoples, people, and places of Africa and the nations in the power of the Holy Spirit.[3]

THE AFRICA ASSEMBLIES OF GOD DECADE OF PENTECOST (2010-2020)

In preparation for this unprecedented missionary advance, the Africa Assemblies of God Alliance (AAGA),[4] has launched a continent-wide initiative from 2010-2020 called the "Decade of Pentecost"[5] (DOP). The initiative's defining goal is to see 10-million new believers baptized in the Holy Spirit and strategically mobilized as Spirit-empowered witnesses, church planters, and cross-cultural missionaries. This goal is at the heart a broader strategy of multiplying Spirit-empowered missionary churches throughout Africa and beyond.

On Pentecost Day this year (May 19, 2013) the Decade of Pentecost emphasis will complete its third year.[6] During these three years, AG churches have taken bold steps to implement the initiative across the continent. Thus far, in twenty-one Acts 1:8 Conferences[7] in all parts of Africa, AAGA-related national churches have committed themselves to, by 2020, plant 40,923 new churches and win 9,123,750 individuals to Christ. Further, they have committed themselves to deploying 1,069 new cross-cultural missionaries and reaching 139 specific unreached people groups in Africa and the Indian Ocean Basin. In order to accomplish this, they have further committed themselves to recruiting and training 25,839 new ministers of the gospel and to seeing from 75-100% of their membership baptized in the Holy Spirit and then mobilized as Spirit-empowered witnesses, church-planters, and cross-cultural missionaries.[8] (Note: For February 2014 update see Appendix 2, p. 233.)

Decade of Harvest Advances

Africa's spiritual leaders view this grand vision of a Decade of Pentecost (DOP) as more than just another church program. They rather envision it as a continuation and natural outworking of the grace God afforded the movement during the previous two decades, beginning with the launching of the now-historic Decade of Harvest (DOH) in January of 1990.[9] This early initiative was the first continent-wide emphasis of its kind in the Africa AG. It was done in concert with AG national fellowships worldwide. During those ten years leading up to the dawning of the new millennium, the African church redoubled its efforts in evangelism and church planting. This evangelistic effort targeted several up-to-then unreached peoples and places of Africa.

During that same twenty-year period, an enhanced missions awareness was birthed in many national AG churches. African leaders began mobilizing their churches for greater missions endeavor. The oft-heard battle cry in those years was "Missions, Africa can to it too!" It was during that time that the Africa Assemblies of God Alliance (AAGA) came into being,[10] along with its subsidiary agencies, including the AAGA World Missions Commission and Africa AG Care.[11] To help facilitate the burgeoning work in Africa, the Africa Office of the U.S. AG Division of Foreign Missions[12] created the Africa Harvest Projects and Coordination Office[13] and Africa Theological Training Services.[14] Other AGWM ministries came into being during this time, notably Africa Tabernacle Evangelism and Africa's Children.

During the DOH the Africa AG experienced unprecedented growth. As the decade began, about 2.1 million believers worshiped in 11,800 Assemblies of God churches in 31 sub-Saharan countries. At its end the number of constituents had nearly tripled to 6.3 million, and the number of AG churches had more than doubled to 24,019. Additionally, the AG had entered into 8 new countries, bringing the total to 39 countries in which AAGA-related national churches were active.

It was, however, during the decade following the DOH (i.e., the first decade of the twenty-first century) that true exponential growth began to occur in the Africa AG. Building on the momentum of the DOH, the pace of missionary activity and church growth was accelerated so that by 2010 the movement had grown to 15.9 million constituents meeting in 65,000 congregations throughout Africa and the Indian Ocean Basin. An ever expanding missional awareness came into the churches along with a growing commitment to reach the remaining unreached tribes of Africa. In addition, several national churches had instituted national missions departments and had deployed missionaries to various places on the continent and beyond. Others were beginning to institute their own programs. During that same ten year period the number of ministerial training institutions increased dramatically.[15]

A Troubling Trend

And yet, while all of this positive progress was being made, another not-so-encouraging trend was being observed in Africa AG churches. While the original DOH declaration had called for a "continent-wide revival accompanied by a resurgence of Pentecostal power" and for the "full spectrum of the Spirit's work in the Church,"[16] (see Appendix 3) and the American mission, citing Acts 1:8, had earlier committed itself to "fervent prayer, fasting, and Pentecostal preaching ... in pursuit of a Holy Spirit outpouring across Africa as a prelude to the Decade of Harvest,"[17] (see Appendix 4) such a continent-wide outpouring had not materialized.

As the Africa AG was becoming ever larger, it was, at the same time, steadily becoming less Pentecostal, at least statistically. Annual reports revealed that the great majority of AG constituents in Africa had not been baptized in the Holy Spirit, and year-by-year the percentage of those baptized in the Holy Spirit was steadily decreasing. Leaders noted with alarm that the message of the baptism in the Holy Spirit was being neglected in the churches, and as a result, comparatively few were being baptized in the Spirit.[18]

The 1993 annual survey done through the Assemblies of God World Mission (AGWM) U.S. Office revealed that only 20% of AG constituents in Africa were reported to have been baptized in the Holy Spirit. This finding was received with varying degrees of concern in the African church and in the American mission. Seven years later, in 2000, another annual report revealed that the percentage had dropped to 17%. The message was clear: *this unacceptable trend must be addressed and reversed.* If the Africa AG was to maintain its spiritual dynamic and fulfill its missionary destiny, the church needed to seek God for a continent-wide Pentecostal outpouring with millions of its members being baptized in the Spirit and empowered as Christ's witnesses to the lost.

In response, in 2000 the AAGA leadership corporately demonstrated their commitment to Pentecostal revival by issuing a continent-wide call for AG churches across Africa to go "Back to the Upper Room" and seek God for a fresh Pentecostal outpouring. Four years later at their 2004 General Assembly in Accra, Ghana, the Acts in Africa Initiative (AIA) was commissioned by AAGA to aid the Africa AG in addressing this critical need. The ministry was mandated by AAGA to assist their 50 national churches in sub-Sahara Africa and the Indian Ocean Basin to mobilize themselves for Spirit-empowered mission by "calling for a powerful Pentecostal outpouring in our churches."[19] According to the AAGA mandate this was to be done, in part, through national and international Holy Spirit Conferences on the continent.

In my talks with several African AG church leaders in all parts of

Africa, I have listened as they passionately spoke of their desire for a such a powerful outpouring of the Spirit on their churches. This thirst for authentic Pentecostal revival is mirrored in the zeal of AG believers to personally experience God's power. Wherever the message of Pentecost is presented and the people are given an opportunity to receive the Holy Sprit, they respond with great enthusiasm. Most are immediately filled with the Spirit evidenced by speaking in tongues and greater zeal to reach the lost with the gospel.

Recent Africa statistical reports reveal that the downward trend in Spirit baptisms may have been reversed.[20] For the first time in two decades the report indicates that there has been an increase in the percentage of AG constituents who are baptized in the Holy Spirit. This report indicates that 19% of AG adherents have been baptized in the Spirit. This increase, we believe, is the result of the strong emphasis on Spirit baptism during the first year of the Decade of Pentecost.

LOOKING BACK: LESSONS LEARNED FROM THE "DECADE OF HARVEST"

As the Decade of Pentecost enters into its fourth year, it may serve the movement well to take a thoughtful look back to the Decade of Harvest of the 1990's, and to learn from the movement's successes and failures in carrying out that initiative. To my knowledge, to date no such published analysis has been done. As has been pointed out, the DOH served as an effective launching pad for a dramatic increase in evangelistic and missionary momentum in the Africa AG. The initiative helped to propel the movement forward, accelerating its missional effectiveness for not just one, but two decades of significant and sustained growth. Below is my attempt at such an analysis. I will seek to answer the question, "What lessons can we learn, both positive and negative, from the Decade of Harvest that will serve us in advancing the Decade of Pentecost?"

Positive Lessons

What then made Africa's DOH of the 1990's such an extraordinary success? I suggest that, among other things, the following five elements contributed to the success of the DOH. They represent five elements that should be emulated during the Decade of Pentecost:

1. Unified Vision Combined with Individual Initiative

The guiding ethos of the DOH was a unified continental vision calling for "every national church to manifest renewed and enlarged missionary vision to send forth laborers claiming the nations for Jesus Christ."[21] This united vision focused on heightened evangelism, aggressive church planting, and increased missionally-focused pastoral training. Significantly, the vision was fully embraced by national churches and partnering missionaries and missions agencies alike.

It is further significant that the unified continental vision of the DOH was coupled to individual initiative. As each national church ran with the vision, they developed their own ways and means for carrying it out. The shared vision produced a continental sense of common mission; the individual initiative facilitated individual buy in, encouraged an entrepreneurial spirit, and served to effectively implement the mission in each nation. The combining of these two elements—united vision and individual initiative—produced a powerful missional synergy resulting in the outstanding results that are now a part of AG Africa's history.

In like manner, if the DOP is to enjoy maximum impact, each of the 50 AAGA-related churches, along with all of the their AGWM partners, must fully embrace the initiative and zealously implement its goals and values into their individual ministry contexts.

2. Synergistic Partnerships

During the DOH powerful synergistic partnerships were formed. As individual entities moved to accomplish common goals, it became natural for them to join hands. Partnerships were formed between national churches, partnering missions and missionaries, Bible schools, para-church agencies, and numerous other entities. These creative partnerships helped to launch new and creative evangelistic, missionary, and training initiatives and served to revive old ones. They became a force in advancing the collective vision of the DOH.

Similar synergistic partnerships will be key to effectively advancing the current DOP initiative. As national churches and missionaries strive together with one heart and one mind to accomplish the common vision of evangelizing all of Africa and the nations in the power of the Holy Spirit, a powerful missional synergy will occur resulting in the greatest missionary and evangelistic advance in the history of the African church: "Five of you shall chase a hundred, and a hundred of you shall chase ten thousand, and your enemies shall fall before you by the sword" (Lev. 26:8).

Significantly, the present DOP offers even greater opportunities for forming synergistic partnerships than did the earlier DOH. New, more universally accessible communications technologies, including the Worldwide Web, e-mail, social media, texting, video conferencing, and other emerging means provide greater opportunity for creative cross pollination and the sharing of ideas and resources that were unavailable during the DOH. If the Africa AG is going to rise to its full potential during the DOP, and the unreached of Africa are to be reached, such synergistic partnerships must be exploited to the maximum. Every AG minister, missionary, and leader will be required to lift up their eyes and look at what God is doing in and through the AG Africa DOP initiative, and then to work together in creative synergetic partnerships in reaching the lost of Africa and beyond in the power of the Spirit. Together we can reap the greatest harvest in the history of the church in Africa, and possibly in the world.

3. Persistent Focus on Evangelism and Church Planting

Another strength of the DOH was its sustained and unwavering focus on reaching the lost through aggressive church planting. While other emphases were initiated, they were almost always connected with church planting. Whether it be Bible school training, lay discipleship training, campus ministries, mass media outreach, youth ministries, children's ministries, humanitarian response, or any other initiative, all was carried out in the context of, and often with the specific goal of, planting vibrant new churches. And everyone knew it.

This unwavering focus on reaching the lost through aggressive church planting continued through the DOH into the first decade of the twenty-first century and resulted in powerful missional momentum and great forward advance. During the two decades from 1990 to 2010 the Africa AG added 13.8 million new adherents and planted 43,000 new churches and outstations, some among formerly unreached peoples. That progress is charted, along with the projected growth of the AG during the DOP, in Figures 1 on the following page.

4. Training for *the Harvest*

The DOH was further characterized by a strong focus on expanded and more effective leadership training. The Africa Theological Training Services (ATTS), led by the late Dr. John V. York, was created to address the need. It was surmised that, if during the DOH the Africa AG were going to plant thousands of new churches, then they must be about training thousands of new pastors and church planters. During the DOH new Bible schools were established and old ones were revamped. Significantly, the decadal focus was not so much on "training to *conserve* the harvest," as some have re-envisioned it, as it was on "training *for* the harvest,"[22] that is, training to advance the harvest. Dr. York's heart-cry was twofold: Our training must be intentionally missional, and it must be thoroughly Pentecostal.

During the DOP our ministerial training institutions must be mandated to critically revisit their mission statements and reevaluate their reasons for being to ensure that they, too, are training *for* the harvest and that their school's guiding ethos is thoroughly Pentecostal and intentionally missional. They must beware of the ever-so-subtle but debilitating shift from training *for* the harvest to training *to conserve* the harvest. Further, faculty, student body, and the national church must together "own" the vision and goals of the school and firmly commit themselves to ensuring that they are implemented.

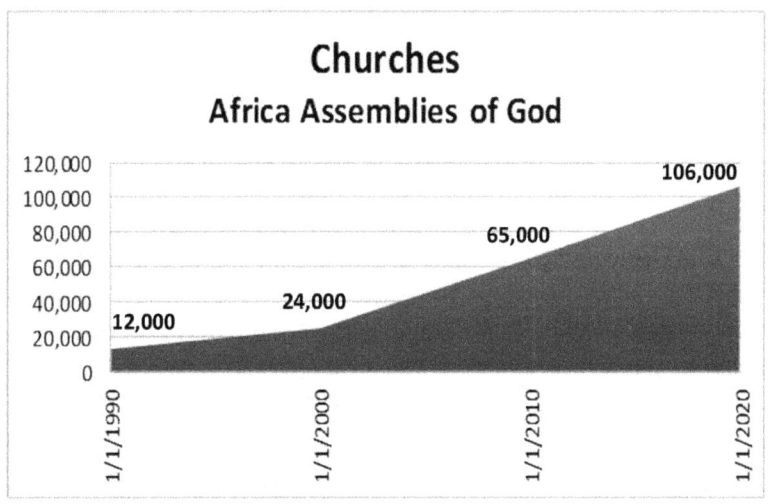

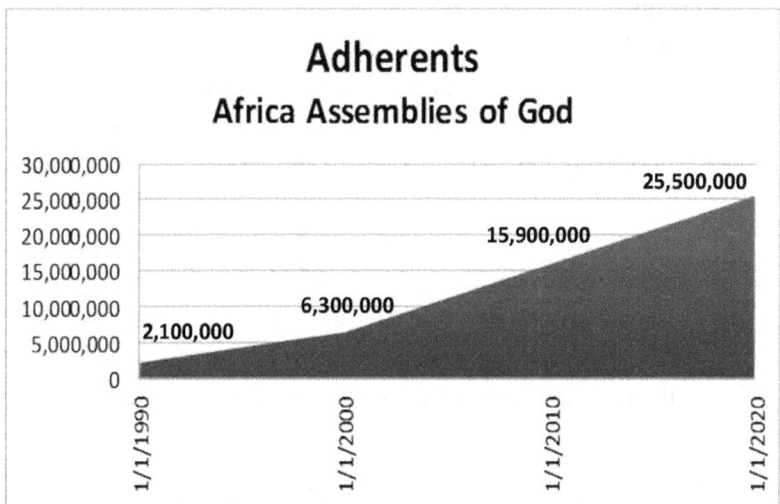

Figure 1: Growth of the Africa Assemblies of God

5. A Spirit-driven Call to Missions

During the DOH and the first decade of the twenty-first century, AG leaders and churches heard and responded to the persistent call of the Spirit to fully engage in cross-cultural missions. This response was nurtured through the Eleventh Hour Institutes (EHI) developed by Dr.

Lazarus Chakwera and Dr. John York and promoted by the Africa Theological Training Services. One stated purpose of the EHI was to serve the African church in mobilizing for greater and more effective missions involvement. These short-term institutes were held in various places across Africa and helped inspire missions consciousness and vision.

During this same period regional coalitions were formed to advance missions,[23] and national missions committees were formulated (or reformulated) to advance intra-country and international missions. In addition, many local churches became increasingly involved in planting churches cross-culturally and in neighboring countries.

During this present DOP the Africa AG can be expected to capitalize on the missional momentum of the previous two decades and to accelerate their missionary advance. This intention is reflected in the "Official Communiqué" developed at the recent AAGA World Missions Commission's first Pentecostal Missions Consultation held in Limuru, Kenya, on February 28-29, 2011. There the gathered delegates from AG churches across Africa cited five pressing areas of need in the Africa AG as they collectively mobilize for strategic missions:

1. The need to strategically focus on *the evangelization of Africa* as rapidly as possible, with a twofold focus on the unreached Islamic peoples of North Africa and the greater Arab World and

    the remaining unreached peoples of sub-Sahara Africa and the Indian Ocean Basin
2. The need to create an ongoing *information database* on these above-mentioned unreached peoples to be shared with our constituent national churches
3. The need to develop *strategic partnerships* across the continent between the national churches affiliated with the Africa Assemblies of God Alliance
4. The need to develop a *strategic prayer network* focusing on the unreached peoples of Africa
5. The need for *missional mentoring* among our national churches as a means of strengthening and building capacity within all of

the national churches of the Africa Assemblies of God
6. The need to develop a truly biblical and missional model for *compassion ministries,* all the while remaining focused on the core mandate of the church, that is, reaching the lost for Christ.[24]

As we address these critical needs, we must, as did the early church, constantly look to the Spirit for power and direction (Acts 15:28).

Two Shortfalls

While such reflection as the above (i.e., focusing on the strengths that helped make the DOH a success) may offer useful insights into how the Africa AG may more effectively move forward during the current DOP, it is also beneficial to examine certain shortfalls that may have mitigated the overall effectiveness of the DOH. In my opinion, two of those shortfalls were (1) the failure on the part of many to consistently emphasize authentic Pentecostal experience and practice and (2) widespread financial impotence in the churches often resulting in aborted mission. If during the present DOP the movement is to fully realize its potential as a effective missions force in Africa and beyond, these shortfalls must be identified and addressed.

1. Failure to Emphasize Authentic Pentecostal Experience and Practice

While the original DOH declaration pointed to the critical need for an Holy Spirit outpouring in preparation for missional advance, both empirical and anecdotal evidence reveal that there was a failure on many fronts to follow through on these early Pentecostal impulses.[25] Admittedly, the need was often emphasized in publications and on a national and corporate level. However, in most cases, it was not sufficiently implemented on the grassroots level. During the DOH many churches were planted, but, in far too many cases, these churches were neither intentionally "Pentecosalized" nor aggressively "missionized."

Further, a strategy for planting Spirit-empowered missional churches was not generally taught in the movement's ministerial training institutions. Unfortunately, in some cases, because an authentic, missional Pentecostalism was not clearly understood nor emphasized, a spurious form of Pentecostalism was instituted in many churches, that is, a quasi-Pentecostalism that inordinately focuses on personal material blessing rather than on fulfilling God's mission in the power of the Spirit. Unfortunately, in my observation, this critical emphasis on authentic Pentecostal experience and practice continues to be neglected by many AG pastors, church leaders, and missionaries.

It was this neglect that necessitated AAGA's calling for a Decade of Pentecost in 2009. What is now required is universal "buy in" on the part of pastors, churches, and partnering missionaries and missions organizations. In the words of the 1988 AGWM Decade of Harvest declaration, we must "consecrate ourselves to fervent prayer, fasting and Pentecostal preaching ... in pursuit of a Holy Spirit outpouring across Africa," fully believing that this emphasis "will inevitably produce the power we need to evangelize (Acts 1:8)."[26]

2. Financial Impotence

A second shortfall mitigating the missional impact of the DOH was the endemic financial impotence of many churches. This financial impotence occurred on both national and local levels. While many churches zealously embraced the goals and vision of the DOH, the lack of financial viability often thwarted effective mobilization. As a result, national church offices went unfunded, local churches struggled in implementing their outreach strategies, and newly-created missions agencies were stymied. In such cases, the all-to-often tendency was to look to external sources for needed funding rather than applying biblical principles of giving and wealth creation. As a result, local, more viable and sustainable means of funding were not generated.

As the Africa AG mobilizes for the DOP, this need must be aggressively addressed and systematically remedied. More biblical, Spirit-driven funding models must be taught in our schools and implemented on all levels. The focus on Western-oriented funding must be balanced by a scriptural, God-focussed, faith-filled African model of funding.

The simple fact is that Africa AG has grown beyond the ability of outsiders to fund its mission. If the task of reaching all of Africa and the yet-to-be-reached peoples of Africa and the world is to continue and thrive, our faith and focus must be squarely on the God of all heaven and earth who stands ready to "supply [our] every need ... according to his riches in glory in Christ Jesus" (Phil. 4:19). Biblical principles of giving must be widely taught and practised. Such principles include a clear understanding of God's mission along with trust in, and application of, the biblical principles of faith-filled sacrificial giving. The newly-formed Africa Financial Empowerment ministry led by AGWM missionary, Ken Krucker, has emerged to serve AG national churches in creating such a model.[27]

A WAY FORWARD: A NEW TESTAMENT "STRATEGY OF THE SPIRIT"

As we mobilize for dramatic decadal evangelistic and missionary advance, we must do so with a keen awareness that we are engaged in a great spiritual conflict "for we do not wrestle against flesh and blood, but against the rulers, against the authorities, against the cosmic powers over this present darkness, against the spiritual forces of evil in the heavenly places" (Eph. 6:12).

We must, therefore, never forget that ours is not a carnal but a spiritual battle and can only be fought and won with spiritual weapons (2 Cor. 10:3-4).

During this DOP, as we boldly advance into the enemy's long-held, previously-unreached strongholds, he will inevitably mount a vicious counter offensive. He will seek to derail, distract, and demoralize the church at every turn. Scripture, however, informs us that we are not to be "outwitted by Satan" nor are we to be "ignorant of his designs" (2 Cor. 2:11). The battle for the soul of Africa will be won only as we successfully engage and defeat these entrenched spiritual powers.

In his letter to the Ephesians, Paul thought it necessary to inform them of the spiritual conflict in which they, and all Christians, must engage (Eph. 6:12-20). Undoubtedly, he wrote in vivid remembrance of the spiritual warfare in which he himself had fought while in Ephesus

(Acts 19:11-41).[28] It was also there that he had seen his greatest missionary success (Acts 19:10).[29] That success was achieved, however, only after he had "fought with [spiritual] beasts in Ephesus" (1 Cor. 15:32, cf. Acts 19:11, 21-41). In his instruction to the Ephesian believers, Paul alerts them to the necessity of employing the "whole armour of God"—or, as Knox translates this passage, "all of the weapons of God's armoury"[30]—as they engage in this spiritual conflict. In the same passage Paul presses his readers to be "strong *in the Lord* and in the strength of *his* might" (v. 10, emphasis added).

This spiritual warfare will not be won in conferences, classrooms, or medical clinics, as essential as these things may be; it will be won in front line hand-to-hand spiritual conflict. It will be won through Spirit-ignited intercessory prayer (Rom. 8:26) and Spirit-empowered proclamation of the gospel accompanied by supernatural manifestations of kingdom power (Mark 16:15-16; Rom. 1:16). Further, Paul's teaching on spiritual warfare should be understood in the context the broader "strategy of the Spirit"

which he employed during his missionary career, a strategy that we will now discuss.

A careful examination and comparison of the missionary strategies of the Heavenly Father in sending Jesus into the world, of Jesus in sending His church to the nations, and of Paul in mounting his Ephesian campaign reveal certain common essential elements of a New Testament Strategy of the Spirit. This strategy, I believe, can—and should—be used as a template today for our DOP missionary and church planting efforts. Let's now examine these strategies of the Father, Jesus, and Paul:[31]

The Father's Missionary Strategy in Sending Jesus

The Heavenly Father *"mobilized"* the Son by sending Him to earth with a clearly-defined strategy: Jesus would come in the Father's name (Luke 13:35; 19:38; John 5:43), and He would carefully execute the plan the Father had given Him (Heb. 10:7; John 5:19; 12:49-50). Before He began His ministry, however, He would need to be *empowered* by the Spirit. Jesus received this empowering at His baptism when "the Holy Spirit descended on him in bodily form, like a dove" (Luke 3:21-22).

Upon receiving the Spirit Jesus immediately "began His ministry" (v. 23). His entire ministry was thus anointed and enabled by the Holy Spirit (Luke 4:1, 14, 16-19, Acts 10:38). In fulfilling His ministry Jesus bore *witness* to the truth by proclaiming the gospel with "authority and power" (John 1:7; Luke 4:18-19, 36) and by performing miraculous signs through the Spirit's power (Luke 5:17; 6:19). Finally, through the same enablement of the Spirit, He offered Himself up for the sins of mankind (Heb. 9:14).

Early on in His ministry Jesus began the process of passing on His redemptive mission to His disciples. He called them (Luke 6:13-16), trained them (Mark 3:14), and empowered them (Luke 3:15-16; Acts 1:4-8; 2:33) to carry on the ministry that the Father had given to Him (John 20:22; cf. Luke 24:46-49). All along, He taught that they were to do it in the same way that they had seen Him do it (John 14:12; 20:21).

Jesus' Missionary Strategy in Sending the Church

In sending His church to the nations Jesus employed the same missionary strategy the Father had used in sending Him to earth. The three key elements of that strategy, as we have seen, were mobilization, witness, and empowering. The Father *"mobilized"* the Son by sending Him to earth to do His will; Jesus mobilized His disciples by training them and sending them out to preach the good news. Jesus bore *witness* to the kingdom by proclaiming the gospel in the power of the Spirit with signs following (Luke 4:18-19; 9:6); He then commissioned His disciples to do the same (Mark 16:15-18). And, just as He, Himself had been empowered by the Spirit before beginning His missional ministry, He commanded His disciples to "stay in the city until [they were] clothed with power from on high" (Luke 24:49; cf. Acts 1:4-5, 8). The disciples obeyed, and on the Day of Pentecost "they were all filled with the Holy Spirit and began to speak in other tongues as the Spirit gave them utterance" (Acts 2:4). This empowering came to them again and again throughout their ministries (Acts 4:8; 31; 8:17-18; 9:17-18).

Paul's Missionary Strategy in Ephesus

In his ministry Paul employed the same threefold Strategy of the Spirit that the Father had employed in sending Jesus to the earth and Jesus had employed in sending His church to the nations. He was simply "working the plan," that is, he was emulating the missionary strategy that he had observed in Jesus and the Heavenly Father. This missionary strategy of Paul's is indicated in both his own description of his ministry in Romans 15:17-20 and Luke's depiction of his ministry in Acts, especially in the Ephesian Campaign (Acts 19:1-11ff).[32]

Paul Describes His Missionary Strategy (Romans 15:17-20)

Paul wrote his epistle to the Romans in preparation for an upcoming visit to their city (Rom. 1:10). His visit was to be an extended stopover on a missionary journey ranging even further westward into Spain (15:28). He wrote to solicit their support for this anticipated missionary campaign (15:23-24). He hoped to prepare them for his upcoming visit by informing them of his missionary plans and by making them aware of the purpose and nature of his missionary ministry.

In 15:17-20 Paul explains to the Christians in Rome how he went about his missionary task. These verses represent his most comprehensive explanation of his missionary strategy, a strategy that relied heavily on the presence and power of the Holy Spirit. Paul describes his missionary strategy in this way:

> [17] In Christ Jesus, then, I have reason to be proud of my work for God. [18] or I will not venture to speak of anything except what Christ has accomplished through me to bring the Gentiles to obedience—by word and deed, [19] by the power of signs and wonders, by the power of the Spirit of God—so that from Jerusalem and all the way around to Illyricum I have fulfilled the ministry of the gospel of Christ; [20] and thus I make it my ambition to preach the gospel, not where Christ has already been named, lest I build on someone else's foundation, [21] but as it is written, "Those who have never been told of him will see, and those who have never heard will understand." (Rom. 15:17-21)

In this passage the apostle reveals three key elements of his missionary strategy:

1. Mobilization: Focus on the yet-to-be-reached

Paul clearly understood his calling and mission; God had called him to be "a minister of Christ Jesus to the Gentiles" (v. 16). He had been sent to preach the gospel "where Christ was not known" (v. 20, NIV) and his eyes were steadfastly fixed on "the lands beyond" (2 Cor. 10:16). It was because of this high calling that Paul had now set his sights on Spain. With these things in mind, he wrote the to Romans to explain to them how he had gone about fulfilling his missionary calling, and by implication, how he intended to do it in the future.

2. Witness: Proclamation + demonstration

At the center of Paul's strategy to reach the Gentiles was *Spirit-empowered witness:* He was committed to boldly proclaim the message of Jesus Christ, the message he believed to be the only means of salvation (1 Tim. 2:5; cf. John 14:6; Acts 4:12). He tells the Romans that "from Jerusalem and around about as far as Illyricum I have fully preached the gospel of Christ" (v.19, NASB). The book of Romans is itself an extended explanation of that message.

When Paul said that he had "fully preached the gospel of Christ," he was not, however, speaking exclusively of content. Nor was he claiming that he had proclaimed the gospel in every locality, or to every person. He was saying that he had included every necessary element and action required for the gospel to be presented in its powerful totality. When Paul says that he *fully* preached the gospel, he is making specific reference to how he had done it "by word and deed" (v. 18). And since Paul clearly defines "deed" as "the power of signs and wonders" he is saying that the gospel has not been fully preached until its truth has been clearly proclaimed and its power has been convincingly demonstrated.

3. Empowering: Reliance on the power of the Spirit

In this passage Paul declares his total reliance on the Spirit of God to enable him in ministry. His ministry had been in "word and deed, by the power of signs and wonders," and he did it all "by the power of the Spirit of God" (v. 19). Throughout his ministry, the Holy Spirit, whom he received when Ananias laid hands on him many years previously (Acts 9:17-18), remained the source of Paul's spiritual power. This fact dramatically influenced the way Paul carried out his apostolic ministry (1 Cor. 2:1-5; 2 Cor. 12:12; 1 Thess. 1:5).

In summary, Paul explained to the Romans that his missionary ministry was Christ-centered, Spirit-empowered, charismatic in nature, and focussed on those who had never heard the message of the gospel. His aim was to "fully preach the gospel of Christ," which for Paul involved both saying and doing, and doing included a demonstration of the power of the gospel through signs and miracles performed through the power of the Spirit.

Luke Depicts Paul's Missionary Strategy (Acts 19:1-11)

In Acts 19 Luke portrays Paul's missionary strategy in much the same way that Paul described it in Romans 15. The emphasis is on *empowering, witness,* and *mobilization.* These three strategic pillars of a New Testament Strategy of the Spirit are charted in Figure 2 below. Let's look briefly at each one as it is presented by Luke in Paul's Ephesian Campaign:

Pillar One: Empowering

Paul arrived in Ephesus with a definite strategy in mind, a strategy that would ultimately produce his greatest missionary success.[33] As we have noted, it was the same strategy employed by the Heavenly Father in sending Jesus to the world and by Jesus in sending His church to the nations. So, just as Jesus began His ministry full of the Spirit, Paul began his Ephesian ministry full of the Holy Spirit. This fact is evident from the nature of his ministry there: he preached with boldness (cf. Acts 4:8 cf. 13, 29-31), prayed with others to receive the Spirit (19:6), and worked "extraordinary miracles" (v. 11). Throughout the book of Acts, Luke consistently portrays Paul and a Spirit-empowered, charismatic apostle (i.e., Acts 9:17-19; 13:4, 9; 16:6-7).

Paul, however, was not only concerned with himself being full of the Spirit, he was concerned with the church being full of the Spirit. To fully participate in the mission of reaching all of Asia with the gospel, the Ephesian church would also need to be empowered by the Spirit. Therefore, upon arriving in Ephesus, he immediately addressed the issue of the spiritual empowerment and vitality of the church. Before he would attempt to mobilize them to reach Ephesus and Asia Minor with the

---

Figure 2
The New Testament "Strategy of the Spirit"

Pillar 1: Empowering	➡ of the missionary
	➡ of the church
Pillar 2: Witness	➡ proclamation
	➡ demonstration
Pillar 3: Mobilization	➡ training
	➡ sending

---

gospel, they, too, would need to be empowered by the Holy Spirit. He, therefore, inquires of them, "Did you receive the Holy Spirit when you believed?" (v. 2). Or, in other words, "Are you spiritually prepared to participate in the upcoming mission?" This same concern likely persisted throughout Paul's entire time in Ephesus. He must have continued to labor to see that those who were constantly being brought into the community of faith were also being empowered by the Spirit. It is also likely that Paul instilled in his disciples this same passion to see their converts filled with the Spirit (cf. Acts 20:20).

Thus, two essential aspects of the first pillar of Paul's missionary Strategy of the Spirit (that is, *empowering*) are revealed: (1) the empowering of the cross-cultural missionary, and (2) the equally important empowering of workers in the church being planted (Fig. 2). This two-fold empowering thus laid the spiritual foundation for the church in Ephesus to become a center of mission activity to reach out to the remainder of the province.

The same is true today. As we advance to fulfill our Decade of Pentecost goals of reaching millions of people for Christ, planting thousands of new churches, and reaching hundreds of yet-to-be-reach peoples and places, we must prioritize two things: the spiritual empowering of the missionaries and church planters we deploy, and the spiritual empowering of the churches we plant. Every church we plant must become a new center of Spirit-empowered missions activity. It must have within itself the spiritual dynamic and clear missionary vision necessary for it to impact its surrounding area and beyond with the gospel.[34]

Pillar Two: Witness

Again following the pattern established by Jesus and the Father, the second pillar of Paul's missionary strategy in Ephesus was *witness*. Paul thus bore witness to the gospel in two ways: through powerful proclamation of the gospel of the kingdom of God and through equally powerful demonstrations of the Spirit's power. This proclamation began when Paul "entered the synagogue and for three months spoke boldly, reasoning and persuading them about the kingdom of God" (Acts 19:8; cf. 8:12; 20:25; 28:23, 31; Matt. 24:14).[35] And Paul's oral witness in Ephesus was accompanied by powerful demonstrations of kingdom power (vv. 11-20). These signs of the kingdom included divine healings and demonic deliverances. Thus, the second pillar of Paul's strategy of the Spirit, like the first, had two components: powerful proclamation of the gospel and a demonstration of its power through accompanying signs. No doubt the witness of Paul's newly Spirit-empowered colleagues included the same two elements.

As we execute our Decade of Pentecost strategies we, like Paul, must be ever vigilant that we clearly and convincingly proclaim the true gospel of Christ.[36] We must beware of distractions and diversions from preaching this God-ordained message, including most notably, the false "prosperity gospel" that has captivated many of our churches, and has diverted many from aggressively reaching out to the unreached with the message of Christ. As we boldly proclaim Christ to the lost, we must pray for and expect God to extend His hand to confirm the message with supernatural signs and wonders wrought by the power of the Holy Spirit (cf. Acts 4:30-33).

Pillar Three: Mobilization

Following the lead of the Father and Jesus, the third pillar of Paul's missionary strategy of the Spirit was *mobilization.* Once the church had been empowered by the Spirit, and as the gospel was being clearly and convincingly preached, Paul began mobilizing the Ephesian church for regional missions. Paul's mobilization of the Ephesian church is indicated in verse 10: "This continued for two years, so that all the residents of Asia heard the word of the Lord,[37] both Jews and Greeks."[38] Without leaving Ephesus, Paul reached the entire province of Asia with the gospel in just two short years. This could only have been accomplished by effectively mobilizing the believers in Ephesus. Paul did this in two ways: First, he trained workers and church planters in the rented school of Tyrannus (v. 9). Note the implicit cause-and-effect relationship between Paul's leadership training and the fact that in the space of only two years everyone living in Asia heard the word of the Lord.[39] Further, the school's curriculum must have included a strong practical emphasis on church planting and evangelism, and the atmosphere of the school must have been saturated with the presence of the Spirit.[40]

Then, once the believers had been trained—or more likely, while they were yet being trained—Paul sent them into every corner of the province to preach the gospel and plant Spirit-empowered missional churches. Doubtlessly, they employed the same missionary strategy as their mentor. The application of this strategy resulted in a spontaneous multiplication of churches throughout the entire region so that in just two years "all the residents of Asia heard the word of the Lord" (v. 10). Paul's strategy clearly included reaching people from all ethnic and cultural backgrounds, for Luke says the gospel was presented to "both Jews and Greeks."

In light of these powerful truths, every church leader, Bible school teacher, and local pastor in Africa must, like Paul and Jesus before them, envision themselves as a mobilizers of the church. They must, as the Spirit leads, acquire the vision and skills needed to train and send their people into the harvest field declaring the message of Christ in the power of the Holy Spirit—and planting His church among every people and in every place until Jesus comes again.

CONCLUSION

On Pentecost Sunday this year the Africa Assemblies of God will enter the fourth year of its Decade of Pentecost emphasis. During the first three years of the initiative the churches have made significant progress in setting and implementing their DOP goals. Already thousands have been reached for Christ, hundreds of churches have been planted, and formerly unreached tribes have been engaged. Others national AG churches are just beginning to mobilize, yet mobilizing they are. With ever-increasing force, the wind of the Spirit is blowing across the continent.

As we move boldly forward in the DOP, we would do well to learn from our experiences of the Decade of Harvest. We must move together with unified vision and purpose; we must cultivate and facilitate synergistic partnerships; we must remain ever focussed on evangelism and church planting; we must train *for* the harvest; we must heed the call of the Spirit moving us to reach the unreached peoples of Africa; we must find biblical, Spirit-driven, Africa-centric means of funding the mission;

and we must persistently emphasize authentic Pentecostal experience and practice in all of our churches.

Above all, as we advance the DOP, we must firmly grasp and effectively apply a biblical, Spirit-driven strategy of mission. Such a New Testament Strategy of the Spirit can serve as an effective framework for African church's mobilizing for effective mission. Therefore, during these final seven years of the DOP initiative, we anticipate the greatest forward advance, and the greatest harvest of souls, in the one-hundred year history of the church of Africa. Let us, therefore, unreservedly commit ourselves to this God-given vision of the Decade of Pentecost.

ENDNOTES

1. Specifically, these early missionaries from the Azusa Street Mission, Los Angeles, California, went to Monrovia, Liberia, and Benguela, Angola. Cf. *The Apostolic Faith,* Vol. I, No. 6, Mar 1907.
2. All scripture references, unless otherwise indicated, are from the English Standard Version (ESV), Wheaton, IL: Crossway Publishers, 2002.
3. A close examination of the five recordings of Jesus' Great Commission reveals three target audiences: (1) "every creature" (Mark 16:5, NKJV), that is, every person; (2) "all nations" (Matt. 28:19; cf. Luke 24:47), that is, every *ethne,* or people group; and (3) to "the end of the earth" (Acts 1:8), that is, every place.
4. AAGA is a multinational coalition of 50 African national churches and the Assemblies of God missionaries working in partnership with them.
5. The Decade of Pentecost website can be accessed at www.DecadeofPentecost.org.
6. Day of Pentecost 2013 will take place on May 19.
7. Acts 1:8 Conferences are missions mobilization conferences conducted by the Acts in Africa Initiative in cooperation with AAGA-related national churches. The Acts in Africa initiative website can be accessed at www.ActsinAfrica.org.
8. "Africa Assemblies of God Decade of Pentecost Goals Summary," as of February, 2014. See Appendix 1. Note: Twenty-seven of the 50 AAGA-related national churches in Africa have not as yet communicated their Decade of Pentecost goals to the Acts in Africa office.

9. In Africa the "Decade of Harvest" was known as "Africa Harvest 2000."
10. AAGA was established in 1990.
11. Both agencies were established by AAGA in 2000.
12. Now called Assemblies of God World Missions or AGWM.
13. Now called Africa Harvest Ministries or AHM.
14. Also known as Africa's Hope or AH.
15. According to Africa's Hope, the Africa AG is presently training 14,000 ministerial students in 251 Bible and extension schools across sub-Sahara Africa and the Indian Ocean Basin.
16. "Declaration of Commitment to the Worldwide 'Decade of Harvest' through Africa Harvest 2000," January 13, 1989, All Africa Leadership Conference of the Assemblies of God, Lilongwe, Malawi. (See Appendix 3.)
17. "Declaration of Commitment—'Decade of Harvest' 'Harvest Africa-2000,'" Feb. 22-26, 1988, Harare, Zimbabwe. (See Appendix 4.)
18. In my ministry travels in thirty-one African countries in all parts of Africa, I have observed the need firsthand.
19. "Africa Assemblies of God Alliance-AAGA, Minutes of the 2004 General Assembly," October 6-10, 2004, Accra, Ghana.
20. Assemblies of God World Mission Office of Statistics, (Reports for 1989-2012).
21. "Declaration of Commitment to the Worldwide 'Decade of Harvest' through Africa Harvest 2000," January 13, 1989, All Africa Leadership Conference of the Assemblies of God, Lilongwe, Malawi.
22. "Training for the harvest" was the original ATTS mission statement.
23. Those coalitions included the East Africa Assemblies of God Alliance (EAAGA) Missions, the Central Africa Assemblies of God Alliance (CAAGA) Missions, the Southern Africa Assemblies of God Alliance (SAAGA) Missions, and the West Africa Assemblies of God Alliance (WAAGA) Missions.
24. Denzil R. Miller and Enson Lwesya, eds., *Globalizing Pentecostal Missions in Africa: The Emerging Missionary Movement in the Africa Assemblies of God* (Springfield, MO: AIA Publications, 2011), 8.
25. Empirical evidence includes statistical data gleaned from "Annual World Statistics" reports completed by national church leaders and submitted to the Assemblies of God World Missions Research Office for compilation and reporting. Anecdotal evidence includes the authors personal experience in training leaders and ministering in Holy Spirit conferences in more than 30 sub-Saharan conferences. During these conferences he has been able to preach in many AG churches and talk with AG leaders on all levels from local to national.
26. "Declaration of Commitment—'Decade of Harvest' 'Harvest Africa-2000,'" Feb. 22-26, 1988, Harare Zimbabwe.

27. The Africa Financial Empowerment (AFE) website can be accessed at www.AfricaFinancialEmpowerment.org.
28. This theme of spiritual warfare in Ephesus is developed further by C. Peter Wagner in chapter 21 of his book, *The Acts of the Holy Spirit: A Modern Commentary on the Book of Acts* (Ventura, CA: Regal Books, 2000), 466-489.
29. Robert P. Menzies calls Paul's work in Ephesus "the chief achievement of [his] missionary carrier" (*Empowered for Witness: The Spirit in Luke-Acts*. Sheffield, Eng: Sheffield, Academic Press, 2005, 220). Robert C. Tannehill calls it "the climax of Paul's missionary work" (*The Narrative Unity of Luke-Acts: A Literary Interpretation*, vol. 2, "The Acts of the Apostles," Philadelphia, PA: Fortress Press, 1994, 236.) Tannehill continues, "Ephesus is not just another stop in a series. It is Paul's last major place of new mission work; indeed, it is the sole center of mission noted in the last stage of Paul's work" and is "meant as a lasting model for the church after Paul's departure" (236).
30. Eph. 6:12, *The New Testament in the Translation of Monsignor Ronald Knox* (Sheed and Ward, 1944).
31. Some of this material is adapted from the author's book, *Empowered for Global Mission: A Missionary Look at the Book of Acts* (Springfield, MO: Life Publishers Intl., 2001), 235-242; 261-266.
32. Paul also describes his missionary methods in 1 Corinthians 2:1-5 and 1 Thessalonians 1:5-8. In both descriptions he emphasizes the central role of the Spirit's powering in advancing the kingdom of God.
33. See note 31.
34. Early twentieth-century Anglican missiologist, Roland Allen, addressed this issue: "There is no particular virtue in attacking a centre or establishing a church in an important place unless the church established in the important place is a church possessed of sufficient life to be a source of light to the whole country round" (*Missionary Methods: St. Paul's or Ours*, Grand Rapids, MI: William B. Eerdmans Publishing, Co., 1962), 12.
35. Paul's ministry in the Ephesian synagogue is reminiscent of the ministries of Jesus and the apostles in Jerusalem, who daily taught and preached in the temple (Luke 19:47; Acts 5:42). Paul's teaching concerning the kingdom of God also reminds us of Jesus' post-resurrection ministry when for forty days He spoke "about the kingdom of God" (Acts 1:3). Jesus' primary kingdom themes during this time were the global mission of the church (Matt. 28:18-20; Mark 16:15-16; Luke 24:46-48; John 20:21; Acts 1:8) and the need for the empowering of the Spirit to accomplish that mission (Matt. 28:20; Mark 16:17-18; Luke 24:49; John 20:22; Acts 1:8). Paul likely emphasized these kingdom themes in his teaching ministry in Ephesus. While in Ephesus, Paul also taught "publicly and from house to house,

solemnly testifying to both Jews and Greeks of repentance toward God and faith in our Lord Jesus Christ" (Acts 20:20-21).
36. In 1 Corinthians 15 Paul defined the gospel: "Now I make known to you, brethren, the gospel which I preached to you ... that Christ died for our sins according to the Scriptures, and that He was buried, and that He was raised on the third day according to the Scriptures, and that He appeared [to many]" (vv. 1, 3-4). The message of Christ's death and resurrection also formed the heart of the apostolic *kerygma* as recorded in his sermons in Acts (9:20, 22; 13:26-33; 14:15; 17:2-3, 17-18). Today, the message of "Jesus Christ, and Him crucified," must remain the centerpiece of our missionary ministries.
37. That is, the message of the *Lord* Jesus Christ, the gospel.
38. Not only did the gospel permeate all of Asia, as is indicated in verse 10, at the same time the gospel penetrated all of the city of Ephesus, for the message of Christ's power "became known to all the residents of Ephesus, both Jews and Greeks. And fear fell upon them all, and the name of the Lord Jesus was extolled" (v. 17).
39. C. Peter Wagner concurs, writing, "What would the curriculum have been like in such a school? Luke seems to suggest a cause-and-effect relationship between this and the fact that 'all who dwelt in Asia heard the word of the Lord Jesus' (v. 10) before the end of two years. This means that the chief foci of the curriculum were likely to have been evangelism and church planting" (*The Acts of the Holy Spirit: A Modern Commentary on the Book of Acts,* Ventura, CA: Regal Books, 2000), 470.
40. Paul's training procedure also seems to have included on-the-job mentoring. This is hinted at in verses 8 and 9 where Paul included the newly Spirit-baptized disciples in his evangelistic ministry. Luke notes that Paul "took the disciples with him" as he reasoned daily in the hall of Tyrannus. This mentoring relationship is further evidenced by the way he remained in close contact with the disciples in Ephesus (20:17-38). Paul presumably mentored his students in his missionary methods. He later wrote Timothy in the same city of Ephesus instructing him, "What you have heard from me in the presence of many witnesses entrust to faithful men who will be able to teach others also" (2 Tim. 2:2).

Comparing Apples with Mangoes: Towards Evaluating the AAGA Missions Enterprise

ENSON MBILIKILE LWESYA

During the last few years there have been rumblings of frustration—and at times outright criticism—in regards to the Africa Assemblies of God Alliance (AAGA)[1] missionary enterprise. These rumblings have come largely from a new generation of U.S. Assemblies of God World Mission (AGWM)[2] missionaries and from certain Africans on the continent.[3] Some of these individuals regard the inspirational and missional messages espoused by such ministries as the Eleventh Hour Institute (EHI), the Acts in Africa Initiative (AIA), and the AAGA World Missions Commissions (WMC) as mere rhetoric.

Interestingly, some of the fiercest critics of the African missionary enterprise have themselves, during these last two decades, been a part of its developmental process. In spite of this, according to the testimony of these critics, the missionary zeal coming from the African church is misplaced, action is absent, and all is fluff. They have further noted that missionary mobilization and deployment do not appear to be commensurate to the missional "preachings" from within the continent. Such criticism calls for serious evaluation and thoughtful response. This I will attempt to do in this paper.

Basis of the Criticism

The 1990s ushered in a new zest for church planting and missions in the Africa Assemblies of God. The Decade of Harvest (DOH), a continent-wide strategic movement, challenged the AG Africa to plant more churches.[4] By 1997, the formation of the Eleventh Hour Institute (EHI) and the East Africa Regional Missions Board (RMB) became examples of the forward advance of the movement and a culmination of various streams of missionary thought and action across the continent. During this time the number of members and adherents in the Africa AG increased from about 2 million at the beginning of the decade to about 13 million at its close. The incremental realization of the growing African church and its place in the economy of God persuaded many to believe that Africa could be a fully bonafide player in the business of missions.

The EHI and RMB were officially launched, initially deploying missionaries from Malawi, Kenya and Tanzania.[5] West Africa also experienced sparks of cross-border missions zeal and activity. Nigeria sent missionaries to Cameroon and Niger, and Burkina Faso sent missionaries into Ivory Coast and other West African nations. The Africa AG theological education systems, largely responsible for ministerial formation, grew stronger and more visionary. Graduate study centers were launched in five countries to augment the successful undergraduate systems the Assemblies of God had been operating for some time.[6]

The number of adherents increased dramatically during the time. Interestingly, while the DOH officially closed in the year 2000, statistical evidence shows that the Africa AG grew even faster in the decade following (2001-2010). This momentum for growth continued for some time; however, following millennial celebrations of 2000, the evangelistic emphasis of the previous decade began to wane somewhat in many national churches as inspirational energy abated, missionary passion and creativity ran low, and many creative promises were relegated to future hopes.

Unfortunately the DOH emphasis failed to catapult the Africa AG into significant and sustained missions expansion. As a result, some critics view the Africa AG missionary enterprise as mostly tokenism, and, when it comes to actual action, merely rhetoric.[7]

But is the criticism valid? Is there any proof of a missionary enterprise forming, let alone growing, in the Africa AG during the last two decades? I contend that while any constructive criticism is welcomed, most of it is misplaced and misguided, for it unfairly compares and contrasts the Africa AG missions movement with other historical and contemporary missions movements.

These comparisons are, for the most part, ill conceived. They are like comparing apples to mangoes, assuming that both are the same. While the correctness of such criticisms is often highly debatable, they may indicate a need for some form of assessment of the Africa AG missions movement. This will help to ensure that the Africa AG, as a collective missions movement, performs at its best. This paper will attempt to show how the Africa AG missions movement differs from other missions movements, and, in doing so, it will survey some of the challenges the movement faces. It will then attempt to offer suggestions on how to jump start the seemingly stalled missionary enterprise of the Africa AG.

THE MISSIONARY TASK OF THE CHURCH

As we proceed, it behooves us to clearly delineate the missionary task of the church. Confusion in defining the mission of God inevitably leads to confusion in the execution of the same. Failure to biblically frame clear definitions of *missions* and *evangelism* mitigates the effective execution of both. Surprisingly, however, defining missions can be both difficult and contentious.[8] Various church-related mission documents of the last four decades attest to this fact—including the Lausanne Covenant (1974), the World Council of Churches' Nairobi Assembly statement on "Confessing Christ Today" (1975), and the apostolic exhortation Evangelii Nuntiandi, (1975).[9]

As in any form of Christian practice, a level of reflection is essential in developing an adequate definition of missions. Unfortunately, missional reflection, being enshrined in time and space, comes with human limitations. To this end, David J. Bosch states that we should never assume to define missions too sharply or to delineate it too self-confidently. A once-and-for-all definition of missions should, therefore, never be held captive to the narrow confines of our own personal predilections. Ultimately, the most we can hope for is to formulate some approximations of what mission is all about.[10]

One recent missional concept is to differentiate *mission* (singular)—sometimes referred to as the *missio Dei*—from *missions* (plural). Mission, according to this view, refers to God's self revelation to the world as the One who loves and seeks to be involved in the affairs of humankind. It refers to the nature and activity of God which embraces both the church and the world, and in which the church is privileged to participate. Missions, on the other hand, refers to the particular ways and forms through which the church participates in the *missio Dei*. Such activities relate to specific times, places, and human needs.[11]

Other scholars have attempted to separate evangelism, semantically and practically, from missions. Evangelism is thus perceived as part of, yet separate from, missions. It is the proclamation of salvation in Christ to those who do not believe, calling them to repentance and faith. Those who will heed the call are invited to become living members of Christ's earthly body and to begin a life of service to others in the power of the Holy Spirit.[12] Missions, on the other hand, is viewed as the whole church bringing the whole gospel to the whole world.[13] With this thought comes an awareness that the church is not the sender but the one sent. Its being sent (i.e., its mission) is not secondary to its being; rather, the church exists in its being sent and in its building up itself for the sake of its mission.[14] These ideas concerning missions have shaped the perceptions of missions in various church communities of the world.

Biblical Foundations

God created humanity with the capacity to know Him and to represent Him to others. In commissioning man as His co-regent, He gave him rule over the earth (Gen. 1:22), and endowed humankind with the ability to care for the earth on His behalf. Tragically, man fell into sin with all of its tragic consequences. At the same time, however, God, in His great love for humankind, set into motion His redemptive plan (Rev. 13:8). Even today He continues to pursue fallen human beings. He has provided the way for man's salvation through the death and resurrection of His Son,

Jesus Christ. Just as the sin of Adam was imputed to all, the righteousness of Jesus is promised to all who will, through faith, appropriate His provision of eternal salvation. Additionally, Jesus founded and commissioned the church, a community of people from all nations, tribes, languages, and peoples who have committed themselves to advancing His kingdom in the earth. The church's primary responsibility is to function as God's missionary community. The church's work of sharing the good news of the redemptive activity of God, the *missio Dei*, is the centerpiece, or the *mitte*,[15] of all Scripture.[16]

Jesus' word and works support His claims and serve as credentials for His ministry. Luke presents His Jordan experience and resultant Spirit-empowered ministry as programmatic model for the Spirit-empowered ministry recorded in the book of Acts (Luke 3:15-16; 4: 1; Acts 10:38). Not only did Jesus teach with authority, He performed signs and wonders (Luke 4:18-19; Acts 2:22). According to John's prediction, Jesus' work was central in endowing the church with Pentecostal power (Luke 3:15-16; Acts 2:33). Jesus Christ viewed the power of the Holy Spirit as the Church's *sine qua non* in doing and accomplishing its mission (Luke 24:49; Acts 1:8).

Mission dictates the development of a missional community. With clear vision Jesus mobilized a His kingdom community to fulfill His goals in the earth. His original band of disciples would launch a church that would ultimately grow it into a world-wide, divinely-commissioned missionary movement. The African Church, including the AG family, is part of this kingdom community. And, just as the apostolic church relied totally on the power of the Spirit to fulfill its mission of proclaiming the gospel to the UPGs of their day, the African church is called to do the same today.

Apostolic Roots and Future Missions

The Spirit's action in setting Barnabas and Saul apart for apostolic ministry, and His directing the Antiochian church to send them out, can serve as a model for the church today (Acts 13:1-5). Noteworthy is the strong emphasis on planting local churches in the apostolic ministries of Paul and his coworkers. Everywhere these apostolic teams went, they powerfully proclaimed the gospel of Christ and mobilized their converts into growing communities where the word of God was taught and the disciples were matured. Very soon these churches themselves became centers of mission and planted other churches of the same kind (Acts 14:21-28). The New Testament mission's movement as depicted in the ministry of Paul becomes the foundation for all missionary endeavors of the future. Thus, the Acts of the Apostles informs the church concerning what it should do, and how it should do it, until Christ returns.

Inevitably, all theological and missiological reflection is carried out in a cultural context. This is one of the great challenges of doing theology, since contextualized self theologizing is never tidy, and can never satisfy everyone. This missiological untidiness can become a significant stumbling block in doing missions work. For example, a common missiological practice today is to view the emerging missionary movements around the world, including the Africa AG missionary movement, through an American missiological lens. Consequently, the New Testament missionary stories are interpreted using an American missiological grid, which is inevitably a reflection of the context out of which it has risen. So, instead of the African church developing its own robust missiology through a rigorous reflection of the acts of God in its own cultural context, it passively relies on missionary philosophies developed by others. Africa thus goes forth and tries to slay its missional Goliaths using the ill-fitting armor of Saul.

Admittedly, missions from Africa's soil has not advanced as quickly as we all would have desired. This could be due to a number of reasons, including lack of commitment, lack of vision, insufficient passion, or poor management of missions organizations. It could also be a result of sheer fear on the part of some Africans in going to the sometimes hostile UPGs in their midst.[17] This paper, nevertheless, contents that a primary reason missions in Africa has not moved forward as aggressively as it could have is because it has been incarcerated in a Western missiological prison which is ill-suited for the continent. Conversely, if Africa will boldly align its missiology with the theology and praxis of the New Testament church, the movement will begin to experience rapid growth.

Some non-Africa commentators, however, use a similar argument to challenge the African church. These detractors charge that many Africa

AG national churches do not truly believe nor practice "New Testament principles" of missions, and they and do not fully appreciate the power and presence of the Holy Spirit as the superintendent of the missions enterprise. While it is true that the African missionary movement, just like any other missionary movement, needs to believe and trust the Word of God more fully and to rely on the power of the Spirit more perfectly, it is also true that accurately evaluating a missionary movement is not always that easy. This is because cultural and ministry contexts differ. Can we really so offhandedly compare and contrast the African missionary movement with that of the New Testament, or for that matter, with that of the culturally-distant Western missionary movement American AG?

Was Paul a Cross-cultural Missionary?

At the heart of the strong criticism of the Africa AG is the notion that Africa is, by-and-large not practicing authentic missions, that is, it is only practicing inside-country evangelism. Based on the Western understanding of missions, a missionary is one who crosses cultural barriers to bring the gospel to others. These barriers include things such as language, color, ethnicity, and so forth. Therefore, according to this view, missions always involves taking the gospel across such barriers to those who have never heard the message of salvation. Missions can only be defined as going to the unreached, those living beyond the cultural frontiers. This way of viewing missions carries with it an implied element of going to distant lands, places out of easy geographical reach.

As a result of this kind of thinking, there is a tendency to devalue those who cross barriers within their own country, and to view them as something less than real "missionaries." Such workers are customarily referred to as simply "church planters." Consequently, despite the tens of thousands of churches the Africa AG planted in the last twenty years—hundreds of which were planted across distinct cultural boundaries—the African church is still deemed to be involved in simple church planting, and not real missions work. But is this a correct reading of the New Testament? Was the New Testament mission always across cultures? Were Paul and his apostolic teams really missionary in the light of the customary definition of missions as it has been formulated by our

Western brethren?

A thoughtful reading of the New Testament reveals that Paul's personal cultural orientation was, in most cases, very similar to that of most peoples in the places where he did his missionary work. Although, by Paul's time, the Romans had ruled for more than 150 years, they had, by-in-large, adopted the philosophies and world view of the Greeks, who had ruled before them. The Greek—or Hellenistic—culture, including the Greek language and customs, thus pervaded the lives of most people living in Western Europe and Asia Minor during that time. Paul and most members of his apostolic team members were born and reared in this culture. Though born a Jew, Paul was raised in Tarsus of Cilicia, a city dominated by Hellenistic culture.[18]

At the same time, Paul regarded himself a Jew. Bruce states that while nowadays Paul is frequently thought of as Hellenistic Jew, he himself would probably not have accepted that description (cf. 2 Cor. 1:22: Phil. 3:6)[19] He was thus a man of two cultures, Jewish and Greco-Roman, and he could move comfortably in both. One thing is clear, Paul was a practical apostle and was never hesitant to use his double cultural orientation to the advantage of preaching of the gospel. Paul was at least bilingual, and probably trilingual, and was able to function comfortably in either setting without consciously "crossing over" from one culture into the other.[20]

As it turns out, Paul often went to places where he understood the culture, where he spoke the language, where he could earn a decent living, and where he would meet people with whom he was already familiar.[21] All of this prompts us to ask the following thought-provoking questions:

- How many cultural barriers did Paul have to cross when he went as a missionary to these Greco-Roman nations and cities?
- What cultural barriers did Paul's apostolic teams cross, since they already knew the Greek language of Asia Minor and West Europe, and they knew their Hellenistic cultures including its distinctive customs and morals?

So, did Paul really cross significant cultural barriers to establish churches in the Roman Empire? And, if he did not cross cultural and linguistic barriers, was he not a real missionary? The fact is, in most of his missionary outreaches Paul did not cross cultural boundaries as we may know it today. On the contrary, the dominant Greek culture in the Roman Empire presented Paul with a ready medium of cultural identification and communication. He was at home in both the Hebrew and the Greek languages, and the biblical text presents no evidence of any attempt to translate the Scriptures into the provincial dialects of Asia Minor by his apostolic teams during their missionary travels.

Paul preached in Greek, wrote in Greek, and expected all of his literate converts to read the Scriptures in Greek.[22] So, if Paul did not cross cultural barriers, can we really call him a missionary using our Western cross-cultural missiological definitions? Should, then, the crossing-of-cultures motif be the determining factor for deeming one to be a missionary, or should it not be the fact that the person is *sent* by the Lord to preach the word to those with little or no knowledge of Him? Echard J. Schnabel states that in the New Testament the determining characteristic of the apostles and other missionaries was not the need to learn other languages or to cross cultural divides but the call and commission of Jesus to proclaim the good news of God's saving action to all people, Jews and Greeks, no matter where they lived—whether in the same city, in the neighboring region, or in another Roman Province.[23]

The Synagogue Factor

Paul's relentless focus on the Jewish synagogue reveals another important component of his missionary practice. His work in new places almost always began at the synagogue (cf. Acts 13:14-15; 43; 14:1; 17:1, 10, 17; 18:4-6; 19, 26; 19:8; 22:19). Upon entering a new city, Paul went directly to this place of worship where he found kinship of language, faith, and Scripture. Even though he was invariably rejected by the leaders of the synagogues, it was not before he had found receptive people. At first the Jewish leaders felt threatened by his new faith; nevertheless, the majority of those hearing his message did not consider it to be entirely new or alien. By visiting the synagogues Paul began his ministry in new places by introducing himself to those who, in significant ways, already believed as he did. Thus, he deliberately sought out people of similar culture, language, and belief.

The faith-distance between Paul and his hearers was thus shorter than in the contemporary context of penetrating UPGs. A modern pioneer missionary often goes to UPGs whose faith has little or no connection or relationship to that of the recipient community. Talk about crossing barriers! In many ways these contemporary pioneers encounter more formidable religious and cultural barriers than did Paul himself. Nevertheless, the truth remains; whether or not one crosses cultural, religious, or philosophical barriers to preach the gospel, he or she must depend fully on the power and anointing of the Holy Spirit since no one can come to a saving knowledge of Jesus Christ except through the Spirit of God.

Paul and the Metropolises

Roland Allen. in his seminal work, *Missionary Methods: St Paul's or Ours,* convincingly demonstrates that, although Paul viewed his mission work through the eyes of provinces rather than cities, the apostle did not himself personally preach the gospel in every place in each province. Rather, his strategy was to establish centers of Christian life in key locations, and then, from those locations, mobilize the disciples to spread the knowledge of Christ into the surrounding region.[24]

The Spirit thus lead Paul into strategic centers from where he launched the work into the surrounding regions. These churches he planted were not feeble, insipid churches, but powerful missionary churches, from which life spontaneously spread into the regions round about (cf. Acts 19:10). Paul invariably located these churches in provincial capitals which were centers of Hellenic civilization and Jewish influence.[25] These capital cities were located on principal trade routes.[26] Paul thus thought regionally rather than ethnically. He chose cities of representative character, and there he laid the foundations for a vibrant Christian community from which churches could be planted into the surrounding towns and countryside.[27]

Paul's missionary strategy, therefore, included the clear intent that a vibrant, Spirit-empowered local assemblies be established in places where many people come and go, not only to hear the message, but to learn it in such a way that they can propagate it into the regions beyond. Through a thoughtful reading of Acts and the Pauline epistles, one discovers that Paul constantly wrestled with the issue of territorial expansion. With these things in mind, the following questions can help us to apply Paul's missionary methods to our day:

- Will the center we are seeking to establish have the innate ability to multiply itself into the surrounding region?
- Will the communities so established, then be able to go out and establish even more communities?
- What value is there in planting a church that does not have the capacity to plant others?
- Why pour valuable resources into a reservoir that will not multiply itself and give life to others?

Paul's missionary method of targeting key cities has huge implications for today's missionary work. Unfortunately, in overemphasizing cross-cultural missions an unhealthy, and sometimes debilitating, notion emerges. It is the notion which implies that doing missions requires that the real missionary relocate to the rural areas of a country where he or she is required to learn the new culture and language of the people. This, however, was not the method used by Paul and his apostolic teams. They saw the cities as the primary targets for their apostolic ministry. Then, from there the gospel would spread to the entire region, sometimes cross-culturally, sometimes within the same cultural context.

Was Jesus a True Missionary?

By the same token, can we, exclusively using the crossing-of-culture motif, view Jesus a real missionary? Since Jesus ministered within the cultural environment of his birth and upbringing, He crossed no significant cultural barriers. "He came to his own" and He ministered to his own (cf John 1:11). Also, during His entire missionary ministry Jesus spoke only Aramaic, the language of His birth and culture. While some may argue that His home was heaven, and that He came as a missionary to the earth, such reasoning ignores the fact that His birth, identity, and upbringing was that of a Palestinian born Jew. Nevertheless, all would agree that Jesus was the greatest missionary who ever lived. However we describe Him, Jesus was a missionary with a clear apostolic mandate (Heb. 3:1). No wonder He commissioned His disciples, "As the Father has sent Me, I also send you" (John 20:21, NASB).

Jesus considered His mission to be all-consuming. He demonstrated this in His words, His life, and His deeds. He then passed it on to His "mission coalition," the apostles. Jesus came "to seek and to save that which was lost" (Luke 19:10). In his gospel and in the Acts, Luke, like the other New Testament writers, links the narratives of Jesus and the apostolic church to all of redemptive history. To do this Luke often cited Old Testament passages and connected the acts of God done in his day to the acts of God he read about in the Hebrew Scriptures.[28] He thus demonstrates how Jesus saw Himself as the Servant, Prophet, and King sent from Yahweh to bring light into the world (Luke 4:18; John 8:12). He accomplished this through the proclamation of the gospel, and He demonstrated it through multiple of acts of compassion. And all was done through the power of the Holy Spirit (Acts 10:38). Jesus truly is heaven's Missionary to earth! And yet, at the same time, He was from the earth. He was the Son of Man, born of a woman and sent to mankind. And as the Son of Man he became the consummate missionary.

Were the Apostles Missionaries?

Today's apostolic reformation movements challenge both the theological presuppositions and practices of contemporary evangelical missions, forcing the church to rethink its concept of "missionary." The English word "apostle" is a transliteration of the Greek work, *apostolos*, which is itself derived from the word *apostellein*, which means to send.[29] An apostle is thus "one who is sent." This meaning is akin to the English word "ambassador" (2 Cor. 5:20) which signifies a messenger sent by one ruler (or government) to another to act on behalf of, and with the full authority of, the sender. Likewise, in our modern English usage, the word missionary also means one who is sent. In the NIV *apostolos* is sometimes translated "messenger" (2 Cor. 8:23; Phil. 2:25). What, then, would warrant the use of this term in both in the New Testament and in our modern context?

In the New Testament the apostles were learners and itinerant evangelists. Their main duties were preaching, teaching, and administration.[30] It is in these areas of activity the contemporary apostolic reformation finds its definition for an apostle. They thus view an apostle as a father, mentor, and supervisor of other ministers.

Despite the gospel's advance across the cultural borders of Jerusalem, Judea, Samaria, Damascus, and Antioch, and from there into Asia Minor and Western Europe, in the New Testament the apostles were not defined by the fact that they crossed cultural barriers, for they, more often than not, ministered within the confinement of their own cultures. It was, however, the fact that they had been sent by Christ, and that leadership responsibility had been thrust upon them, that defined them as apostles.

In those days, disciples routinely ministered wherever they went. Even while fleeing from persecution in Jerusalem, Philip ministered Christ cross-culturally to Samaritans. Interestingly, Luke refers to Philip—who was likely a Gentile or Hellenized Jew and clearly crossed cultures to preach in Samaria—as an "evangelist" and not as an apostle (Acts 8:4-8; 21:8). Could it be that these definitions are more descriptive of a person's giftedness than of the fact that they were crossing cultural barriers? It seems, therefore, that even the twelve apostles and Paul do not always measure up to our contemporary evangelical definition of a missionary.

The recent trend of describing apostolic nature by employing the concepts of calling and giftedness helps to relieve some of the tension created by missiologists in describing the work of Peter and Paul. Without realizing it, these interpreters unwittingly portray Paul as a better apostle than Peter, since Paul crosses more frontiers than his colleague. However, as we have demonstrated, Paul himself did not cross any significant cultural barriers. Paul thus describes apostleship more in terms of calling and of being sent out than in crossing cultures. He writes, "God, who was at work in the ministry of Peter as an apostle to the Jews, was also at work in my ministry as an apostle to the Gentiles" (Gal. 2:8).

Scripture indicates that every disciple of Christ has been sent to preach the gospel. Jesus sent out the Twelve and the Seventy-two to evangelize within Israel (Luke 9:1-6; 10:1-17). Later, He commanded His church go in power of the Spirit and proclaim the good news to the "end of the earth" (Acts 1:8). In the Acts of the Apostles all kinds of people go out to preach. Despite their unique giftedness, prophets, teachers, and evangelists all go out as missionaries (Acts 8:4-8; 11:19-24; 15:31-33). Some, like Philip mentioned above, evangelize even as they flee from persecution (Acts 8:5). The New Testament emphasis is not so much on which particular individual goes for mission, but on the fact that the church goes out to accomplish God's work. Everyone is a minister, and in this sense, every member of the Jesus community is commissioned as a missionary to the entire world to make disciples of all nations (Matt. 28:18-20; Mark 16:15-16).

What Then is Missions?

In Luke 24:47-48 Jesus emphasizes the twin themes of proclamation and witness. Whether presented as "proclamation" *(kēruchtēnai)*, meaning the announcement of good news, or "witness" *(martures)*, the missionary's primary activity is to tell the world about God's redemptive work in Christ. Missions should then be viewed as the conscious effort of the church in its corporate capacity, or through voluntary agencies, to proclaim the gospel (and all it implies) among peoples and regions where Christ is not known or where He is inadequately known. Missions is not a mere department of the church, but the church itself in its complete expression, that is, in its identification of itself with the world.

Some, including many Western missiologists, insist on defining missions as the establishment of Christ's work across cultural and language barriers, with planting the church into that culture as the main thrust. Evangelism, on the other hand, is the activity of proclaiming the gospel to people among which the church already exists. It thus involves church growth activities in places where the gospel has been for some time. It appears to me, however, that these hard distinctions between missions and evangelism, are superficial and cannot be substantiated by biblical reflection as has been demonstrated above. Missions, therefore, should be understood as global evangelization.

The Frontier Missions Movement (FMM) is another missions organization that advocates the position that missions is the redemptive activity of the church in societies where the church is not found.[31] Thus, according to the FMM, a missionary is one who crosses over cultural boundaries from a society with an existing church movement into a society where the church does not exist to proclaim the good news of Christ. The FMM maintains a sharp distinction between evangelism—which they define as the work of the church among its own people in the same cultural group—and missions, which they define as the crossing of cultural boundaries to bring an initial penetration of the gospel among an unreached cultural group. These cultural boundaries that must be crossed to bring the gospel to a new group become the new "frontiers" of mission, thus the name of the movement.[32]

Further, Ralph Winter, who initiated the frontier missions philosophy through his 1974 Lausanne presentation, defines missions in terms of what is known as the E-Scale, with "E" meaning evangelism. According to Winter, the expansion of the Christian movement begins with E-2 evangelism (i.e., evangelism in a different but similar culture) or E-3 evangelism (i.e., evangelism in a radically different culture). Both of these forms of evangelism represent efforts to cross cultural barriers into new communities, and to establish strong, on-going, vigorously evangelizing denominations. Once that is accomplished, then that national church is to carry the work forward on the really high-powered E-1 level (i.e., evangelism within one's own culture).

We are thus enjoined to agree that until every tribe and tongue has a strong, resident, powerfully evangelizing church, cross-cultural (i.e., frontier) missions remains urgent.[33] What Winter often stresses is that in the missiological reality of today, most missionaries who are crossing cultural boundaries do so in order to work in a culture where a Christian movement already exist. He terms this kind of missions as "regular" missions." This kind of missions involves many kinds of good works in assisting a growing national church, including works of compassion, disciple making, and leadership training. He reserves the term "frontier" for the kind of cross-cultural work where there is no existing church movement among a particular people.[34]

I agree that, for the sake of practical mission work, the distinction between "regular" missions to already-reached peoples and "frontier" missions to unreached peoples needs to be maintained. While missions can be deemed as any form of world evangelization, cross-cultural evangelism (E-2 and E-3 evangelism) demands special emphasis. If E-3 missions, which is the more challenging of the three, is not emphasized, the tendency is to neglect it altogether, and to work among people with whom the missionaries are more comfortable. Thus, because the practical implications outweigh the debate over theological terminologies, it is necessary, and useful, to accept these debatable missiological demarcations. This being said, however, it is also unwise to push them too far, or to stress them too rigidly. It may be helpful at this point to "deconstruct" the crossing-cultures missions motif.

Rethinking Our Definitions

The deconstruction of the crossing-cultures motif is significant on three accounts: First, it reveals that our commonly-held definitions of who is, and who is not, a missionary are not necessarily biblically informed. This realization can be disheartening since it can engender arguments over the endeared term of "missionary," and concerning the true nature of apostolic work. Second, it brings us to the realization that missions may not necessarily always include the crossing of cultures but may, after all, include traveling long distances and crossing geographical boundaries to minister to those who may or may not share the culture of the missionary. Paul was indeed a missionary to the Jews and Gentiles of Ephesus, even though he shared the language and culture of both. Similarly, an African who preaches the gospel and starts a church in London among diaspora Africans is no less a missionary than Paul.

Third, the deconstruction of the crossing-cultures motif challenges the idea that Paul was sent out by the Antioch Church, at least in the commonly-held sense (cf. Acts 13:1-4). What, then, does it mean to be sent in this regard? "Sending theology" is the philosophy and practice of mobilizing personnel and funds for missions; it is a concept that, through the years, has grown with distinction through Western missionary enterprise. It infers that every missionary has a home community who recognize him as their representative to the nations. Through this community, prayer and financial support is mobilized.

In his paper in this book, "Missionary Care: The African Church's Challenge in Its Missions Enterprise," Malawian missionary Milward Mwanvani contends that the commonly held view that the practice of the Antioch church in Acts was such a sending base for Paul's apostolic teams is inadequate. He states that Acts 13:1-4, which confirms and amplifies the apostolic motif earlier practiced by Jesus (John 20:21), reveals the true nature of the church's sending function. Although our English Bibles use the word "sent" in both verses 3 and verse 4, the Greek uses two separate words. Verse 3 uses the word, *apelousan,* which means "to free fully or dismiss" (cf. Matt. 14:22; Mark 8:9; Luke 8:38), while verse 4 uses the word *ekpempthnentes*, which means "to dispatch or send forth" (cf. Acts 17:10),[35] indicating that the Holy Spirit sent forth Saul and Barnabas while the church simply set them free to go.

Furthermore, in Mwanvani's estimation the reception by the church of the apostles on their return journeys seems to reveal the church's responsibility and participation in the sending out of the apostles. Just as Jesus prepared a time of debriefing for His disciples on their return from ministry (Luke 10:1-20), Paul and Barnabas were debriefed on their return (Acts 14:26-28). Mwamvani thus deduces that there should be some kind of continuous link and ongoing care for the sent by the senders.[36]

I, nevertheless, contend that any rigid philosophy that insists that the missionary's support must come from the home church finds its basis, not in Scripture, but primarily in historical Western missions practice and experience. Although Paul strongly believed in a sending community for missionaries (Rom. 10:13-15), there is no scriptural evidence that the Antioch church provided ongoing financial support for the apostle. They did, however, serve the apostles as a community of rest and accountability.

Of course, the Antiochian church may have contributed financially to Paul's support; however, neither Luke nor Paul make any mention of such a practice. On the contrary, Paul's tentmaking texts reveal his passion to raise his own funds for his gospel outreaches (Acts 18:3; 1Thess. 2:9; 2 Thess. 3:8; 2 Cor. 11:8-9). Melvin Hodges concurs, stating that in pioneer missions work, unless the national evangelist receives help from neighboring churches, it may be necessary for him to find secular employment until such a time that the church is fully established.[37] Admittedly, others contributed financially to Paul and his apostolic team, including the church in Philippi (Phil. 1:5; cf. 2 Cor. 8:1-9). A missionary, then, may legitimately financially partner with the receiving community in doing missions. Earlier, Jesus applied the same principle when He sent out the Twelve to preach. He instructed them to depend on the recipients of their message for their financial support (Matt. 10:1-11; Luke 10: 1-8).

The fact that Paul never crossed any significant cultural barrier to carry out his mission only causes us to respect more those who do so today. Cross-cultural work is no mean feat, and requires years of hard labor. Before penetrating the host culture with the gospel, the missionary must become a member of that community and learn to culturally adapt to its particular customs and mores. The fact that one can be an authentic missionary without pioneer missions activity; however, does not justify the African church's slowness in such mission involvement.

While it is true that the Africa AG needs to increase its efforts and effectiveness in missions work, it is equally true that the movement should critically reflect on the missiological assumptions of the past, and of the "fathers." It is true that movements often become trapped by the philosophies of the past. Africa's missiologists, like all missiologists, should, therefore, be wary of well-intentioned definitions and descriptions that create the impression that missions can only be done by am expert "career missionary" supported by huge budgets from the sending agency.

THE AMERICAN AG FELLOWSHIP

Some missiologists and missions practitioners[38] have unfairly compared the American AG at the beginning of the twentieth century with the Africa AG at the beginning of the twenty-first century. They note, and rightly so, at the very founding of the American AG in 1914 it set itself to creating the infrastructure needed to mobilize and send missionaries to the nations. This comparison, then, begs the question, "Why has the

Africa AG taken so long to become actively involved in missions?" This question can be answered by looking at the distinctive histories of both movements. There were conditions in the America historical context very different from those in the African context. These two movements, therefore, cannot be directly equated. Allow me to explain what I mean.

First, the religious and social contour of America at the turn of the twentieth century had been seeded by a rich Christian and missionary tradition of close to two hundred years. Christianity was brought to the New World from Europe by the Pilgrims, who were committed Christians. Periodically throughout its history America has experienced spiritual awakenings. One such awakening occurred during the last half of the nineteenth century. Then, at the beginning of the twentieth century, America experienced the greatest awakening in its history. This awakening has come to be known as the Pentecostal Revival. Today, one hundred years later, the Pentecostal church has girded the earth. The American AG was birthed out of this revival. The revival began with the fabled Topeka Outpouring of 1901 and spread to the nation and the world through the Azusa Street Outpouring of 1906-1909. As the flames of Pentecost spread, hundreds of new Pentecostal congregations were planted across the nation.

The challenges the Church faced at that time are not issues of indigenization and contextualization. These movements and churches that eventually became the Assemblies of God already had a degree of maturity. They also shared a common missions vision growing out of the Radical Evangelical context of their time. For these ministers and communities theological and missiological reflection was not new. Self-theologizing was an intrinsic part of their society. In fact, the church had already created theological systems and missions societies championing such activities.

Contrast this with the beginnings of the Africa AG. In the beginning the neophyte national churches constituting the Africa AG were new fields established by pioneering missionaries who crossed both oceans and cultures to establish them. As the gospel entered into Africa, the emerging churches needed time to develop and mature within their cultural context. At the same time, the church needed to confront and "Christianize" various aspects of the African culture before it was ready to cross significant cultural barriers to minister to others who had never heard the message of Christ.

At that time, Africa could not boast of a rich and long history of Christianity and Christian tradition, as could America at the turn of the twentieth century. The church of Africa was thus required to confront legions of dark powers from within their own cultures and in the surrounding fields and cultures. Also, in order to create a missions movement on the continent, the African church needed to first birth a movement towards the formation of missions sending organizations and structures. This required a time of conversation about missions. The American church did not have to struggle with these historical issues.

Second, the American and African AG churches differed in their formative communities. The America AG began as a collaborative or a fellowship of various congregations and individual believers who had already experienced the fruit of the grace of salvation and the infilling of the Holy Spirit. Of the approximately 300 persons who attended the first General Council of the Assemblies of God in April of 1914, 128 registered as ministers and missionaries. The list of the attendees looks like a "Who's who?" of early Pentecostal missions. Present at the council were F. F. Bosworth, A. B. Cos, J. Crouch, R. E. Erdman, Cyrus B. Fockler, J. Roswell Flower, H. A. Goss, S. A. Jamieson, John G. Lake, B. F. Lawrence, T. K. Leonard, Jacob Miller, D. C. O. Opperman; M. M. Pinson, Fred Pitcher, E. N. Richey, and John Sinclair. Others who soon joined and served the movement were E. N. Bell, A. P. Collins, J. W. Welch, W. T. Gaston and R. M. Riggs. The America AG thus began as a strong fellowship with a significant number of ministers with immense skills and a strong missions vision.[39] The Africa AG, on the other hand began with first generation Christians with little understanding of the work of the church in reaching the nations with the gospel.

Third, the two movements differ in the processes employed to establish them. The American AG began as a fellowship, a cooperative of mature groups and persons whose driving force among many others was to organize a system to mobilize and send missionaries to the nations. Their long-standing Christian faith endowed the original members with a knowledge of the lostness of humanity and the church's responsibility of reaching them. The prevailing pre-millennial beliefs of the early members and their dramatic reception of the Holy Spirit prepared a fertile seed bed and strong foundation for the call to develop a system to mobilize and send missionaries to regions beyond. The Africa AG, on the other hand, began with a penetration of animistic and paganistic cultures. This required a long, and sometimes tedious, process of basic discipleship and ministerial training.

From the very beginning, among the five major reasons that lead to the founding of the American AG fellowship was strong desire to develop a workable system for the mobilization and support of missionaries.[40] Although the vision of establishing the mission infrastructure took a bit longer, the American General Council of the Assemblies of God began with missionaries already on the field. According to Edith Blumhofer, "When the first roster of General Council workers was published in the fall of 1914, it contained the names of sixteen missionaries representing seven fields. By 1915, the affiliated missionaries numbered 54 representing nine fields."[41] It was instantaneous and phenomenal; even as the organization was being established, it was supervising missionaries.

Thus, in retrospect, those who wonder why Africa has taken more than five decades to consider sending missionaries to the nations, must consider its history. While this is no time for Africa to make excuses concerning its slowness in mobilizing for missions, we must, nevertheless, humbly ask, "Is this comparison between the American and African church really necessary or useful?" Is it not comparing apples and mangoes. The two movements have distinctly different formational histories, contexts, and resource bases. Would it not be better to simply begin where we are, and together, march into the future of African missions endeavor? The African missions movement must be allowed to develop and grow as the Spirit Himself guides and energizes it. The leadership required for Africa AG the mission movement must be allowed to emerge and develop.

CHALLENGES OF PIONEER MISSIONS

The Pentecostal missionaries who came to Africa at the turn of the twentieth century were pioneer missionaries penetrating new cultural frontiers. Such pioneer missions endeavor was a extremely difficult, challenging the limits of human endurance. At that time the continent did not have the social and economic amenities it has now. Thus their pioneer missionary work was excruciating, and often took decades to bear significant visible fruit. Pioneer missionaries from the West thus endured many hardships when they brought the gospel to Africa.

Unlike these pioneer missionaries to Africa, the Christian Pilgrims who emigrated to America came, not as missionaries, but settlers. And, over the years they came in large numbers bearing their Christian faith. Most of them did not come to America to evangelize the indigenes but to find a good life for themselves and their progeny. However, the missionaries who came to Africa to penetrate the darkness with the light of the gospel often came in small numbers, sometimes as a small missionary band or as lone couples. Their way of life was thus significantly different from the Pilgrims and those who followed them to settle America.

Additionally, those early African missionaries had to create the educational and health infrastructures that helped to bring a better life to the Africans. In these pioneer missions fields the missionary was the preacher, teacher, and health worker. Before the Pentecostal missionaries arrived in Africa missionaries from the historic sending agencies—such as the Catholic, Presbyterian, Baptists and Anglican—poured their efforts and resources into a three-pronged approach of establishing churches, schools, and healthcare facilities. A mission center was deemed successful only when all three institutions were functioning well.

Missiologists have criticized the mission compound-based approach used by these missionaries, suggesting that it was evangelistically introverted in that, in order to find Christ, seekers were expected to trek to the compound instead of the missionaries and believers going out to aggressively proclaim Christ to the lost. Contextually, however, the missionaries did these things for three good reasons:

- First, the missionaries knew that it would be impossible to mature a recently-reached people and to develop them into a strong indigenous church, unless they were taught to read and understand the word of God for themselves. This reality

necessitated the initiation of school systems. Sometimes pioneer missionaries even had to create an alphabet, develop a written languages and then set up an elementary school system to teach the people how to read. All of this took time and cost a lot of money. Nevertheless, these early missionaries worked tirelessly to create workable education systems in Africa.
- Second, when the missionaries saw the poor physical condition of the people, they realized that they had to do something. As a result, they worked to lay down the infrastructure of Africa's health system. They realized that the people could not be left sick and dying without addressing their health needs.
- Third, the church, and the church building itself, became the center of everything that was done at the mission station. This is where the people came to assemble every week and learn the word of God.

Despite the difficulties of laying these foundations, the pioneer missionaries' desire was for the transformation of Africans into devoted followers of Christ. When the American AG missionaries arrived on the continent at the turn of the twentieth century, they followed the pattern set by those who had preceded them. These "late comers" to pioneer missions in Africa, seeing the same needs, often themselves created mission centers with the same threefold emphasis.

In the late 1950s and into the 1960s, as African independence movements began to throw off the chains of imperial of Europe, changes began to occur in missions philosophies and policies. It was during this period, for example, that the American AG mission in East Africa began to move away from the practice of the heavy subsidizing of schools and clinics. By this time, however, the infrastructures of schools and clinics were stronger and had already began to create a new breed of more educated people working with missionaries.[42] In addition to these challenges were the ones of creating workable missions stations, learning new languages, and helping to facilitate the creation of indigenous national churches. As with the other developmental processes, these processes also took time.

Although any Spirit-formed local assembly can create a missions movement, such a movement is best achieved through efforts of a mutually accountable collection local churches, that is, an indigenous national church. The fact that some local churches are attempting to act as their own missions sending agencies demonstrates their lack of understanding of the failures of the past. The sheer magnitude of the work of resource mobilization, coordination, and supervision of missions activities demands the establishment of a special and separate agency. Samuel Metcalf avers that a desire to frame a local church as a mission's agency clearly reveals a missiology and ecclesiology that are deficient theologically, historically, and practically.[43]

Notwithstanding the current criticisms of Africa's AG pioneer missionaries, and the growth of the Africa AG missions movement, the truth is that the disciples of the early American missionaries to Africa themselves learned their "fathers" ways. While the American missionaries effectively went about crossing cultures, learning new languages, and preaching the gospel, they often did not teach their disciples to reach out to the UPGs themselves. Should we, then, consider them to have failed as missionaries? Think of it. To initiate and sustain a concerted missions movement where hundreds of missionaries are mobilized out of a receiving context would have required huge sums of money to pay for the travel and living expenses needed to settle them in faraway places. It would have demanded the formation of organized systems while these pioneer American missionaries were sometimes still hacking their way through the jungles to set up mission stations.

Experience has taught us that national churches only come to a missionary-sending level of competency once they have significantly progressed through the five stages of the indigenous church philosophy: self-governing, self-propagating, self-supporting, self-theologizing, and self-missionizing. One critical issue is the timing of such an evolution. This timing will depend on unique issues within various national church environments, including leadership, discipleship, mission sensitization, financial strength, and other factors. In retrospect, the Africa AG may only now at the beginning of the twenty-first century be theologically and missiologically at the stage where the American AG was at its beginnings. I am not saying that the system must be fully functional to start missions. Nevertheless, history teaches us that there is always a "fullness of time" in the history of any national church when the availability of certain critical elements is present to launch a missions movement (cf. Gal. 4:4). The great challenge, then, is to discern those times and to respond to them.

Therefore, to claim that the Africa AG has taken too long to fashion itself as a mature missionary church could be an matter of not understanding the process and challenges of developing an indigenous Christian movement. Not all African national churches began at the same time, nor did they emerge out of the same contextual realities. Although hindsight may be 20/20, it also tends to over simplify, especially when all of the historical, social, and economical contexts are not considered. In his evaluation of the Frontier Missions Movement, Allan Johnson discusses what Ralph Winter and other missiologists identify as four distinct stages of growing a church on a newly penetrated mission field.[44] Each state takes time and the amount of time taken depends on varying environmental conditions. Those conditions are as follows:

- *A Pioneer stage*—where the gospel first is brought to a group with no existing Christians or church movement.
- *A Paternal stage*—where expatriates train national leaders as a church movement is emerging.
- *A Partnership stage*—where the missionary and the national leaders work as equals.
- *A Participation stage*—where expatriate missionary are no longer equals, but work only at the invitation of the national church.[45]

One would wonder, could a church be in the "pioneer stage" and simultaneously be functioning on a "participation" level of missions involvement? In principle—and ideally—every established church should be involved in evangelistic and church efforts from the beginning. However, the reality is that new, unorganized, and immature churches, which have not progressed through the developmental stages identified above, may be too weak to launch into E-2 and E-3 (i.e., cross-cultural) missions. An indigenous movement becomes ready to launch into serious mission work only when it has successfully grown through all the five "selfs" that make an indigenous church strong.

AFRICA'S DIVERSITY: CHALLENGES AGAINST CORPORATE MISSIONS

One criticism of the Africa AG missions movement is the general lack of cooperation and coordination in mobilizing for missions observed among national churches with one another and with their Western partners. Among the possible reasons for this missional malaise is Africa's vast cultural diversity. This cultural diversity would naturally mitigate against effective cooperation. It is represented by hundreds of uniquely different people groups speaking hundreds of languages across the continent. This circumstance is exacerbated, at least in part, by Africa's conflicted identity, an identity intrinsically wrapped in the continent's colonial history. As Africa struggles to nationalize its organizations in both the secular and sacred realms, its dreams of self-governance are dogged by this serious lack of self understanding.

The cultural perceptions and philosophical differences between Africans and the Western mission agencies with which they partner inevitably create tensions which spill into various sectors of African life. One big challenge is that Africans often derive their self perceptions from their cultural environment rather than from a scriptural understanding of the *imago Dei* (i.e., image of God) motif.[46]

Who, then, is the typical African? This question cannot be easily answered, since it is impossible to generalize about Africa. The continent is vast, occupying 20% of the earth's land mass, and its people are staggeringly diverse. The more than one billion people who reside in Africa live in 53 countries and comprise 2000+ tribes, each with its own language, traditions, beliefs, and history. Any generalizations we make about Africa's people are bound to be myopic, and at best, an oversimplification.

Africa's History and Beliefs

The above being said, there are still some common things that can be said about all Africans. The appellation "African" can apply equally to the Arabic speaking residents of the north, the Nilotic peoples of the Horn, the Bantu peoples of West, Central, and Southern Africa, the Pygmies of Africa's central rain forests, the San people of the Namib, and the Afrikaner of South Africa.[47]

Africa's historical and geographical realities cast long shadows across the continent impacting its perilous journey into the future. Significant events from pre-colonial and pre-Africa independence eras have combined to shape the present identity of Africa and its people. The slave trade, colonialism, and subsequent neocolonialism have left their indelible marks on the continent. The nineteenth century "Scramble for Africa" irrevocably impacted life on the continent. The national boundaries somewhat arbitrarily chiseled out by the Western colonial powers shaped Africa into what it is today. Understanding these facts can help us to better understand why Africa sometimes lags behind other continents economically, intellectually, and creatively.

African world views also help to determine Africa's development. World views are the basic assumptions about reality which lie behind a people's beliefs and behaviors, thus determining their conception of reality.[48] Thus, to a certain degree, Africa's world views create and determine its identity and destiny. This involves more than the "colonization of the mind." World views determine how we perceive "reality." In many ways Africa is shackled by its perceived realities.

Another facet of the African world view is its approach to religion. Africans are by nature very religious. In Africa Christianity has the most followers (59%), followed by Islam (28%), and then animism. Animism, nevertheless is pervasive in all facets of African life. Animists believe that nature is pregnant with spiritual forces, and from time immemorial Africans have embraced such beliefs. Although some claim that only about 7% of Africans are animist, the animistic world view still pervades the African psyche. It is, in fact, so pervasive that people carry it along with them when they become Muslims or "Christians." This trend can be easily observed in how millions of Africans are captivated by Africa's numerous "prophetic movements" with their dubious theological concoctions. In fact, animism is the basic philosophical and spiritual foundation of nearly all African UPGs. Other religions such as Hinduism, Baha'i, and Judaism account for about 6 % of Africa's population.

Various solutions have been proposed to liberate Africa from its past and to mobilize for economic and missional progress. Some have suggested that accelerated market reforms will lead to Africa's liberation. Unfortunately, many attempts as such reforms have failed. In my book, *Why Africans Fail to Lead*, I describe five proposed economic solutions that have been tried, all with dismal results.[49] Others, like Robert Guest, suggest that the solution to Africa's problems is political. He believes that Africa is economically shackled because it is poorly governed, and that, if Africa was better governed, it would be more prosperous, and therefore, liberated from bondage.[50]

African presidents, Obasanjo of Nigeria, Mbeki of South Africa and Wade of Senegal have all called for a visionary revamping of the economies of the continent, and the late Muammar Gaddafi called for the unification of Africa based on the vision, desires, and philosophy of the founding fathers of the Organization of African Unity, later renamed the African Union.[51] With varying emphases, most African leaders believe that economic integration is the future hope of the continent. Many believe that Africa's hope lies in the right leadership. These new leaders must genuinely pursue democracy, good governance, sound fiscal policies, and the genuine observance of human rights. The NEPAD initiative and the Africa Peer Review Mechanism evolved as part of the realization that an ill-governed continent cannot sustain economic progress.

Certainly the answer to Africa's perceived backwardness and slowness is not easy to find. Many attempts have been made, but to no avail. Part of that answer, I am convinced, must include Africans' coming to terms with who they really are before God and of their God-ordained destiny. Africans must realize that they, like all other peoples of earth, have been created in the image of God. And, because of this they stand equal before all other men and free to follow God in doing whatever He has called them to do.

Ethnicity, Teams, and Collaborative

Africa is rich in people diversity. Rightly understood, and rightly exploited this great diversity could become one of Africa's great strengths. Unfortunately it has become one of Africa's great stumbling blocks. Rather than energize, it has tended to immobilize the continent. Tribalism, regionalism, and nepotism has rocked and unraveled African society again and again. This same diversity has slowed the developing missions movement of the Africa AG.

The difficulties of developing a united front of missions from among national churches and across Africa lies in part to the challenges created by Africa's ethnocentrism. Most continental, or even regional, initiatives result in failure because of the propensity on the part of many to protect their own nationhood or national sovereignty. Part of the answer to the divisive nature of tribalism is found in a clear and convincing articulation of the need for AG national churches and missions departments to work collaboratively in teams.

Such an approach will accomplish at least two things: First, it will open us up to an understanding of the intra-personal differences essential for team building. Second, it will reveal to us approaches that will help us to develop working teams, Collaborative, and organizations despite the evident and visible cultural and national differences. The Africa AG continues to move painfully slow in developing a multi-national missions Collaborative. This is, at in least part, because our national churches are often self-centered and care little about what happens beyond their own national boundaries. This self-centeredness is often cloaked in the guise of national sovereignty. It is unfortunate that many national leaders fail to see the great missional benefits of multinational collaboration.[52]

Effective team work is dependent on mutual recognition of the unique strengths and giftedness of the individual members. In this context, individual brilliance only becomes meaningful when it is anchored in the collective efforts of all. In the Pauline passages that speak of the giftedness of individual believers, the context is that of the human body with its various and functioning members. Each member is significant and serves an essential function (1 Cor. 12:12-27; Rom. 12:3-6; Eph. 4:7-16). The function of each is for the common good. The success of leadership thus lies in the success of the community.[53] This philosophy must be applied on the continental level where individual national churches bring specific strengths for continent-wide missions, and where success is measured, not only in the success of the individual national church, but in the successful advance of the continent-wide missionary movement of the Africa AG.

Teamwork and leadership are not only essential to the welfare of a local community of believers, these qualities are also at the heart of the maturation and impact of larger institutions. Organizations that perfect the art of working and leading by teams are more successful than those that do not. This includes churches and missions organizations. These successful organizations invariably emphasize and appreciate the unique role and giftedness of each member. In light of this fact, African church leaders must seek to develop a "beyond" mind set. They must not only think of missions that functions within the geographical boundaries of their own countries, but they must learn to work together in multi-national Collaborative. They must develop cooperative links and missions networks with leaders and missions organizations from other nations.[54] It is a mistake to think, however, that such teams develop automatically.

African communities struggle with team development for a number of reasons. First, Africa's diversity, as discussed above, poses an ongoing challenge to the creation of teams, at least at the beginning. Second, Africa's tribal understanding of culture tends to lessen the desire to develop multi-cultural working teams. Tribalism, that is, the negative inward-looking bigotry practiced by tribesmen, naturally destroys the essence of team building. This societal cancer tends to grow even in contexts that it should not, even in the church itself.[55] Spiritual leaders should be committed to the fact that the church is a community of people from all tribes, languages, and peoples. And yet, they still stumble over the issue of ethnicity. One solution for this unacceptable situation is the intentional development of leaders with a world vision.

The success of collaborative leadership lies in the biblical truth that leadership is for the benefit of the believing community and the lost nations of the world. We must never forget that the church exists for the purpose of "seeking and saving that which is lost" (Luke 19:10).

MISSIONS ORGANIZATIONS OF THE AFRICA ASSEMBLIES OF GOD

The missionary involvement of the Africa AG is slowly growing stronger. Admittedly, progress is sometimes painfully slow, and at times even seem to retrogress. Over the last twenty or so years various national churches and regions of the Africa AG have attempted to initiate various missions organizations and projects. AG national churches from West Africa, such as the AG Nigeria, have sent missionaries into Cameron, Niger, and other places. The Burkina Faso AG has sent missionaries into Ivory Coast and Guinea Bissau. National churches from other regions such as the Malawi, Kenya, and Tanzania AG, have done likewise.[56] These attempts have, almost exclusively, been on the national level. In addition to national churches sending out missionaries, other missions initiatives were started with the aim of inspiring, sensitizing, and coordinating the work of AG missions across the continent:

Eleventh Hour Institute

In 1997, during the East Africa Leadership II meeting, a call was issued for the formation of a mobile missions school.[57] This school was to serve as a vehicle to raise awareness for missions and to inspire the Africa AG to become more aggressively involved in spreading the gospel to the nations. The first Eleventh Hour Institute (EHI) was held in Lilongwe, Malawi, in July-August of 1999, with 165 East African AG leaders in attendance. Following that meeting, the AAGA Executive Committee requested that the EHI should become a continent-wide initiative. With the strong backing of Africa Theological Training Services (ATTS, sometimes called Africa's Hope), over a period of ten years EHI's were conducted in more than 15 African nations. These institutes encouraged national churches to institute their own missions organizations.

Interestingly, the outstanding success of the EHI spawned one of the major criticisms concerning the slowness of missional growth in the Africa AG. This criticism stemmed from the evident passion exhibited by delegates in the various sessions of EHI across the continent. Further, the creation of national missional departments following these EHI's created an expectation in the hearts of many of a mass missions mobilization movement in the Africa AG. Then, when such a movement failed to materialize, disillusionment set in. Some continue to think that the missional impact of the Africa AG missions movement has not been commensurate with the number of missionaries deployed.

While these criticisms contains seeds of truth, they are, I believe, misplaced. A correct evaluation of any project's success must always begin with a clear understanding of its original purpose. The EHI was never meant to be an agency to mobilize and send out missionaries. Its aim was to raise awareness and to sensitize the churches to greater missions involvement.[58] In retrospect, the EHI was extremely successful in this area. It has, indeed, successfully sensitized many Africa AG national churches to their need to fully participate in the *missio Dei*.

In its present configuration—which is a loosely-knit association of national churches—it is impossible for AAGA to create a continent-wide sending agency. EHI's often included strategy sessions that sought to lead the participants to develop missional goals, including the creation of national missions departments. It then became the responsibility of these national mission departments to develop their own strategies for mobilizing and deploying missionaries.

World Mission Commission

The AAGA World Missions Commission (WMC) was provisionally instituted in January of 2000 during the AAGA Executive Committee meeting and later ratified at the Indianapolis AAGA General Assembly in August of the same year.[59] The agency's creation was a reflection of the deep desire in the hearts many African and American AG missionary leaders to channel the tremendous impact of the just-completed Decade of Harvest emphasis into the formation of a powerful African missions movement. This desire lead to the call for the creation of an organization to coordinate the growing missionary activity of the Africa Assemblies of God under the oversight of AAGA. The WMC was thus created to fulfill three main purposes:

- First, it was to work towards prioritizing efforts to reach Africa's unreached peoples by the national churches of Africa. This work was to include the conducting of research into the location and nature of these unreached people groups. This database would then serve as source of accurate and useful information for the national AG missions agencies across Africa. The commission could also help in allocating primary missions responsibility for specific unreached peoples to interested national missions departments.
- Second, the WMC was to help coordinate existing and new missionary endeavors across the continent. As a service to the national AG churches of Africa the WMC was to (1) maintain a data base of current missionary endeavors being actively pursued across the continent, as well as those missionary endeavors projected for future implementation, (2) provide an official listing of all missionaries representing A G national churches, including their place of assignment, ministry activity, and length of service, and (3) serve as a forum for discussion, strategic planning, decision-making, and conflict resolution concerning the deployment of national church missionary personnel across the continent.
- Third, the WMC was to encourage the establishment and function of regional missions departments along the geographical divisions of the official AAGA regions (a total of five at the time) with two primary intentions: First, the regional missions departments were to facilitate the ongoing implementation of the "Eleventh Hour Institute" concept of mission training in each region of the continent and in individual countries requesting the same in close collaboration with ATTS as the leading agency in this function.[60] The resolution further called for a timetable for the implementation of the EHI program, which was to be established as a first priority of the WMC. Second, the regional missions departments were to aid in the development of an AAGA Research effort, focused upon world missions efforts, but not limited to that function.[61]

Unfortunately, during its first decade of existence, the WMC failed to adequately fulfill any of its three major purposes. Its only noteworthy effort during this time was a missions meeting held in Burkina Faso in 2005.[62] Then, in 2010 at the AAGA General Assembly held in Johannesburg, the Africa AG leaders moved to rekindle a new zeal for the original vision and mission of the WMC. Following that meeting the new WMC leadership resolved to improve, and began to conduct regular meetings occurring in three year cycles, as follows:.

- During the first year of the cycle the WMC conducts *Pentecostal Missional Consultations* for missiologists and reflective practitioners. During these consultations well-written papers on missions issues affecting the Africa AG are presented and discussed. They later published in book form. The first such consultation was held in Limuru, Kenya, in April of 2011. The book, *Globalizing Pentecostal Missions: The Emerging Missionary Movement in the Africa Assemblies of God*, containing the presentations from this meeting was subsequently published by the Acts in Africa Initiative.
- During the second year, *Regional Missions Meetings* are conducted in the AAGA-related regions aimed at empowering national missions departments and leaders.
- During the third year of the cycle, WMC organizes a triennial *World Missions Congress* which brings all of the AG national leaders and national missions leaders from across the continent for a time of envisioning and vision casting for missions. This paper was presented at the first such congress which was successfully conducted in February-March of 2013 in Limuru, Kenya.

It is hoped that the rest of the purposes of the WMC will be engaged in the near future. During the AAGA General Assembly in 2010, the AAGA leadership further resolved to find means for effective data collection, storage, and dissemination on missions-related issues.

Acts in Africa Initiative

In 2004, at their General Assembly held in Accra, Ghana, the AAGA leadership commissioned the Acts in Africa Initiative (AIA) to help the movement achieve its missionary goals. The stated purpose of AIA—"to help inspire a new Pentecostal awakening in the Africa Assemblies of God resulting in the greatest evangelistic and missionary advance in the history of the continent"— meshed well with the philosophy and missionary goals of AAGA.

At first glance the overall growth statistics of the Africa AG are very encouraging. They reveal that the movement is experiencing exponential growth and has now grown to about 17 million constituents attending more than 65 thousand churches in 50 countries in sub-Sahara Africa and the Indian Ocean Basin. This is up from about 2 million constituents and 12 thousand churches in 1990. A closer look, however, reveals a troubling deficit in the Africa AG. These same statistics also reveal that, continent wide, only about 19% of the church's constituents have been baptized in the Holy Spirit according to the scriptural pattern shown in Acts 2:4 and 1:8. In this context AIA serves AAGA-related national churches in helping them to achieve their Decade of Pentecost goals, which I will discuss in the next paragraph. The leaders of AAGA and AIA share the belief that the only thing that will shift these figures upward is a powerful Pentecostal revival sweeping through the AG Africa. Without such a revival the Africa AG will never become the Spirit-empowered missions movement God intends for it to be.[63]

One of the major roles of AIA has been to raise awareness across the continent concerning the need for Spirit-empowered missions resulting from believers being baptized in the Holy Spirit according to the prescription of Acts 1:4-8. In 2010, AAGA officially launched its "Decade of Pentecost" emphasis extending from Pentecost Sunday 2010 through Pentecost Sunday 2020. During this 10-year period the Africa AG is believing God for 10-million new believers to be baptized in the Holy Spirit and mobilized as Spirit-empowered witnesses, church planters, and missionaries. AIA seeks to implement this grand strategy through Acts 1:8 Conferences and Schools of the Spirit conducted throughout Africa. To date, the ministry has conducted 31 such conferences in 21 African countries. The ministry is also working to raise up 100,000 Spirit-filled disciples who will intercede daily for a Pentecostal outpouring on the continent, and for the more than 900 unreached people groups on the continent. The ministry as a publishing arm called AIA Publications.

MATURING A MISSIONAL ORGANIZATION

Despite the stirring missions-oriented preaching heard each week in AG churches across Africa, the movement's national missions departments have not developed to the point where they can mount an effective missions mobilization effort in their countries and beyond. Thus, despite the phenomenal numerical growth of the African church in the last twenty years, most of its national churches do not have mature missional departments. Tony Pedrozo and Brad Walz have pointed out that missions maturity is not the result of an instantaneous miracle, but rather the deliberate and intentional application of sound organizational principles and practices. Pedrozo and Walz, who have helped to develop the exemplary Argentina AG missions department, state that a strong missions department takes time to mature. They cite two important factors contributing to that growth:

- First, they note that everything of real value takes time to develop. On the way to organizational maturity, missions leaders will make many mistakes, they will confront enemies and win many battles, and they will gain needed experience. Such things are impossible to get from books or theory alone.
- Second, in order to achieve organizational maturity, a missions department must have the right leaders in place. Many times, a country is ripe for blessing, but the right leader has not been found. Another real challenge for most of national churches with emerging missions departments is that they have no missions leaders with real missionary experience.[64]

The greatest missionary challenge our Africa AG national churches face is lack of mature missions departments. Nevertheless, like any developing organization, missions departments must progress through certain growth cycles.⁶⁵ Pedrozo and Walz discuss five critical stages in a missions department's path to missional maturity:

1. In the *Pioneer Stage* growth is very slow.
2. The *Battle Stage* is filled with challenges that sometimes frighten the church leadership.

3. The *Growth Stage* is characterized by increased fruit and permanence, which is observed by the Christians in a national church.
4. The *Consolidation Stage* is when a solid structure is organized in anticipation of future growth.
5. The *Respect Stage* comes when the agency and its leadership have earned a good name in the national church.⁶⁶

The duration of each stage depends on the long term vision, patience and determination of the national church leaders, and on their ability to stay the course despite the challenges that come their way. To compound this situation, a number of national churches in Africa have not themselves sufficiently matured, let alone their missions departments. These and other contextual challenges have slowed the progress of the Africa AG missions movement.

AFRICA'S NEW PENTECOSTALS

As we discuss the Africa church doing missions, it is helpful if we understand that the contours of Africa's Christianity are rapidly changing. The continent's Christianity is progressively becoming distinctly "Pentecostal," and this transition is affecting both the historical and mainline and evangelical movements. With the center of gravity of Christianity shifting from the Global North to the Global South, the churches of Africa, Asia, and Latin America have become decidedly larger and more vibrant than those of the North. Africa, with its more than a billion people, is quickly becoming the epicenter of the Global South church.

I should hasten to point out, however, that, as "Pentecostalism" in Africa is becoming bigger, it is also becoming more fluid, and sometimes more difficult to define. In this fluid context various forms of Pentecostal churches aggressively do missions within and outside of Africa. At one time Classical Pentecostals where the only ones in Africa branded as Pentecostals. However, today, depending on how one defines Pentecostalism, there are at least three other forms of Pentecostals on the continent. These three forms can be categorized based on their origin, their modes of governance, and their doctrinal positions. The first group of churches come under the category of Classical Pentecostals; the other three have been categorized as AICs, as I will explain below.

Classical Pentecostals

Africa's Classical Pentecostals are those historical Pentecostal denominations that were begun, or were strongly influenced, by Classical Pentecostal missionaries coming from North America or Europe. These churches often look to the West as the place where their "fathers" came from, and therefore, where their vision and control come from. Most of these churches believe that speaking in tongues, according to Acts 2:4, is an essential sign that one has been baptized in the Holy Spirit.

Although some of these churches trace their origin back to the Azusa Street Revival that occurred in Los Angeles in 1906-1909, most were started in localized revivals. Classical Pentecostals entered Africa between 1908 and the early 1950s. Some "late entry" Classical Pentecostal missionaries coming from Latin America and southern Asia began to show up in Africa in the 1980s and 1990s. Classical Pentecostal denominations in Africa include, among others, the Assemblies of God, the Apostolic Faith Mission, the Four Square Baptized Church, the Full Gospel Church, and the Church of God.

AICs and Pentecostalism

The next three forms of Pentecostals in Africa are regularly called AICs. AIC is an abbreviation with overlapping meanings and may variously stand for

- African Independent Churches,
- African Initiated Churches, or
- African Indigenous Churches.

The designation depends largely on the researcher describing them.

The basic identifying characteristic for any AIC is that it is a Christian church that was independently started in Africa by Africans independent of any expatriate missionary. Although disagreements arise about which characteristics are most significant and which taxonomy is most accurate, scholars attempt to group them according to common traits. These radically different "insider movements" have challenged the historic Christian beliefs and practices of the Classical Pentecostal churches started by Western missionaries. I see three forms of AICs:

AICs-1: Africa Independent Churches

AICs-1 include "Pentecostals" who began on the continent with no Western connection or headquarters to look to. These AICs mushroomed in Africa around the turn of the twentieth century and were founded on the desire for independence from missionary domination.[67] They began as political and administrative reactions to European mission churches. While they established their own governing structures, some, nevertheless, retained vestiges of European ecclesiastical practice, such as infant baptism, oral liturgies, European hymnody, and European-style clerical garb. These vestiges may also include forms of church organization, hermeneutical approaches, and a non-emotional worship styles. Although the words "African" or "Ethiopian" are usually absent in their names, they have an implicit "Ethiopian ideology" in that they highlight God's preferential treatment of Africa in Scripture (cf. Psalm 68:31; Acts 8). They often celebrate Ethiopia's successful resistance of European colonialism when she defeated Italy in the Battle of Ardua. In varying measures, different regions of Africa saw the rise of this type of AICs.[68]

While some Africa Independent Churches have aligned with historic evangelical or mainline churches, many have followed a "people of the Spirit" format. And, some have an inordinate Old Testament orientation, with an attachment to Sabbath observance, the use of holy water, the garbing of the priests, and the use of various temple-related paraphernalia. As "people of the Spirit" they often invoke the Spirit of God. The most prominent example of this type of AIC is the millions-strong Zion Christian Churches of South Africa.

AICs-2: Africa Initiated Churches

AICs-2 are Christian movements of African origin who have a propensity of redefining evangelical doctrine and of emphasizing a strong primal African quest.[69] These represent the largest AIC community in Africa. Although they began in Africa, unlike the AICs-1, they did not begin on the premise of independence from foreign mission domination. They more often began because of a unique theological emphasis. Some scholars have labeled them as the "Prophetic Movement" because most of the founders viewed themselves as prophets and established the churches with a prophetic ministry emphasis. The teachings of these particular AICs have diverged significantly from the teachings of classical evangelical and Pentecostal churches. They often combine various aspects of African animism and ancestral worship into their "Christian" liturgy. However, because these are "people of the S(s)pirit"—at least in their style of worship—and they exhibit a predisposition to invoke the "spirits," many scholars add them to the list of Africa's "Pentecostals." This grouping of AICs includes such groups as the Apostolos of Zimbabwe, the Mutumwas of Zambia, Kimbanguists of Congo, and the Celestial Church of Nigeria.[70]

Because the traits between the Africa Independent Churches and Africa Initiated Churches sometimes tend to blur into one another, most social historians categorize the two groups as one.[71] For example, Chris Armstrong places both into one group calling them "prophetic independent churches."[72] I prefer, however, to split them into two distinct groups. I do this because of how differently they view the advent and nature of the S(s)pirit(s). AICs-2 tend to believe in the variegated-spirit who comes in different spirits, mostly as the reincarnation of the spirits of the old prophets and human ancestors. Therefore, people in this community are usually filled with the spirits of Elijah, Moses, Samson, and the like. AICs-1, however, are more orthodox in their view of the Spirit of God, and believe in the one Holy Spirit who is part of the Trinity.

AICs-3: Africa's Indigenous Churches

AICs-3 are in essence Classical Pentecostals churches and networks that have been started by Africans on the continent. Scholars call this group by different names. C. Peter Wagner sees these movements as part of what he calls the New Apostolic Reformation.[73] Allan Anderson at first called them Independent Pentecostal Churches, but later began to call them New Pentecostal Churches (NPCs).[74] A few northern hemisphere scholars commonly call these churches Africa's New Pentecostals. They do not, as I am doing, refer to themselves as AICs, for they see themselves as Pentecostals. And yet, while they do, indeed, subscribe to the same theology as the Classical Pentecostals, they do so with a radically different form of practice. These networks are deeply contextual and aggressively utilize present day cultural-social tapestries. Like the two previously mentioned forms of AICs, AICs-3 are also "Spirit-led" and "prayer-focused." They may have roots and ties in Western Pentecostalism; however, they always function with an entirely indigenous leadership and style. Some of these of churches began in the late 1950's; however, the majority are of more recent creation, from the 1970's onwards. Most of the founding leaders of these networks were either at one time associated with Classical Pentecostalism or else they were raised under the umbrella of such churches. The fact is, however, they were locally bred and birthed with no direct organizational connection to the church from the West.

Rather than classifying AICs based on their doctrines, some classify them according to their origin or the nature of their leadership, as follows:

- *Ethiopian Churches* are those churches that arose out of the Ethiopian Movement of South Africa in the late nineteenth century which taught that African Christian churches should be

under the control of black people. Most of these retained the doctrines of the mother churches from which they broke away.
- *Zionist Churches,* such as the Zion Christian Church of South Africa, trace their origins to the Christian Catholic Apostolic Church in Zion City, Illinois, USA, founded by John Alexander Dowie.
- *Messianic Churches* are AICs with venerated founders who focus on the power and holiness of their leaders. These founding leaders are believed by their followers to have possessed Christ-like powers and virtue. These Messianic AICs include the Kimbanguist Church in the Democratic Republic of Congo.
- *Apostolic Churches* are those that boldly call themselves apostolic, including the Amapostole of Zimbabwe.
- The *Aladura Churches* have their origin in Nigeria and rely on the power of prayer and in all effects of the baptism of the Holy Spirit. Examples include such churches as Cherubim and Seraphim, Celestial Church of Christ, and the Church of the Lord (Aladura).

Before leaving the discussion on AICs, a few comparisons of the groups are useful. Generally, Classical Pentecostals and the Africa's New Pentecostals (AICs-3) would now regard the AICs-1 and 2 as being true Pentecostals despite the fact that some Northern Hemisphere scholars insist on this. Allow me to make three concluding observations about AICs:

1. It should be noted that all three categories of AICs, including most of Africa's Classical Pentecostals, are oriented toward the belief in a personal devil and the reality of demonic powers at work in Africa—especially through African traditional religion. Further, they all believe that prayer is the key to all problems in this world and that God continues to heal and deliver people today as He did in the days of the apostles.[75] AICs, nevertheless, are more supernaturalistic in their ontological orientation than the Classical Pentecostals who are more likely be influenced by a Western, rationalistic worldview.

2. Unlike the semi-literate founders and leaders of the prophetic churches (AICs-1 and 2), the leaders of Africa's New Pentecostal Churches (AICs-3) are more educated and intensely gifted in managing their institutions. They focus more on media and literature than do the prophetic churches, who focus more on "prayer tangible" items like staffs, crosses, holy water, gourds, and so forth.
3. The AICs-3 are fond of crusades, revivals, and other large open-air meetings, choosing them over the smaller-group, more communal style meetings of the prophetic groups[76]

It should be noted, however, that the stereotype of "illiterate leaders" among AICs-1 and 2 is being broken down. There is now an increasing number of educated leaders from these groups. It should also be noted that, at times, it is very difficult to clearly classify the AICs, for one church may likely fit in more than one category. However one describes these AICs, one fact remains, Africa's Christianity has been forever changed by these fast growing insider movements.

What Makes the New Arrivals Different

The existence and aggressive growth of the different types of Africa's Pentecostals outlined above, especially the last three, strengthens Ogbu Kalu's contention that African Christianity does not have its origin in the Azusa Street Revival, nor is African Christianity a product of Western missionary enterprise. It is, rather, an authentic outworking of Africa's religious quest for life.[77]

So, we now come to the important question, "How does the missional theology and practices of the Africa AG differ from other segments of African Pentecostalism?"

Although in the Africa AG national churches have done fairly well in advancing the work within their own national boundaries, unfortunately, most have not done so well in crossing cultural and national boundaries to preach the gospel to those who have never heard the good news of Jesus Christ. It seems, however, that Africa's New Pentecostal Churches have readily been able to extend themselves to various countries of the world. It appears to me that it would be a profitable exercise for Africa AG missiologists to ask another question, "What is the missing link in the Africa AG approach to missions?"

I will attempt to at least begin to answer that thought-provoking question. First, as stated in the *Eleventh Hour Institute Missions Reader* and in other recent publications, the indigenous philosophy articulated by AG missionaries worldwide failed to clearly emphasize a strong missional DNA. Although the three components of the indigenous church, namely, self-government, self-propagation and self-support did indeed include the planting of other churches in other regions and among other cultures, the churches and their founding missionaries did not sufficiently emphasize active participation of the national churches in frontier missions.[78]

Also, the ministerial training systems, which is one of the great success stories of the Africa AG, for many years did not have—and to some extent, still does not have—a strong missional core curriculum, that is a curriculum that compellingly emphasizes the biblical philosophy, theology, and practices of missions. It is true that people teach the way they were taught; and therefore, most graduates from our Africa AG Bible schools emphasize, not corporate continental missions, but the independence of the local and national church. Little effort is expended to proactively engage the "regions beyond." The New Pentecostals, however, tend to begin with an incredible sense of world vision. Whether or not these leaders are moving with pure motives is not the issue at hand. The issue is that, for whatever reason, Africa's New Pentecostals consistently look to the nations. Additionally, these New Pentecostals do not (yet) subscribe to the indigenous philosophy. The daughter churches planted in foreign fields still report to the "mother church" located in the African country where the church originated.

Second, the missionary strategy of the Africa's New Pentecostals is intensely Spirit-based and Spirit-led. At the core of the missions strategy is a strong belief in, and an aggressive practice of divine healing and signs and wonders. The authenticity of their miracles is not the question here. What is important to this discussion is the understanding that they connect with the deeply spiritual and experiential primal instincts of Africa. Being filled with the Spirit accompanied by speaking in tongues is not a debatable issue; they are part of the accepted identity of a missionary.

Third, the profile of a New Pentecostal missionary is radically different from that of the Africa AG. These missionaries receive basic training and are then sent to plant churches abroad like the ones at home. They may receive a meager support from home; however, most go as tentmakers who are expected to grow their congregations until they are able to leave their secular vocation and begin pastoring full time. Others continue as tentmakers until another "vocational minister" comes to receive the baton of leadership. The Redeemed Christian Church of God (RCCG) of Nigeria and the Christian Missionary Fellowship of Cameroon both use this method well.[79]

A common characteristic of the New Pentecostal missionaries is that they receive their salaries from the churches they establish. Unlike many Africa AG missionaries, who go back to their home countries to raise support for ministry, missionaries from the New Pentecostals raise their support locally. Significantly, they sometimes accomplish this even in poverty-stricken countries.[80] Although they do not insist this is the only way to raise funds—because some do rely on income from their home churches—they have come to believe that this to be a biblical mandate. They point out how Christ commanded His disciples, "Take nothing for the journey— no staff, no bag, no bread, no money, and no extra tunic. Whatever house you enter, stay there until you leave that town" (Luke 9:3-4).

Fourth, though the training formats of these New Pentecostal missionaries contain definite theological elements, they are highly practical and intensely personal. Mentorship, internships and apprenticeships are embedded in the New Pentecostal ministerial training formats. The strong emphases on prayer and discipline in these training networks helps to shape leaders with a strong sense of vision and achievement. Nigerian Missionary, Ayuk A. Ayuk, observes that missionaries from RCCG are able to succeed in the United States of America and other parts of the world because of two strong factors: spiritual discipline and assertiveness. Furthermore, he states that Nigerian missionaries from the RCCG are devoted to the Word of God and prayer. They do not take these two spiritual disciplines lightly, and, as a result, they pray daily and fast often to maintain their spiritual fervor. These missionaries are assertive and do not allow circumstances to deaden their spirits. They are not easily intimidated when it comes to the sharing of the gospel.[81] The Africa AG missionary enterprise would do well to learn from the strengths of these newer Africa insider movements. Fearing or caricaturing their theologies and practices will not help. Learning from the things they do well will.

LEADERSHIP AND MISSIONS IN THE AFRICA ASSEMBLIES OF GOD

Pedrozo and Walz reveal the critical place of strong leadership along with stable structures in the development of the missionary vision of a national church.[82] These two elements are symbiotically related. The Africa AG suffers from ineffective leadership models, especially in the area of developing a grass-root missions movements. Nevertheless, the fact is that mature and visionary leaders are key to effective, functioning sending structures.

Paradoxically, the indigenous philosophy, a hallmark of AG theological foundations, can create its own dark shadows. The drive to make local and national churches self-sustaining can create aggressive and independent-minded cultures and influence communities to be self-focused and unable (or unwilling) to see beyond their own national boundaries. Unless, leaders develop a world vision, they see only the nearby and convenient ministry opportunities. The Africa AG desperately suffers from a lack of strong visionary leadership at three levels:

Local Leadership

First, the Africa AG suffers for lack of local pastors who are able to inspire vision and raise up local missionary communities. As I have already stated, our ministerial training systems in Africa must be transformed to reflect the missionary purpose of the church. The Africa AG, in conjunction with Africa Theological Training Services (ATTS), have, through their endorsement process, tried to improve the focus and quality of their ministerial training institutions. However, additional emphasis on ministerial formation is the need that will lead to a leadership training paradigm in the schools. For too long it has been wrongly assumed that every trained pastor will have the capacity to lead. This is both theoretically and practically incorrect. Leadership ability is gained from both calling and training. There is always a need to train for the challenges of leadership. It is therefore essential that ministers be intentionally equipped with leadership skills.

Most AG ministerial training systems in Africa, however, are geared towards producing pastors and preachers, not leaders. Thus, the majority of our ministers can care for a flock, but they do not really know how to lead a church. By and large, the majority of the Africa AG pastors need to be radically re-trained as leaders. Only then will they be able to lead the church in the expansion of the kingdom of God across political and cultural boundaries. Not only must the pastor be seen as a missional leader, he or she must be equipped to raise up local missional lay leaders. As leader of the local church, the pastor is the inspirer-in-chief and must be willing and able to instill missionary vision into the church.[83]

National Leadership

Second, the Africa AG suffers from a deficiency of truly missional national leaders. National church leaders must learn to lead their constituents to look beyond their countries' geopolitical borders. As God's missionary people, the church must see those nations and people who do not have the gospel as their *raison d'etre,* their reason for existence. However, just as in the case of local church ministers, our indigenous philosophy sometimes unwittingly influences national leaders to focus almost exclusively on the development of national church functions, while neglecting the need to look to the fields beyond their national borders. If the church's purpose is to "seek and save the lost," then national church leaders must deliberately move their churches beyond a conserving mentality to embrace a sending theology and to initiate structures for the same. Such a sending vision will require leadership on both local and national levels.[84]

Pedrozo and Walz contend, and rightly so, that creating a "sending vision" in a church requires developing leadership capacity within a community. They observe that many times a country is ripe for missionary outreach, but the right leaders have not been formed, or are not willing, or have not been selected to take up the challenge.[85]

The formation and operationalization of the missions department is also a leadership issue. Missional leaders engender the creating, casting, and communicating of missions vision. They are necessary not only to initiate the process, they are needed to maintain its momentum. The inspirational tone of the various Eleventh Hour Institutes conducted across Africa has all-to-often been dampened by leaders who fail to maintain the process. One aspect of maintaining missional momentum in the church is efficiency in managing the processes and systems of a sending vision. This is done, at least in part, by assuring the financial contributors of financial accountability and by ensuring the missionaries of continued support. Leaders of effective missionary sending systems are needed if Africa is to move into full participation in the *missio Dei*.[86]

Continental Leadership

Third, on the multi-national and continental level, the Africa AG desperately needs to demonstrate leadership in corporately envisioning missions and in developing a theology of collaboration. Unlike the New Pentecostals, who, when they arrive on a new field, assume that there will be no national church, and therefore work aggressively launch one, when Africa AG missionaries arrive on fields, AG national churches usually already exist. This, therefore, necessitates immediate collaboration from both the sending and the receiving communities. AG missionaries, therefore, do not go to other countries to plant churches which will be controlled by the mother church at home; they plant indigenous churches, churches that will be led by the nationals themselves, and which will relate to their own local national church. Although this scenario is counter-intuitive to a pioneer missionary ethos, it is an intensely New Testament philosophy and practice. It has great benefits, for it anchors the work in the hearts and hands of the nationals who, above all others, are suited to lead the church.

The AAGA World Missions Commission (WMC) is strategically placed to inspire and coordinate continent-wide missions collaboration among the Africa AG. Two obstacles, however, exist mitigating the effective development of such collaboration. First, many national churches lack vision for international and cross-cultural missions. The WMC cannot coordinate work that does not exist. Its existence only becomes meaningful when multiple AG national churches want to take the message of Christ to other nations, and when they are prepared to cooperate with other Africa AG national churches in doing so. Second, for the WMC to become effective, it must be empowered with resources it needs to get the job done. These resources will logically come from its constituent members, the AG national churches of Africa. However, as long as member national churches remain intensely independent and self-focused, and as long as WMC has no power to compel its member churches to contribute to its support, this situation will continue.

CONFLUENCE

Although it is difficult to evaluate a movement as diverse as the missionary enterprise of the Africa AG, it is nevertheless essential that we try. In order to do this some form of yardstick needs to be employed to gauge our performance. As we consider the confluence of ideas from our previous discussions, one thing becomes clear. The Africa AG must follow the New Testament missionary pattern as it attempts to become a church that truly pursues Jesus' mandate to seek and save the lost. Yet, it is also true that what we sometimes call the New Testament pattern is "contextualized" by specific missions communities.

The Africa AG lives under the long shadow of the American AG, and it is thus unconsciously influenced by America's missions model. Like a son imitating his father, the Africa AG often imitates the America AG in how it approaches the missionary task. While many things can be learned from our American counterparts, one great problem with this scenario is the inherent contextual challenges involving the great diversity of Africa and of the Africa AG. The national churches making up Africa AG are not one continental church. They are, rather, 50 very diverse, multi-cultural churches. Due to fact that the Africa AG is influenced by of hundreds of cultural and tribal variables, the Africa AG can never be a single monolithic missionary community like the American AG. Its constituents can, therefore, never see things in the same way, nor act in the same way in their pursuit of fulfilling the *missio Dei*.

Complicating the situation is the Africa AG's attempt to too closely follow the very challenging America AG missionary model. Over the last one hundred years the American mission has developed certain ideas in regards to cross-cultural missions and UPGs. It is essential, however, that each ecclesiastical community, including the African church community, self-theologize and self-contextualize the missional precedents found in Scripture. In doing this, the African church must also remain ever cognizant of the historical precedents from other global church communities.

Interestingly, the same biblical antecedents do not always produce identical philosophies and practices in every cultural context. This is what makes practicing theology so challenging—and promising. It tends to spawn different contextual practices. In his book *Transforming Mission*, David Bosch highlights this challenge by pointing out that, from the very beginning, there have been differing theologies of mission and that "there are no immutable and objectively correct 'laws of mission' to which exegesis of Scripture give us access and which provide us with blueprints we can apply in every situation".[87] It is true, then, that missions philosophies are as much influenced by their proponents' cultural context as they are by sound biblical exegesis. I, therefore, suggest that Africa be permitted to practice missionary methods that are more "do-able" in the African context while remaining biblically informed.

How do we do this? One way is to adopt more flexible, culturally-relevant missionary categories. The Latin American AG categories listed in Table 1 below can serve as a good starting point.[88] In addition to the challenges of organizing a workable mission-sending structure within a national church, is the greatest challenge of all, that is, the challenge of resource mobilization. Generating the required financial resources for supporting missions is a challenge that the Africa AG must squarely face and resolve.

Not every national church within the Africa AG boasts of financial stability, much less financial viability within their missions departments. Because of these perennial financial challenges, and lack of proper organization in missions departments, Categories 3 (short-term missionary) and 6 (bi-vocational missionary) are possible ways of sending missionaries from the Africa AG at this point in time. Categories 4 (missionary pastor) and 5 (ministerial support) also hold promise. One challenge, however, is that there is still a stigma against these categories coming from within both the Africa AG and some American AG missionaries.

Each of the four missionary categories mentioned above poses unique challenges for the African church. For instance, the challenge of sending short-term missionaries (Category 3) is the lack of the necessary infrastructure to raise the needed funds. This is exacerbated by the high unemployment rate in Africa which makes people fearful of resigning from a job for a year. It is likely that, on their return from the one-year missionary work, they may not find another job. Bi-vocational missions (Category 6) is both innovative and biblical. Paul used it extensively. However, like Categories 3 and 4, this missionary category carries with it significant stigma in the African context. For instance, certain leaders from the Malawi AG (some even in the national missions department) have not come to the place of accepting some of their own successful tent-making missionaries as being real missionaries. This is because to most Africa AG leaders, only Category 1 and 2 missionaries—that is, fully-appointed missionaries and missionaries in training—are considered real missionaries. To these leaders the rest of the categories appear to be aberrations.[89]

Categories 4 (missionary pastor) and 5 (ministerial support) are the most flexible of the four likely categories for missions mobilization in the Africa AG. In these two categories missionaries are allowed to receive financial support from the churches they plant and pastor on the mission field. With this option available it becomes easier for an experienced and effective minister to consider planting a church in a metropolis of another African country. I submit that the utilization of these categories of missionaries is part of the answer to developing a strong missionary enterprise in the Africa AG. Such a strategy has the potential of immediately releasing the most qualified and effective ministers into mission work with least the financial investment.

Two criticism are often voiced against this possibility. First, the pervasive idea that a missionary must acquire his or her support from a "sending base" requires that the missionary raise huge amounts of money before being deployed to the field. If a missionary does not raise such funds, but goes to the field and plants a church, and is then supported by that church, he is deemed not to be a true missionary. This position, however, cannot be scripturally sustained. As I have already demonstrated, Paul was indeed a true missionary, and yet he often received income from within the context of his field ministry, either through tent making or from partners. Africa's New Pentecostals, especially the Winners Chapel, are sending missionaries by the droves as full-time pastors who receive their support from the churches they pastor on the field and as tentmakers who rely on the income they receive from their professions. The Africa AG would be wise to adopt some form of this method, in keeping with indigenous principles, as one of their missionary strategies.

A second criticism against sending missionaries to be local pastors who find their support on the mission field among already-reached peoples is the fear that such workers will become wrapped up in pastoring their churches instead of penetrating UPGs. This fear, however, is unwarranted. In his missionary strategy, Paul himself targeted the great centers of population where he planted Spirit-empowered churches as centers of mission who then reached out to outlying places. For example, Paul stayed in the city of Ephesus for two years planting a church that became a powerful center of outreach to the entire province (Acts 19:10). After a consistent pastoral ministry of house to house and public ministry, all of Asia received the word of God (20:20). Even though Paul himself never sought out UPGs, he instilled into the missions center in Ephesus the vision and capacity to send the gospel into all of the surrounding areas.

A key component of Paul's strategy of establishing powerful missions-sending churches was his emphasis on the church being empowered by the Spirit. He insisted that believers be filled with the Holy Spirit, for this empowerment ensured the effective penetration of that great population center with the gospel. It also ensured that unreached peoples and places surrounding that population center would be penetrated with the gospel (Acts 19:1-10 cf. 1:8).[90]

CONCLUSION

Along with the church worldwide, the Africa AG shares the awesome responsibility of taking the message of Christ every nation, tongue, tribe, and people on the face of the earth. The AG missionary movement in Africa must, therefore, under the guidance of the Holy Spirit, employ every strategic means possible to accomplish that end. In doing so, it must prayerfully and humbly reflect on the biblical model as to how it will approach the task. And it must align itself with what the Spirit is doing in the world today. Like Jesus, the church must learn to do only what it sees the Father doing (cf. John 5:19). This will call for courage in order to resist outside pressures and to boldly follow the Lord for the harvest. May the Africa AG fully do its part in fulfilling Christ's command to take the gospel to all nations before He comes again—when "the kingdom of the world has become the kingdom of our Lord and of his Christ, and he will reign for ever and ever" (Rev. 11:15).

Table 1 Latin American AG MISSIONARY CATEGORIES					
Category Type	Economic Relationship	Time on the Field	Time of Deputation	School of Missions Required	Observations
1. Fully appointed missionary	Fully supported from sending country	3 years, 4 years possible on request	6-12 months	Required during deputation	
2. Missionary in training	Fully supported from sending country	3 years first term	6-12 months	Required during deputation	First term: under supervision of a mentor. After: promoted to fully appointed

3. Short-term missionary	Fully supported from sending country	1 year. Renewable for a 2nd year	6 months	Required before leaving	Must be under the supervision of a missionary
4. Missionary pastor	Support beings shared by the local church they pastor	5 years and then renewable	Flexible according to need & situation	Required once at least every 5 years	Must be submissive to DNM and not just to receiving country.
5. Ministerial support	Support can be shared by the local church they pastor	5 years and then renewable	Flexible according to need & situation	Required once at least every 5 years	Must be in full time ministry without secular employment
6. Bi-vocational missionary	Receives most of their support from work.	5 years and then renewable	Flexible according to need & situation	Required once at least every 5 years	Though they do not depend on sending country, they can receive offerings
7. Missionary to ethnic groups in country	Can receive support from churches	Ongoing as need requires	Flexible according to need & situation	Required once at least every 5 years	Is within the country but to another culture or ethnic group

---

ENDNOTES

1. Throughout this paper references to the Assemblies of God is abbreviated simply AG. References to the Assemblies of God constituency in Africa is abbreviated as the Africa AG.
2. Throughout this paper the references to the Assemblies of God constituency in America is abbreviated as America AG.
3. Elder statesmen, such as Dr. Lazarus Chakwera, Dr. Charles Osweke, Dr. Peter Njiri, and others, have received the harshest criticism,

describing their work in missions as "more noise than action."

4. The "Decade of Harvest" was an America AG initiated grand strategy to see the church's greatest ever evangelistic results from 1990-2000. During the Decade of Harvest, the Africa AG grew from about 2 million members and adherents to about 13 million. During the same decade many changes occurred in theological and ministerial formation, missional awareness, etc. That strategy greatly impacted the growth of the Africa AG.

5. The Regional Missions Board (RMB) was initially set to become an agency to organize, send, and supervise the missionaries sent from the East Africa region of Africa AG. Initially, the Malawi AG sent three missionary couples to Sudan and the Kenya AG sent one. Also, the Tanzania AG deployed one couple to Rwanda. While, this was a great start, national church leaders underestimated the power of national church sovereignty as opposed to participation in a regional association. Because the RMB lacked legal cohesion, the results were not encouraging. It was left to the national churches to support each missionary in contradiction to the original idea of mobilizing funds from all regional nations to support regional missionaries.

6. Graduate Schools opened in Lomé (Togo), Capetown (South Africa), Nairobi (Kenya), Lilongwe (Malawi) and Jos (Nigeria).

7. Effective leaders understand the power of organizational assessment. Organizations mature and increase in effectiveness in proportion to their capacity to evaluate themselves. Similarly, great organizations learn from their failures, while zealously pursuing the satisfaction of their customers. In this regard, the church has two main "customers": God and humankind. God, the Maker and Creator of the universe—the Master of the very mission the church executes—stands as the primary focus of the church's activities. Next, human beings, whose needs and demands constantly influence the delivery modes of the gospel, are the church's daily customers. These two customers, however, are not of equal value. Therefore, as the church in general, and the Africa AG in particular, evaluates its effectiveness, one crucial question in must ask is, "To whose music shall we dance?' God is owner of the mission; therefore, the church's passion must be to satisfy God's desire for humanity. The critical question, therefore, is "What does God want the church to be doing in the earth?" One way to evaluate the performance

of the church is to check its alignment to the mission of God. This form of evaluation assumes, since God is the Creator, Owner, and Lord of the church, His demands supersede the needs of humanity, however colossal they may appear.

8. David Bosch, who was called the "bridge" between the Ecumenical and the evangelical movements of the world, provides a fuller description of missions, including all the various elements and nuances usually demanded of by either camp.
9. For a fuller review of these documents see James Scherer and Stephen B. Bevans, eds., *New Directions in Mission and Evangelization 1: Basic Statements 1974-1991* (Maryknoll, NY: Orbis Books, 1992).
10. David Bosch, *Transforming Mission: Paradigm Shifts in Theology of Mission* (Maryknoll, NY: Orbis Books, 2011), 9.
11. Ibid., 10.
12. Ibid., 10-11. The "Conciliar Ecumenical Statements" and the "Evangelical Protestant Statements" of the last four decades all reveal the same essence of differences and connections between missions and evangelism.
13. This statement is a summary of many statements of several international missionary conferences; however, the words are a summary from "Confessing Christ Today," a statement from the World Council of Church's Fifth Assembly held in Nairobi in 1975.
14. Karl Bath, *Church Dogmatics IV/1.* (Edinburgh: T and T, 1956), 725.
15. The word of for "center' in Germanic language.
16. Enson Lwesya, *Missions at the Workplaces.*
17. A "people group" is a significantly large sociological grouping of individuals who perceive themselves as having a common affinity for one another because of their shared language, religion, ethnicity, residence, occupation, class, caste, situation, or combinations of these elements. From the viewpoint of evangelization, a people group is the largest possible group within which the gospel can spread as a church planting movement without encountering barriers of understanding or acceptance. An "unreached people group" (UPG) is a people among whom there is no indigenous community of believing Christians with adequate numbers of resources to evangelize the rest of its members without outside cross-cultural assistance. A "reached people group" is a group with adequate indigenous believers and resources to

evangelize this group without outside cross-cultural assistance.
18. Paul was a man of two cultures (Hebrew and Hellenistic) and two "nations" (Israel and Rome). He was bilingual, extremely talented, and passionate about taking the gospel to where Christ was not known.
19. F. F. Bruce, "St. Luke's Portrait of St. Paul," available on the Internet as http://www.biblicalstudies.org.uk /pdf/ffb/luke-portrait_bruce.pdf, accessed on January 2, 2013.
20. Eckhard Schnabel, *Paul the Missionary: Realities, Strategies, and Methods* (Downers Grove: InterVarsity, 2008), 329.
21. Ibid.
22. Roland Allen, *Missionary Methods: St Paul's or Ours?* (Grand Rapids, MI: World Dominion Press, 1962), 14.
23. Echard J. Schnabel, *Paul the Missionary: Realities, Strategies and Methods* (Downers Grove: InterVarsity, 2008), 439.
24. Allen, 12.
25. Bosch, 16.
27. Ibid., 130.
28. Larry D. Pettegrew, *The New Covenant Ministry of the Holy Spirit* (Grand Rapids: Kregel Publications, 2001), 20.
29. Everett F. Harrison, Geoffrey W. Bromiley, and Carl F. Henry, eds., *Wycliffe Dictionary of Theology* (Peabody, MA: Hendrickson Publishers, 2000), 57.
30. Ibid, 58.
31. Ralph Winter, "The Meaning of 'Mission," in *Mission Frontiers Bulletin* (March-April 1998): 15.
32. Alan Johnson, "The Frontier Mission Movement's Understanding of the Modern Mission: Part 1" in *International Journal of Frontier Missions* (18:2 Summer 2001), 82.
33. Ralph Winter, "The Highest Priority: Cross-Cultural Evangelism," in *Let the Earth Hear His Voice*, ed., J. D. Douglas (Minneapolis, Minnesota: World Wide Publications, 1975), 220
34. Alan Johnson, "Major Concepts in Frontier Missions: Part 2," in *International Journal of Frontier Missions* (18:2 Summer 2001), 90.
35. Milward Mwanvani, "Missionary Care: How Is The Two-Thirds-World Church Doing?" vol. 3. Issue 1. Available on http://www.antsonline.org/Vol1I1a4. html. Accessed on 01 January 2013.

36. Ibid.
37. Melvin Hodges, *The Indigenous Church*, (Springfield MO: Gospel Publishing House, 1953), 87.
38. It is necessary to differentiate between missiologists and reflective practitioners. Ideally all missiologists should be practitioners, but sadly, that is not always the case. Sometimes eloquent missiologists have never been missionaries themselves, and have never been on the front lines of missionary work. While philosophizing from the ease of academia, these speak with feigned authority; however, they know little about the real challenges of being in the trenches where missionaries wrestle with issues of life.
39. William W. Menzies, *Anointed to Serve: The Story of the Assemblies of God* (Springfield, MO: Gospel Publishing House, 1971), 97.
40. Edith Blumhofer, *The Assemblies of God: A Chapter in the Story of American Pentecostalism, Vol. 1., To 1941,* (Springfield, MO: Gospel Publishing House, 1988), 201.
41. Ibid., 288.
42. Gregory Mvula and Enson Lwesya, *Flames of Fire: The History of the Assemblies of God and Pentecostalism in Malawi*, (Blantyre, Malawi: AGLC, 2005), 115.
43. Samuel Metcalf, "When Local Churches Act Like Agencies: A Fresh Look At Mission Agency—Local Relationships" in *Mission Frontiers The Bulletin for the U.S. Center for World Missions.*
44. Ralph Winter, "Four Men, Three Eras," 20; and Ralph Winter, "Frontier Mission Perspectives" in *Seeds of Promise: World Consultation on Frontier Missions, Edinburgh '80,* ed., Allan Starling (Pasadena, CA: William Carey Library, 1981), 59; and Ralph Winter, "The Long Look: Eras of Mission History" in *Perspectives on the World Christian Movement: A Reader*, eds., Ralph Winter and Steven Hawthorne (Pasadena, CA: William Carey Library, 1981), 170.
45. Alan Johnson, "Major Concepts in Frontier Missions: Part 1" in *International Journal of Frontier Missions* (18:2 Summer 2001), 83.
46. A major part of this section is gleaned from Lessons 2 of Enson Lwesya, *Emerging Leadership Issues from Africa: Doctoral Study Guide (Prototype).* Lomé, Togo: Pan-Africa Theological Seminary, 2008.
47. Ibid., 15.

48. Paul Hiebert, *Anthropological Insights for Missionaries* (Grand Rapids, MI: Baker Book House ,1985), 45.
49. In the book, *Why Africans Fail to Lead* (Springfield, MO: CLEAN Consult Resources, 2009), I describe five economic ways already tried on the continent with dismal results. These include (1) *modernization,* which regards the developing countries as doing catch-up to the industrialized nations; (2) *dependency* (or underdevelopment theory), which assumes a struggle between the North and South in a stratified world; (3) the *state-centric theory,* which postulates that governments and public institutions have a decisive role in managing domestic change and international relations; (4) the *state-society theory,* which recognizes the independent role of the societal groups in political dynamics; and (5) the *eclectic approach,* which focuses on domestic, social and political factors, rather than on international linkages as central factors in the process of change, x-xiii.
50. Robert Guest, *The Shackled Continent: Africa's Past Present and Future* (London: McMillian Publishers, Ltd, 2004), 25.
51. Gaddafi was killed and became a victim of the Arab Spring Uprising (2011-) when he failed to manage the need for change within his country.
52. Lwesya, *Emerging Leadership Issues.*
53. Ibid.
54. Ibid., 15-16. Teams or Collaborative, however, do not just happen. They emerge as a result of a distinct process of team development. One important aspect of team development is that the team's cohesion and effectiveness tend to grow worse before they reach peak performance levels. While the previous Africa AG missions Collaborative have not worked well, could it be that certain aspects of team development have not been considered? As teams develop, they experience growing pains. Many levels are reached in the team development cycle. Effective teams exhibit certain common characteristics. Patrick Lenciano in his book, *Five Dysfunctions of a Team,* explains that functioning teams are vibrant and active. Members of such teams (1) trust each other, (2) give attention to agreed upon results, (3) are not afraid of conflicts that arise among them, (4) are passionate and committed to the mission and vision of their organizations, and (5) are accountable for their individual behavior,

results and the direction of the organization. Strong and well-performing teams are grounded on the premise that teams work well when the qualifications, responsibilities, and expectations of members are well articulated.
55. Ibid.
56. Originally the East Africa countries formed the Regional Missions Board (RMB) as a mobilization and sending agency for the participating national churches. Even though it never worked well, the RMB managed to send missionaries from Malawi (three families), Kenya (one family) and Tanzania (two families).
57. Dr. Lazarus Chakwera called for the formation of a mobile mission institute when he challenged the AG leaders of East Africa while preaching from the parable of the "Eleventh-hour Laborers" (Matt. 20). The following year, in 1998, he and the late Dr. John V. York assembled a curriculum whose individual lessons where written by missions practitioners. Chakwera used the "Eleventh Hour Institute" (EHI) concept as the practical design for his doctoral project.
58. Chakwera and York originally envisioned that mobilization would be a part of the EHI process; however, during the first EHI held in Lilongwe, Malawi, in 1999 it was decided that a the mobile institute was not the right vehicle for mobilization.
59. Don Tucker (AAGA General Secretary), John York (ATTS Director) and John Ikoni (Nigeria AG, General Secretary) sponsored a letter that called for the formation of the World Missions Commission (December 1, 1999). The sponsors of the resolution asked for a provisional creation of the World Missions Commission (WMC) and the appointment of a chairman even before a full discussion took place at the upcoming General Assembly in Indianapolis in August of 2000. Therefore, the resolution asked that the WMC be provisionally formed in January of 2000 and later ratified in a General Assembly.
60. ATTS is an acronym for Africa Theological Training Service, also known as Africa's Hope (AH). This ministry was launched in the early 1990s at the beginning of the Decade of Harvest strategy. Its purpose was to facilitate, coordinate, and encourage the efficiency of theological training in the Africa AG. Dr. John V. York, a visionary and intense missiologist, set it up and oversaw its rapid expansion. It has become a great and influential organization within the AG.

61. For copies of the letter calling for the WMC resolution, the WMC Resolution and the WMC Constitution, see *Globalizing Pentecostal Missions in Africa,* eds., Denzil R. Miller and Enson Lwesya (Springfield, MO: AIA Publications, 2011), 185-192.
62. The WMC Executive Leadership meeting held in Limuru, Kenya, in 2011, concluded that lack of commitment by the leaders, and inadequate financial resources for its operations, contributed to the WMC's lack of success.
63. The Acts in Africa Initiative has been commissioned by AAGA to champion the "Decade of Pentecost," a continental strategy of the Africa AG calling on all of Africa's 50 national AG churches to emphasize the baptism of the Holy Spirit with the goal of seeing ten million new converts empowered and mobilized as witnesses for Christ. Denzil R. Miller discusses the Decade of Pentecost in his paper in this book entitled "Power for Mission: Africa's Decade of Pentecost and the New Testament 'Strategy of the Spirit'." The AIA website can be accessed at www.ActsinAfrica.org. The Decade of Pentecost website can be accessed at www.DecadeofPentecost.org.
64. Tony Pedrozo and Brad Walz, "Missional Mentoring: How National Churches with Strong and Effective Missions Outreaches Can Mentor Those Without" in *Globalizing Pentecostal Missions,* eds., Denzil R. Miller and Enson Lwesya (Springfield, MO: AIA Publications, 2011), 91.
65. Pedrozo and Walz identify ten characteristics of mature missions agencies worth noting:
    a. *Long-term missionaries.* A mature missions sending department will have sent long-term missionaries outside of its country who speak the languages of the people they are working with. They will have overcome the barriers of time (short-term-only missionaries), distance (just going to near-by nations), language (speaking only the language of the sending country) and religion (reaching people within the same or similar religious context). Each barrier requires a greater effort than the previous.
    b. *Income.* Their income is constantly growing and has possibly even surpassed the income of the general headquarters. You know that you have a mature missions vision when this condition no longer bothers church leaders nor causes jealousy among them.

c. *Pastoral care.* The department provides pastoral care to the missionaries in the field. The missionaries are understood and ministered to. This can also be done by local churches. A missions agency should never be seen to take the place of the local church in loving and caring for missionaries on the field.
d. *Executive director.* They have full-time administrative personal with one or more members of the executive team dedicated full-time to missions. If the executive director is married to both his church and to the full-time job of leading the missions department, he will be severely limited in his ability to move the work forward.
e. *Good reputation.* The missions department has a good image and a positive reputation when it comes to the administration of financial resources. Because those administering the finances are transparent in their use of money, there are no legitimate questions about their integrity.
f. *Savings.* The department is not living day by day but has savings in the bank which will allow it to respond effectively to emergencies.
g. *Decision-making team.* The responsibility of making decisions does not fall on one person only, but there is a team who constantly decide, execute, and evaluate decisions.
h. *English competency.* To ensure that international communication is not limited, there is one or more persons in the team who speak English.
i. *Missionary training.* There are training programs to prepare and orient future missionary candidates to the work.
j. *Promotion.* There are programs to motivate and mobilize the churches in all areas, including children, youth, intercessory prayer, promotion, and information sharing to the local churches. (Pages 91-92).

66. Ibid., 92.
67. Chong, H. Kim, "Another Reformation on the Horizon" in *International Journal of Frontier Missions,* 23:1 Spring 2006.
68. Chakanza. J. Chaphadzika, "The Independency Alternative: A Historical Survey" in *Religion in Malawi* No. 4, (February 1994), 32-33.

69. These descriptions of AICs are mine, others define them differently. Usually most scholars put AICs 1 and 2 together, essentially having three two groups with AICs-3.
70. Many African Pentecostal scholars do not recognize the African Initiated Churches as Pentecostals, while scholars from North America tend to do so. The greatest challenge is their doctrines. Most do not believe only in the existence of one divine Holy Spirit, they believe in a reincarnation of the spirits of the prophets of old. This belief is not accepted under an evangelical-pentecostal theological grid.
71. Most African Indigenous Churches, even though they began as African Initiated Churches, have progressed on their journeys towards evangelicalism. While, many do not necessary aspire to evangelicalism as the ideal, nevertheless, global influences, such as literature and travel, have helped to shape such churches into what they are today.
72. Chris Armstrong, "Do Nigerian Miracle Ministries Discredit the Faith?" Accessed at http://www.christianitytoday.com/history/newsletter/2004/ may21. html.
73. C. Peter Wagner, *Churchquake! How the New Apostolic Reformation Is Shaking the Church as We Know it* (Ventura, CA: Regal Books, 1999).
74. Allan Anderson, *Bazalwane: African Pentecostals in South Africa* (Pretoria: University of South Africa, 1992); *African Reformation: African Initiated Christianity in the 20th Century* (Trenton: Africa World Press, 2001).
75. Ibid.
76. Ibid.
77. Ogbu Kalu, *African Pentecostalism: An Introduction* (NY: Oxford University Press, 2008).
78. During the EHI the additional two indigenous pillars were proposed, that is "self-missionizing" and "self-theologizing" While these concepts have been vigorously discussed, they have not yet found their way into the textbooks of the Africa AG.
79. Interviews with Rev. Ngo, a Cameroonian missionary to Malawi with the Christian Missionary Fellowship, and Rev. Jacob a missionary to Malawi with the Redeemed Christian Church of God. These men indicated that the majority of their missionaries are sent as tentmakers, and most regularly depend on income from the churches the pastor on

the mission field.
80. Ayuk A. Ayuk, "Portrait of a Nigerian Pentecostal Missionary." Available at http://www. apts.edu/reimages/File/AJPSPDF/ 05-1-AyukAyuk.pdf. Accessed on 28/12/2012, 124-125.
81. Ibid.
82. Pedrozo and Walz, 115.
83. Ibid., 106.
84. Ibid.
85. Ibid, 114.
86. Enson Lwesya, "Missional Mentoring: A Response" in *Globalizing Pentecostal Missions in Africa,* eds., Denzil R. Miller and Enson Lwesya (Springfield, MO: AIA Publications, 2011), 114.
87. Bosch, 8.
88. Pedrozo and Walz, 182.
89. In 2011, during their Executive Meeting, the AAGA World Mission Commission adopted the Latin American list of the missionary categories. They will encourage the agencies affiliates to consider developing policies and infrastructure for sending missionaries from within these categories.
90. Denzil R. Miller, in his book, *Empowered for Global Mission: A Missionary Look at the Book of Acts,* discusses the New Testament "Strategy of the Spirit" that Paul employed in his missionary ministry, pp. 235-242. He also discusses this strategy in his article on "Power for Missions: The Decade of Pentecost and the New Testament Strategy of the Spirit" in this book.

Four Pillars for Successful Missions

ARTO HÄMÄLÄINEN

In Jesus' parable of the two builders, their two buildings experienced vastly different outcomes (Matt. 7:24-27). The one, because it was built on a rock, withstood the pressure of the storm, while the other, because it was built on sand, was destroyed. The moral: the future of a building whose foundation is strong can be ensured, while the future of one whose foundation is weak cannot. If the African church is to expect lasting results in its missionary work, it will need to build on a firm foundation. This foundation will include a biblical recruiting process, an effective training program, a well-structured sending system, and a cohesive partnering network. On these four foundations we can build our missionary work with confidence and assurance.

Pillar 1: A Biblical Recruiting Process

When Jesus saw the crowds, He was deeply moved. He understood their spiritual emptiness and physical needs. This understanding prompted Him to tell His followers to pray to the Lord of the harvest for workers (Matt. 9:38). The laborers were too few then, and they are too few today. In starting a missionary work, the first thing the church must do is to pray for workers. All successful missionary movements have been prayer movements. The Moravians conducted a chain prayer meeting lasting more than 100 years.[1] The global prayer campaigns of the 1990s opened the doors for focus on unreached people groups. Behind the fall of the iron curtain were effective prayer movements. In my country, Finland, every church was assigned a certain city in the USSR for which to pray. As a result, huge change came to the USSR. One example of such change was evident in the recent training session on world missions I gave in Vladivostok, Russia. In our Finnish Pentecostal church we prayed for 100 more missionaries to be raised up in the five years starting in 1988. God accomplished this in just four.[2]

Why, then, are not all churches praying for more missionaries? Sometimes the church has not really understood its very purpose of existence. The church exists for missions. Jesus promised the Holy Spirit to empower the church for witness to the very ends of the earth (Acts 1:8). This purpose of missions characterized the early Pentecostals one hundred years ago. Their "personal Pentecosts" made them mission minded. Gary B. McGee notes that the history of the Pentecostal church "cannot be properly understood apart of its missionary vision."[3] If any Pentecostal church is not involved in missionary work, it must ask itself if it has not lost its Pentecostal fire, or if in spite of the fire, its eyes have not been opened to the unsaved world.

Some pastors wrongly interpret the geographical progression of Acts 1:8. They believe that they must first reach their "Jerusalem" before going on to Judea; then they may reach their "Judea" before going to Samaria, and so on. However, Jerusalem and Judea were not fully reached before Paul left Antioch, nor was Samaria fully reached when he dreamed of going to Spain. In Acts the fulfillment of 1:8 occurred simultaneously. If you ask, "When should I start missionary work in my church?" The answer is, "Now!"

One reason for some of the misunderstanding concerning missionary work is the terminology used. The word *missionary* is not found in the Bible. Its origin is in the Latin word *missio,* which means "to send." This word is synonymous to the Greek words *apostellō* and *pempō*. In the gospel of John, Jesus uses the sending expression often. He Himself was a missionary sent by God. Today we use many words describing the work of the missionary, such as teacher, trainer, coordinator, mentor, and the like. And in many cases, the use of such words is necessary, since using the word missionary would prohibit entry into some countries. A current widespread practice is to use the word missionary for a person working in a cross-cultural context whether in their own country or abroad.

Workers doing outreach within their own cultural context are known rather an evangelists. However, we must keep in mind the spiritual meaning of the word. Jesus told His disciples, "As the Father has sent me, I am sending you" (John 20:21).

Further, some use the word missionary to describe people working in a pioneer effort. Others connect it to people working abroad, and some use it for anyone working in a cross-cultural context. Paul and Peter were different types of apostles. The former was sent to the Gentiles, while the latter was sent to the Jews. In many ways Paul was trained to work among people in other cultures.

Today, because of their missionary receiving history, many pastors in the Majority World understand missionary work to be a Western enterprise. They wrongly connect missions to money, and thus believe that only more affluent countries and churches can be missionary. This shallow concept of missions is far from biblical. It is, nevertheless, held in spite of the fact that colonialism often engendered harmful materialistic concepts in the minds of Majority World people. Paul praised the generosity of the poor Macedonians (2 Cor. 8). Even though they were poor, they gave abundantly. Following the Second World War, Finland was an impoverished country; however, the Christians did not allow their poverty to hinder them. Finland has become the European country sending out the most Pentecostal missionaries. Missions is vision-driven, not money-driven.

Even in Paul's time the mission-minded church model inspired others. Thus, Paul wrote to Thessalonians, "You became a model to all the believers in Macedonia and Achaia" (1 Thess. 1:8). The Thessalonians were known everywhere for their missionary zeal. In mobilizing for mission, it is crucial to ignite a missionary fire which will then quickly spread to other churches. Churches naturally imitate one another. We must, therefore, seek to light a fire for missions in key pastors and churches who will then inspire others. Many times the igniting persons have themselves been missionaries. In the history of our Finnish Pentecostal Mission, it is easy to point to those who have been instrumental in motivating others to get involved in world missions.

Our focus naturally turns to those who will go. However, we must also recruit senders: Paul asks, "And how can they preach unless they are sent?" (Rom 10:15). Every believer must find their place in the work of missions.

As Pentecostals we have the privilege of trusting in the leadership of the Holy Spirit. He calls both those who will go and those who will send. None are to be lazy. We must challenge believers by boldly teaching what the Bible has to say about world missions. In doing this, we must paint for them a vivid picture of the spiritual condition in the world. When this is done with the anointing in the Holy Spirit, people's hearts are touched. I received my missionary calling in my home when, as a ten year old boy, the Holy Spirit spoke to me. And, thank God, I was not the only Finnish child to be called by the Holy Spirit in the early years.

Pillar 2: An Effective Training Program

Pentecostalism is characterized by the urgency of missionary work. The success of missionary work and the return of Jesus Christ are closely linked in the Pentecostal consciousness.[4] Without doubt, this is a strength of the movement. However, at times, this same mind-set can become a weakness. Some missions candidates, along with their senders, become so eager to get on with the work that they view training as an unnecessary delay in their getting to the field. A principal in a Brazilian mission school once told me that many in his country see training as a waste of time; however, 80% of those who go to the field without training come back home within two years.

Patrick Johnstone contends that effective missionary training demands a close cooperation between local churches, the missions sending organization, and the missions training institution.[5] Unfortunately, however, these entities often go about their business never knowing nor appreciating the importance of the others. Each of them, however, should be mission-minded and mutually supportive of one another. Further, training for missions should be multifaceted. Both senders and goers need training. Short-term ministries are ineffective without it, and long-term missionaries to other cultures need it even more.

Ethnocentrism is one of the great hindrances to successful missionary work. Our missionaries must move from ethnocentric pitfalls to ethnorelative approaches.⁶ This issue must, therefore, be addressed in our missionary training. In order to understand the host culture and effect biblical change, missionaries must be taught to dig below the surface of cultural behavior to the differences in world view.⁷ Cultural training should thus encompass a large portion of missionary education.

Based on decades of Finnish missionary experience, we have developed seven theses concerning mission training:

1. *The mission training curricula should support the mission path.* Short-term missions can often be recommended as a first step. This gives both the "short-termers" and the senders a chance to test their calling. Nevertheless, without training short-term experience is much less profitable. This training should include feedback and evaluation following the journey.
2. *A proper balance between academic concerns and praxis is needed.* In His missionary training model Jesus combined theory with praxis.
3. *Training should be tailored to the field of service.* Missionaries should be made aware of cultural differences, not only on the surface, but also on a deeper level.
4. *The senders must receive training.* One good tool for such training is the Kairos Course" which is available on every continent.⁸
5. *The trainers themselves must be trained.* Like with Paul, our aim should be multiplication (2 Tim. 2:2).
6. *All theological training should be missional.* The Bible is the book of God's mission. Sadly, however, even some Pentecostal theological institutions lack courses in world missions.
7. *Mission training should be Pentecostal.* We must appreciate and emphasize the powerful Pentecostal dynamics which have moved the center of gravity of Christianity from the north to the south.⁹

Another essential element in missionary preparation is the screening of those who are interested in being trained. Effective screening will help expose potential issues which may forecast the fact that the candidate is likely to leave the missionary task early and return home. According to a survey by Peter Brierley, the top five reasons missionaries prematurely return from the field are (1) lack of home support, (2) lack of call, (3) inadequate commitment, (4) disagreement with the agency, and (5) problems with the peers.[10] Most of these issues are related to the attitude and maturity of the candidate, and can be brought to the surface through proper screening. Many of these problems can be addressed and remedied through proper training. Additionally, proper screening might predict impropriety on the part of some candidates. It is not impossible that some may seek missionary status for the wrong reasons.

Pillar 4: A Well-Structured Sending System

In his abovementioned survey, Brierley found that the number one reason for missionaries leaving the work early was lack of home support. This fact points out the need for a well-structured and effective sending structure. Too many times our eagerness to do missions is greater than the structure necessary to support the work. We Pentecostals have learned to trust in the leadership of the Holy Spirit, and we must retain this trust at all costs. However, it is also important to accept the fact that structures are not an enemy of the Holy Spirit. Soon after the outpouring of the Spirit at Pentecost, the early church in Jerusalem developed structural forms aimed at advancing the mission. The apostles took the leading roles. Very soon, however, deacons were added, and the church continued to expand. It soon began sending people out. Some who went out established the church in Antioch, which itself became an effective sending church.

The Bible is a strategic book. Even the business world has adopted many concepts from its pages. Many companies today have formulated missions statements to keep them on track. The Bible gave to the church a mission statement long ago. Our mission statement is the Great Commission of Jesus Christ!

Avant-garde companies also have vision statements. As a church and mission, we need them even more. What would we like to achieve through our activities? What kind of church or mission would we like be in the future? Should we not put that vision into words and communicate it to our churches? We should thus clearly and forthrightly state that we want to be a mission-minded church focusing on the unreached people groups in Africa, or that we seek to change the spiritual climate of postmodern Europe.

Clearly articulated values statements have also become important in the business world. If we want to win souls and change the world, we too should ask which values are crucial for the church and mission. We also need to think about what foundational principles we want to use in our work, and what will be our success factors. These ideals and principles can be found in the Bible.[11]

Paul was goal oriented in his missionary work. He had geographical goals. For instance, in Romans 15 he mentions Illyricum as one of those goals (v. 9). In the same passage he notes that he was aiming to go to westward into Spain (v. 24). Paul also had spiritual goals for his work. He wanted the churches he established to become dependent on the Lord, not on himself. Today we still speak of the self-governing, self-supporting and self-propagating Pauline churches.[12]

DeLonn Rance expands on this three-self emphasis in Pentecostal church planting. He believes that our missionary work should further be Spirit-governing, Spirit-supporting, and Spirit-propagating.[13] The resources of the Holy Spirit are unlimited, and it is to our benefit to be open to His influence.

Paul was also holistic in his missionary work. He saw both spiritual and material needs. To the Galatians he wrote, "Let us do good to all people, especially to those who belong to the family of believers" (6:10). This attitude focuses on the well-being of the whole person. In spite of the fact that we will not see this goal fully realized before the King has establishes His kingdom on earth, we can have a foretaste of it. The original "shalom-harmony" of the Garden of Eden was spoiled by sin. The Messiah, through His atonement, reestablished a new shalom relationship between man and God. With Him, we already live in this new kingdom, and have a foretaste of the shalom-harmony of the future world. On the other hand, as we await the return of the King, this condition is not yet enjoyed in its fullness. This eschatological tension is felt in our holistic missionary ministry.

What kind of processes or activities are then necessary to reach the goal of the holistically serving persons and communities? Like Paul, we have to preach the crucified Christ, that is, we must proclaim the gospel, the *euangelion* or good news. According to Matthew's version of Jesus' Great Commission, proclamation alone is not enough. We must "make disciples" of all nations (28:19). Teaching, training, and establishing churches was the method of Paul used to guarantee the healthy growth of every believer.

Historically, the role of social ministry has not been without problems in world missions. Some have seen it as the one key to spreading of the gospel. Others have seen it as an important component of missions that must, nevertheless, be submitted to the preaching of the gospel. More and more, Pentecostal missions are understanding that humanitarian concern is an integral part of the whole gospel message. In the Great Commandment, Jesus implied that loving of God and loving one's neighbor are an indissoluble relationship. He states that our most important relationship is to love God, but we must also have an equally loving relationship to our neighbor. In other words, if you do not love those around you, there is something wrong with your relationship with God.

Often, in non-Western cultures, a holistic approach to life is normal. People in such cultures do not separate body from soul as do most Westerners. Spiritual, physical, and social needs belong together. Caring for others is not a matter of how much money one has, and loving one's neighbor is not dependent on financial resources. It is an attitude of the heart.

In our missions work we may be very effective in our evangelizing, discipleship, and social programs; and yet, we may still fall short if we have not tended to the necessary supporting activities.[14] To remain effective we as a mission need personnel, resources, communications, leadership, and management. And among our first needs is information and marketing. Communication not only needs to be between us and those involved in mission; it also needs to with those who *should* be involved. When Jesus wanted to get more workers He started with information sharing: "The harvest is plentiful," He stated. We must motivate the people and utilize the tools of motivation.

Then, once we have recruited workers—the human resources—we must properly care for them. One area which we often inadequately address is the care of the children of missionaries. We must find ways to meet their basic educational needs. And, of course, we must adequately deal with the salaries of the missionaries. The local church and the mission organization are equally responsible for these missionary care issues.

Further, leadership is a central issue in missions structures. The following leadership questions must be asked and answered: Who is to take responsibility for which aspects of the work? To whom is the missionary accountable? Who is giving support on the field? What is the role of the partnering national church while the missionary is on the field? In all of these management areas we must be transparent. Nothing can harm the work more than the misuse of money, and to gather sufficient funds, we must apply good biblical guidelines for raising and handling money.

Pillar 4: A Cohesive Partnering Network

There is no country in the world without a Pentecostal witness. Thus, as we expand our work, we face a big theological question. Our Lord prayed that we would be one (John 17:21); however, many times in the past each Pentecostal mission has established its own national work, reflecting its own style. And this was done in spite of the fact that a Pentecostal church already existed in the country. Has this practice truly emphasized the theology of the unity of the body of Christ? This is an especially pertinent question as we focus our efforts on reaching the unreached people groups of Africa and the nations. With almost 7,000 such groups remaining in the world, will we as Pentecostals go together to reach them?

Pentecostals are benefitted by the fact that we are almost everywhere. The Pentecostal World Fellowship (PWF) represents some 57 million Pentecostals worldwide, and the World Assemblies of God Fellowship (WAGF) represents more than 60 million. What a wonderful potential network of cooperation we have through these fellowships! There are also the Pentecostal mission networks in Europe (PEM), Asia (PAM), and

Latin America (AG missions). Something similar also exists in Oceania. In Africa the Africa Assemblies of God Alliance World Missions Commission (AAGA-WMC) provides a relevant network for continent-wide missional cooperation. These continental networks can serve us in useful ways as new senders are deploying their missionaries. Should we not each be linked to our sister churches and missions organizations across Africa and the world? Together we can find and reach the needy places and peoples of the world.

Further, if we really want to receive maximum benefit from our networks, we must develop effective tools. New missionaries will need the support of experienced ones. And it has become clear that it is not enough for new missionaries to have a good national partner. The unique challenges faced by new missionaries raise special types of questions. In many cases the best advisors are those who have already gone through the same missionary challenges. It is difficult to understand culture shock if one has never gone through it. Therefore, cooperation between new missionaries, experienced missionaries, and the national church is important. Unfortunately, up to now, this kind of structure has not yet been adequately developed.

CONCLUSION

As the African Assemblies of God missionary movement continues to develop, it faces many challenges. The starting point is the mission-minded church. The Holy Spirit wants to make every church a sending church. The church's real reason for existence is missions. God is a missionary God, and His church should be a missionary church. Pentecostal pastors are in a key position to ignite the fire of mission in their congregations; however, in this missionary enterprise every believer is needed. Therefore, every believer in Christ should be recruited, either as goer or as a sender, and both need training.

As Africa sends missionaries to the world's unreached people and places, adequate sending processes and structures will be crucial. Without such structures our efforts will evaporate like water in the Sahara. As we go, we must seek to be Spirit-governed, Spirit-supported and Spirit-propagating. This, however, will not nullify the importance of the proper structures. Missionary educator DeLonn Rance summarizes well: "To be the church of Jesus Christ every church must be a missionary church, every pastor a missionary mobilizer, and every member a missionary sender."[15]

ENDNOTES

1. Ruth Tucker, *From Jerusalem to Irian Jaya* (Grand Rapids, MI: Zondervan, 1983), 71.
2. Arto Hämäläinen, *Leadership: The Spirit and the Structure* (Helsinki: Fida International, 2005), 269.
3. Gary B. McGee, Gary, "Early Pentecostal Missionaries," in *Azusa Street and Beyond*, 2nd ed., Ed., Grant McClung (Alachua: Bridge-Logos, 2012), 35.
4. Grant McClung, "Try to Get People Saved," in *Azusa Street and Beyond*, 2nd ed., Ed. Grant McClung (Alachua: Bridge-Logos, 2012), 5.
5. Patrick Johnstone, *The Church is Bigger Than You Think* (Fearn: Christian Focus Publications, 1998), 210.
6. Hämäläinen: *Leadership,* 150.
7. Paul G. Hiebert, *Transforming World views.* (Grand Rapids, MI: Baker Academic, 2008), 32-33.
8. You can find out more about the Kairos Course on the Internet at http://www.kairoscourse.org/about-kairos.
8. Arto Hämäläinen and Pasi Parkkila, "Synergy for Designing Mission Training: Finnish Reflections." *JEPTA,* Vol. 32.2. (2012), 157-163.
10. Peter Brierley, "Missionary Attrition," in *Too Valuable to Loose,* Ed., William D. Taylor (Pasadena, CA: William Carey Library, 1997), 94.
11. Hämäläinen, *Leadership,* 271-291.
12. Arto Hämäläinen, *How to Start Missionary Work in New Sending Countries* (Kerava: Fida International and Avainsanoma, 2003), 42-47.
13. DeLonn Rance, "Training Pentecostal Missionaries: Getting Properly Wired: Hearing and Obeying the Voice of the Spirit." *JEPTA,* Vol. 32.2 (2012), 189.
14. Hämäläinen, *How to Start,* 53-64.
15. Rance, 189.

The Nigeria Experience—Part 1: The Challenges and Joys of Developing A Missions Agency

ANTHONY E. OGBA

> *Jesus said to them again, "Peace be with you! As the Father has sent me, I am sending you." (John 20:21)*
>
> *I will not venture to speak of anything except what Christ has accomplished through me in leading the Gentiles to obey God by what I have said and done—by the power of signs and miracles, through the power of the Spirit. So from Jerusalem all the way around to Illyricum, I have fully proclaimed the gospel of Christ. It has always been my ambition to preach the gospel where Christ was not known, so that I would not be building on someone else's foundation. Rather, as it is written: "Those who were not told about him will see, and those who have not heard will understand." (Romans 15:18-21)[1]*

Growth is a process and every stage of the process has its own unique challenges. The African Assemblies of God is no exception. It has gone through various stages of growth. As I see it, the movement has past the adolescent stage and is now in the young adult stage. Like a young adult, the movement is bubbling with ambition, full of life and vigor. The Africa missions movement is ready to conquer new mountains and explore new worlds.

Missions leaders the world over believe that this could be Africa's greatest moment. It is our time to utilize our God-given opportunities and ministries to bless the nations. As we think about how much we have received from the Lord through our friends in the West, we must remember the words of our Lord, "Unto whomsoever much is given, of him shall be much required" (Luke 12:48, KJV). Many territories remain to be conquered for Christ. Even much of Europe is today post-Christian. These truths highlight the relevance of the subject of this paper. We will discuss the challenges that emerge as the African church rises to face its missionary responsibility.

PRELIMINARY CONSIDERATIONS

Before we consider some of the necessary elements of developing a missionary-sending agency in the African context, let's discuss some preliminary philosophical considerations.

The Primacy of the Missionary Ministry

For the church, missions is of first importance. Paul says that Christ has given to the church, and to every believer in Christ, "the ministry of reconciliation" (2 Cor. 5:18). Our primary job is to join Christ in reconciling the lost world to God. It has been noted that for the church to carry out this ministry effectively, it must engage in two main functions: its self-continuity function and its reason-for-being function. The church's self-continuity function involves all of the ministries in which it engages to remain alive. All of this is done, however, so that it can effectively carry out its reason-for-being function, that is, outreach to a dying world.

Missionary ministry should thus receive priority in the church's budgeting and planning. The missionary responsibility of the church must takes pre-eminence over every other ministry in the church. What was of highest priority to the Father when He gave His only begotten Son to redeem the world must be of highest priority to the church. It must command our highest degree of attention. It cost Jesus His own life blood and it must be for His church the pearl of greatest value. Nothing is of more value than the souls of men, and nothing is more important than reaching them for Christ. The Lord Jesus is our perfect example, and He assigned highest priority to salvation of sinners. Matthew notes how

Jesus went through all the towns and villages, teaching in their synagogues, preaching the good news of the kingdom ... When he saw the crowds, he had compassion on them, because they were harassed and helpless, like sheep without a shepherd. Then he said to his disciples, "The harvest is plentiful but the workers are few. Ask the Lord of the harvest, therefore, to send out workers into his harvest field." (Matt. 9:35-38)

Jesus' parables of the Sower, the Hidden Treasure, and the Pearl of Great Price suggest the primacy of missions (Matt. 13; Mark 4; Luke 8). We are all the products of missionary work. Without missions there would be no local churches, no Districts and no General Council.

Again, our Lord emphasized the primacy of missions when He said to His disciples, "My food ... is to do the will of him who sent me and to finish his work. Do you not say, 'Four months more and then the harvest'? I tell you, open your eyes and look at the fields! They are ripe for harvest'" (John 4:34-35). The African Church should follow the footsteps of her Lord and Master.

Evangelism remains the supreme task of the church. It is the only means by which people come to know Christ as Savior and it is the central and indispensable component of the Great Commission. Evangelizing the lost is central because all other ministries and activities of the church arise from it. It is indispensable because it is the process of offering salvation in its fullest meaning to lost people. The good news that we preach is the only message that addresses man's deepest and most profound needs both in this world and in the world to come. Let the African Church arise and make every effort to bring the message of eternal salvation back to the front burner of our church life and ministry.

Application of Pauline Method of Missionary Service

In his letter to the Roman church Paul made two significant missionary assertions. First he said, "I will not venture to speak of anything except what Christ has accomplished through me in leading the Gentiles to obey God" (15:18). Then he said, "It has always been my ambition to preach the gospel where Christ was not known" (v. 20).

These statements are insightful and challenging. They give us insight into what the apostle viewed as the primary objective for missionary service, that is, to lead people into obedience to the commands of Christ (cf. John 14:15, 21-23) and loyalty to constituted authority. These are the acid tests of true discipleship. Secondly, these statements reveal Paul's guiding principle in field selection. To him highest priority must be given to the regions where there was no Christian presence. Paul thus intentionally and systematically targeted unreached people groups for evangelization.

He then explained his motivation for doing so. Quoting Isaiah he said, "As it is written: 'Those who were not told about him will see, and those who have not heard will understand'" (v. 21; cf. Isa. 52:15). Given this fair-minded Pauline principle in field selection, it follows that an associated principle must be equity in the distribution of resources—human, financial, and practical.

DEVELOPING A MISSIONS AGENCY

Let's now turn our thoughts to practical matters, namely, the development of a missions sending agency in an African context. Our times are characterized by a proliferation of ministries and organizations in both religious and civic society. In view of this trend one might ask, "Do we really need another missions agency?" My answer is a resounding, "Yes!"

The Necessity for A Mission's Agency

A missions agency is an organization of people with a shared passion to reach the world with the gospel of Jesus Christ. The body may be an arm of a church denomination or a para-church organization. For example, the Missions Department of Assemblies of God, Nigeria (AGN) is an example of a denominational agency. It is the official missions agency of the fellowship. There is also in Nigeria a para-church missions agency known as the Nigeria Evangelical Missions Association. This association's mandate is to facilitate active involvement of churches in Nigeria in world evangelization.

Catalyst to Frontier Missions Vision

Missiologist Ralph D. Winter quotes from Billy Graham's final talk at the Lausanne meeting in 1974:

> While some people can be evangelized by their neighbors, others and greater multitudes are cut off from their Christian neighbors by deep linguistic and political chasms. They will never be reached by near neighbor evangelism, that is to say, normal evangelism. To build our evangelism policies on near-neighbor evangelism alone is thus to shut out at least a billion people from any possibility of knowing the Savior. Many sincere Christians around the world are concerned for evangelism. They are diligent at evangelizing in their own communities and even in their own countries, but they may not yet see God's big picture of world needs.[2]

Throughout Scripture God placed this global responsibility on His people. The Christians of Nigeria, for example, are not just to evangelize Nigeria, nor or the Christians of Peru, just to evangelize Peru, both have a global responsibility. God's heart beats for the nations. Each year the world's need for Christ increases; therefore, there is an ever-growing need for missionaries from every church in every land to every people in all the world. The nations' unreached billions await the message of God's salvation.

Winter's quotation highlights the need for missions agencies to help the church develop a frontier missions vision. The apostles were with the Lord for quite a while, and yet they knew little about the needs of the entire world. Their world was Judea, Samaria, Galilee and a few neighboring areas. However, the Master wanted them to see the Father's big picture. They needed a global vision; and more importantly, they needed to begin focusing their efforts on "the regions beyond," where His name was not known. Jesus had challenged them, "Do you not say, 'Four months more and then the harvest'? I tell you, open your eyes and look at the fields! They are ripe for harvest" (John 4:35). Missions agencies are needed to help sensitize and mobilize the church to embark on frontier missions reaching across ethnoliguistic and geopolitical borders.

Mobilization of the Entire Harvest Force

Missions is a collective responsibility of the entire church, and for any church in any land to make a significant impact in world evangelization, it must mobilize the entire church to participate actively in God's mission. This is one area in which a missions agency can play a significant role. It can serve the church as a catalyst for inspiring and enabling the church to organize and mobilize for Great Commission ministry. It can implement programs and activities aimed at mobilizing the entire church to participate in missions. Its aim should be to mobilize every minister, layperson, and local congregation to be actively involved in helping to evangelize the remaining unreached people groups in their own nation, across Africa, and beyond.

CHALLENGES OF DEVELOPING MISSIONS AGENCY

We have stressed the role and importance of a missions agency. It is the organization charged with the responsibility of mobilizing the church and inspiring her to implement the Great Commission. In carrying out this role it faces some significant challenges. Here are some of the challenges which the AGN Missions Department had to face and resolve as it emerged as the Nigerian church's missions mobilization agency. Any emerging missions movement in Africa can expect to experience similar challenges.

Policy Challenges

For a missions organization to effectively move forward it must establish clear organizational policies. Policies are advance decisions used to guide future actions of a group in a number of prescribed areas. Policy statements detail how an organization intends to carry out its set goals and objectives. By prayerfully establishing prudent policies, a missions organization can spell out in clear terms how they believe God wants them to go about accomplishing the missionary mandate. A wise missions agency will develop policies covering a myriad of issues including doctrine, relationships, personnel, leadership, finances, discipline and much more.

Fund Raising Challenges

Someone has said that missions and money are companions. Raising the needed funds to carry out the missionary task is one of the chief challenges of a missionary agency. The agency must, therefore, come up with an effective and clearly defined strategy of generating missions funds. While no one policy will work in every nation, in the AGN every first Sunday of the month is called Missions Sunday and is dedicated to missions. In every local church the day is set apart for missions education and missions fund raising. The missions agency in every AAGA-related national church should formulate a viable financial policy that is effective, culturally understandable, and acceptable to the people. The national funding policy should also include guidelines on how missions money must be used and how it will be properly accounted for.

Missionary Care Challenges

The need for the pastoral care of missionaries cannot be over-emphasized. Every mission should consider this as a vital component of its missionary policy. Missionaries are like solders on the war front. They often face hostile environments in terms of weather, language, unfamiliar cultural practices, and attacks from demonic forces. Missionaries often feel inadequate because of the enormity of their task and because of unrealistic expectations from the home front. These and a myriad of other factors contribute to missionary attrition.

A good pastoral care program will go a long way in reducing missionary drop out. It is therefore vital that the emerging missions agencies in the Africa AG include pastoral care for missionaries in their mission policy and practice. We could look to our Western missionary partners for advice and help us in this area, since they have a great deal of experience in this area.

Medical Care Challenges

One critical area of missionary care is meeting the medical needs of serving missionaries. Commenting on this need, Denis Lane notes, "Physical and emotional health equip the missionary to give full attention to his work. A person who is dragging himself around often drags others behind him. A missionary community cannot afford to be a convalescent home."[3]

It is therefore essential that our missions policies include some level of health care for our missionaries and their families. In the AGN, for example, the missions department pays medical bills for our missionaries. While other missions may do it differently, the important thing is that provision is made for missionaries' health matters.

Missionary Family Challenges

From the time of Abraham till now the whole family has been involved in responding to the call of God. No issue touches the heart of a missionary more deeply than the welfare of his children. His children's education, and their prospects of a future good life, may, to a large extent, determine the missionary's ability to perform effectively on the field. Denis Lane contends that the education of missionaries' children should be a matter of great concern to mission leaders.[4] Our policy in the AGN is for the missions department to take responsibility for the education of up to four children of every foreign missionary. The mission will pay their school fees from nursery through the secondary or high school level. Our missionaries serving at the home front, however, do not enjoy this benefit.

Cooperation Challenges

As we have already stated, missions is the collective responsibility of the whole people of God. National and local AG churches in many nations have caught the vision of world evangelization. Like the church in Antioch (Acts 13:1-4), they have come to realize that it is their responsibility to take the gospel to the lost and perishing people at home and in foreign lands. There is need for these churches to come together as one united entity in order for them to make a greater impact. Again, national and international missions agencies can help in this area. Confirming the ability of missions agencies to facilitate such cooperation in missions, the *Missions Manual* of the U.S. AG Division of Foreign Missions recounts its missionary history,

> The newly formed General Council of the Assemblies of God was intensely missionary. In November 1914 the leaders met at the Stone Church in Chicago, and in that meeting declared, "As a council, we hereby express our gratitude to God for His great blessing upon the Movement in the past. We are grateful to Him for the result attending this forward movement, and we commit ourselves and the Movement to Him for the greatest evangelism that the world has ever seen. We pledge our hearty cooperation, prayers, and help to this end..." One of the resolutions of the November 1914 meeting was to lead eventually to the establishing of the Division of Foreign Missions ... The solution that the presbytery found for accomplishing nationwide cooperation in missions ... was to form what is now called the Division of Foreign Missions.[5]

In addition to forming national missions agencies, national Africa AG churches agencies should direct their missions departments to seek full cooperation with the Africa Assemblies of God Alliance World Missions Commission (AAGA-WMC) and the regional missions departments of which their national churches are a part.[6] Together we can do more.

CONCLUSION

Time is running out. The eternal destiny of millions of people in the unreached places of Africa and the world now hangs in the balance. Let the church in Africa rise up to the challenge of completing the task of harvesting the ripened fields of our beloved continent ere the Master returns. This will require the untiring effort of every national and local Assemblies of God church in Africa. Our mandate is not only to set up functional national missions departments, but to empower the same to mobilize every local congregation in their constituencies in order to facilitate nationwide cooperation in missions. By so doing the national missions agency will be able to lead the national church into greater participation in world evangelization. With God's help, and through the power of His Spirit, the ripe fields of Africa shall harvested.

ENDNOTES

1. All Scripture quotations, unless otherwise indicated are from the New International Version.)
2. Ralph D. Winter, "Frontier Missions Perspective," in *Seeds of Promise: World Consultation on Frontier Missions, Edinburgh '80,* Allan Starling, ed. (Pasadena, CA: William Carey Library, 1981), 45.
3. Denis Lane, *Tuning God's New Instruments: A Handbook for Missions from the Two-thirds World* (Singapore: World Evangelism Fellowship, 1990).
4. Ibid., 71-79.
5. *Missions Manual* (Springfield, MO: Assemblies of God Division of Foreign Missions, nd).
6. The four regional divisions of the Africa Assemblies of God Alliance (AAGA) are the West Africa Assemblies of God Alliance (WAAGA), the East Africa Assemblies of God Alliance (EAAGA), the Central Africa Assemblies of God Alliance (CAAGA) and the Southern Africa Assemblies of God Alliance (SAAGA).

The Nigeria Experience—Part 2: The Challenges and Joys of Missions Participation

PAUL M. OGANYA

> *Those who sow in tears will reap with songs of joy. He who goes about weeping, carrying seed to sow, will return with songs of joy, carrying sheaves with him. (Psalm 126: 5-6)*

As missionaries go about their activities, they experience a combination of challenges and joys. The Assemblies of God Nigeria's (AGN) involvement in Missions Cameroon has resulted in both and has become a motivation for even more missions endeavors. The purpose of this paper is to present the personal experiences of my wife's and me as pioneer African missionaries, and through this presentation to create greater missions awareness in the African church. I further hope to sensitize and inspire fellow Africans, African churches, and African missions organizations to look beyond the daunting challenges of cross-cultural missions to renewed missionary commitment and engagement.

This presentation will be in three parts: First, I will offer my personal testimony as a pioneer missionary. Then, I will enumerate and analyze some of the challenges and experiences of African pioneer missionaries on the field. And finally, I will issue a challenge to the church of Africa to mobilize itself for greater missions involvement.

PERSONAL TESTIMONY

As Nigerian AG missionaries to Cameroon, my wife, Cecilia, and I have had many experiences, some rewarding, some challenging. I will highlight a few of those experiences from the early days of our ministry. I will also talk about our call to missions, reflecting on the necessity of a personal encounter with God, the role of prayer, the Holy Spirit, and family in the missionary calling.

The Missionary Calling

The call of God to missions is a profound revelation of divine intention. It reflects God's intention to redeem all the nations through Christ, and it heightens the awareness of the committed disciple to the need for cross-cultural ministry in fulfilling the divine mandate. The call to missions does not normally come as a "bolt out of the blue." It is rather, in the words of William E. Goff, "the fruit of our habitual, positive response to his [God's] voice, with a longing to know and be obedient to his plan for our lives."[1] In calling the missionary, God first reveals to him or her the "big picture," that is, His plan to redeem the nations through Christ. The individual then earnestly seeks the face of God to discover the specifics of his or her personal call. To grasp the full picture of one's missionary call thus requires repeated encounters with God.

Personal Encounter with God

A personal encounter with God constitutes the bedrock to effective missionary ministry. It becomes the anchor that stabilizes the missionary in the midst of great challenge. It also serves as a reference point that guards him against giving up and leaving his post of duty.[2] The missionary, Paul, often made references to his "Damascus vision" (Acts 22:5-11; 26:6-12; 2 Cor. 11:32; Gal. 1:17). For him that encounter with Christ was the compass that guided and guarded his missionary ministry. The need for a personal encounter with God in the life of the missionary cannot be overemphasized.

Convictions concerning their missionary calling may differ from person to person, yet it is essential that any missionary be certain of his or her call to missions. While the calling ultimately rests "upon the foundation of the *missio Dei,*" nevertheless, "the missionary calling is an individual matter."[3]

This emphasis on a personal encounter does not mean, however, that all who participate in missions must have a dramatic encounter with God. Some legitimately go out as volunteer missionaries based on the general calling on all believers to participate in the *mission Dei*. However, due to the great challenges that the missionary will inevitably encounter both at home and abroad, one would insist that the African career missionary persist in prayer until he or she receives their own Damascus experience.[4] It is important to personally hear the voice of God because experiences on the field and encounters with leaders can tempt the missionary to lose focus. However, missionaries who have had memorable encounters with God will persist even in the face of great difficulty. They have heard from God and, in times of trial will turn again to God for inspiration and strength. In addition, the constant need for funds will send the missionary back to God again and again.

At various times I have received specific directions from the Lord for the work in Cameroon. Our personal assurance of God's call has played a foundational role for whatever successes my wife and I may have achieved as missionaries to Cameroon.

My specific call into cross-cultural ministry came early on, even before my Bible college training. The call came again and again during my days in Bible college. Finally, while serving as a pastor in Nigeria, the Lord confirmed the call and gave to me more detailed direction about the call to missions. It is during one of those divine encounters, while my wife and I were preparing to go as missionaries to Gabon, that the Lord directed us to the Republic of Cameroon instead. These revelations confirmed the general call to Cameroon. With time they became more detailed and specific. The assurances and specific directions that came from these revelations were great preparation tools and armed us for the challenges and experiences ahead.

The Role of Prayer in the Missionary Calling

One's success or failure as missionary is predicated on prayer. The missionary's prayer life demonstrates his or her dependence upon God, the owner of missions. God is the source of all wisdom, knowledge, and authority. In prayer we admit our weakness before Him and fall back on Him "who is able to do immeasurably more than all we ask or imagine" (Eph. 3:20). For the missionary to succeed, his life and ministry must revolve around prayer. Like a soldier in battle, the missionary cannot ignore his supply lines. The battle is often lost or won depending on the supply from the cantonment.[5] When the supply line is cut, the enemy rejoices and redoubles his attack. Prayer is the spiritual supply line for the missionary.

Three potential sources of prayer support are available to the missionary: the home front (or sending agency), the missionary himself, and the field. While prayer is needed from all three sources, it is absolutely essential that the missionary himself develop a consistent and disciplined prayer life. He must develop a personal culture of prayer that goes far beyond his normal prayer habit. Sometimes it is required that the missionary add fasting to his prayer.

In prayer the missionary discovers God's will concerning where he will serve. Prayer then prepares him for his coming time of service. Prayer also helps to ensure effective missionary service on the field. During prayer the missionary faces the demands and challenges of the work, and he receives strategies on how to tackle those challenges.

Cecilia and I almost chose the wrong field of service. During an early visit to Dr. Charles Osueke, the then General Superintendent of the AGN, I told him of my call to a Francophone African country. He recommended that I go to Gabon or Congo Brazzaville. At first, without much thought, I chose Gabon, due to my previous personal interests in the country. Cecilia and I then began telling our friends about our intentions to go to Gabon as missionaries.

Then, one day my wife asked if I was sure that this choice was from God. After that, for about a week I prayed and fasted seeking to discover from God specifically where He wanted us to go. Two days after I had finished my time of prayer, while I was resting in the bedroom, a sudden revelation came to me. It became clear that we should not go to Gabon but to Cameroon. This revelation from the Lord gave us clear directions and great assurance that we were moving in His will.

In addition, prayer calls the presence of the Holy Spirit into our day-to-day missionary activities. Through prayer my wife and I have survived critical times on the field. During times of discouragement, God has always renewed our strength. The challenges in the life of the missionary on the mission field require prayer above all other resources. The fervent and persistent prayers of the missionary are the foundation of effective missionary service (James 5:16).

The Role of the Holy Spirit in the Missionary Calling

The presence and power of the Holy Spirit is indispensable in every aspect of the missionary's life and work. According to Denzil R. Miller, a clear "Strategy of the Spirit" is revealed in the New Testament, and the work of the Spirit at the heart of this strategy.[6] The Spirit empowers the missionary and the new church, He inspires witnesses through the preaching of the gospel accompanied by demonstrations of divine power, and He helps the missionary to mobilize the church for widespread outreach through training and sending. It is a complete cycle. At times during our missionary ministry in Cameroon, the presence of the Holy Spirit was manifested through signs and wonders as the gospel was preached. These manifestations of divine power confirmed the word of God in the hearts of the people.

During our time in Cameroon we always insisted that new believers be baptized in the Holy Spirit in order that all might be equipped for effective service. Consequently, from the beginning, the church in Cameroon had a Pentecostal formation. It became "out of fashion" for a new believer not to be baptized in the Holy Spirit. This Pentecostal foundation resulted in the Assemblies of God Cameroon (AGC) becoming a missionary church from the beginning. Immediately new believers became partners and team members in reaching out to their own people with the gospel of Christ. My first evangelistic team in Cameroon was made up of Cameroonians who had caught a vision for missions. Ignoring the discomforts, we went into the nooks and crannies of the land.

Many of the converts gave freely to the work of expanding the gospel, not waiting for funding from the mission. Locals were taught to sponsor their own missionary activities as they were motivated by the Holy Spirit. This strategy made sponsoring missions a bit lighter for the sending church, and it helped to instill a missions vision into local Cameroonian believers. During his visit to Cameroon, the AGN General Superintendent was amazed at the rapid development of work in Cameroon.

The Holy Spirit also advanced the work in Cameroon by demonstrating His power to deliver both people and their lands from Satanic bondage. The survival of the AGC can be contributed, at least in part, to the manifestations of spiritual gifts. He did these things, not that man might receive glory, but for the advancement of the work.

Sometimes God revealed things to us before they came to pass. On one occasion the young church conducted an open air revival at Mbaimboum. While I lingered in prayer, the Lord revealed to me a certain spirit that called itself "the mother of the Mboums." Embolden and empowered by the Spirit, I took authority over that territorial spirit in the name of Jesus. Once we arrived at Mbaimboum, many unexpected things happened. There the Dongari, the village chief, gave us a 1.5 hectare plot of land to build our first church. The church built on that plot thus became a permanent witness to what the power of God could do in a demon-infested land. Today, from that one church several other churches have been planted in the land of the Mboums.

We further insisted that there be a strong Pentecostal emphasis in the training of all of our pastors. As a result our AGC churches became centers where people can be touched by the power of God. Many oppressed people have been, and are still being, set free from demonic bondage. Our goal is to raise a Spirit-empowered church that is relevant to the daily needs of Cameroonians.

The Family in Missionary Calling

Often, as preparations are being made for going to the field, the missionary's family is forgotten. The sending agency sometimes only deals with the men and forgets their wife and children. This is unfortunate since the entire family is engaged in the missionary calling. For instance, while the leaders were working with me alone, my wife objected. She insisted that she would not follow me to the field based solely on my own convictions, she needed convictions of her own. This opened my eyes; she needed her own experience with the Lord and her own God-given conviction that she would cling to during her difficult moments. As a result we took a retreat together. At the retreat center, God gave her very detailed revelations about the missionary calling. When we arrived on the field, these revelations helped to sustain her during the great challenges we had in coping with the culture of Cameroon.

Language was another difficulty faced by my wife. I could manage in French, but, because she could speak little French, she was often embarrassed and had difficulty coping in certain situations. On occasions she even considered leaving the field and returning home to Nigeria. She once referred to herself as "an educated illiterate." But, because she had previously heard from God, she endured, and today the entire family feels at home in Cameroon.

ANALYSIS OF FIELD CHALLENGES AND EXPERIENCES

Let's now consider certain challenges the African missionary may face on the field. In this section I will address three related issues: (1) I will seek to analyze the challenges inherent in the field; (2) I will discuss some key experiences of a pioneer African missionary, giving special attention to the specific place of calling and the building of an indigenous church; and (3) I will attempt to evaluate the challenges and experiences in working with the sending agency, the indigenes, and fellow missionaries.

Primary and Field Challenges

Some of the challenges we had were particular to my own family, others related to the field. The first challenge was our leaving Nigeria amidst many open doors for ministry. For instance, as we were preparing to go to Cameroon, we received a scholarship grant to study at the West Africa School of Theology (WAAST) in Lomé, Togo. During the same period, the church we were pastoring was able to secure a large piece of property which had begun to develop. At the same time, the district presbytery had assured me of no transfer until I had developed my vision for the church. We were thus tempted to abandon our missionary vision in favor of these seemingly bright ministry opportunities.

Next came the language challenge, as mentioned above. When we arrived in Cameroon my wife had no knowledge of French whatsoever, so coping on the field was not easy. Also, during those early days, she struggled to adapt to the environment. The concurrent devaluing of the Nigerian currency posed yet another challenge. Although the AGN valiantly strove to care for their missionaries, when exchanged in other currencies, the allotted Nigerian naira did not go as far as before. As a result, sustaining the missionaries in the field became a burden on the sending church. The devaluing of the naira also mitigated much the missionaries wanted to achieve, and many envisioned projects had to be curtailed or delayed. In addition, missionaries on the field lacked a means of transferring money, so we had to look for other, more involved, means of securing our funds.

Finally, among the challenges we faced in Cameroon was one of being accepted by the host culture as missionaries from Nigeria. Unfortunately, there is a general belief in Cameroon that all Nigerians are dishonest. As a result, even a missionary from Nigeria is looked upon with suspicion. Over time, however, we were able to prove our integrity and love for the people. Rather than stopping our missions work in Cameroon, all of these challenges caused us to run back to God whose call and love for us was never in doubt.

Specific Place of Calling

God, who made us, knows what abilities He has put in us. He also knows where each person can serve Him best. Understanding this truth enables a church to maximize its complementary ministries and to expedite the evangelization of the world. I believe that God has mapped out for every missionary a specific place for a specific moment of time. C. Peter Wagner concurs, and posits that such strategy and timing is essential. He lays out four essential components of an effective missionary strategy: (1) the right goals, (2) the right time and place, (3) the right methods, and (4) the right people.[7]

When the right missionary is in the right place, the missionary effort is maximized. It is like setting the round peg in the round hole! The sending church and the missionary ought, therefore, to work with the Holy Spirit in deploying missionaries to their various fields of service. God will give the increase, but we must do the harvesting. In like manner, the right person must be present to conserve the harvest.

The superintending role of the Holy Spirit in missionary placement is demonstrated when He directed Paul and his companions to Macedonia (Acts 16:6-10). Even in the business world, successful companies carefully focus on people selection.[8] Sending churches must beware, for whatever reason, of sending out the wrong people, even when it's to the right place. Most setbacks on the field are due to the deployment of certain individuals to places where they do not fit. The sending churches, as well as missionaries, must be prompt in replacing or relieving persons who are not in the right places. Such prompt action will save cost and sometimes even the work itself.

Building an Indigenous Church

One key challenge for the missionary is to build an indigenous church. The indigenous church planting strategy points the people away from dependence on the missionary to dependence on themselves and on God. It helps them understand from the onset their role as members of the body of Christ and calls for wisdom on the part of the missionary. In our world today, with so many "prophets" striving to attract people to themselves, the work of building a truly self-supporting, self-governing, self-propagating church can be like rowing a boat against the wind.

From the start of the Nigerian effort in Cameroon the plan was to establish an indigenous Cameroonian Assemblies of God. From the beginning local Cameroonians were used to launch the work. Even when problems were encountered and more Nigerian missionaries were sent to enhance the work, the AGN mission never lost its focus on establishing an indigenous church. Thank God, today a strong, self-reliant work is emerging in Cameroon.

Self-propagating

Very early in Cameroon the newly-founded church was encouraged to partner with the missionaries in multiplying other local churches. They joined the work early enough to become evangelistic and missions-minded from the beginning. Local churches embraced their responsibility of planting other churches around them. Individuals took up projects of taking the gospel to their families, villages, and to other regions. Right now, one Cameroonian brother has embarked on raising what he calls "mega-churches" for the AG Cameroon. He began his work last year and has already personally invested about 10 million Central African Francs (approximately $20,000 U.S.) in just one church.

In the same spirit of propagating the gospel, the AGC has trained a pastor from the Central African Republic and has sent him back to his country to plant a church in Bangui. Though still young, the church in Cameroon is bent on being a missionary church.

Self-supporting

Before we were sent to Cameroon we were warned that they were not good givers. We agreed, however, with the late John V. York that all people are created in the image of God and can therefore do business with and for Him. So, from the beginning, while still receiving sponsorship from the sending church, believers in the new church were taught to support the work themselves. As a consequence, some structures at the new Bible college have been built by individual Cameroonian believers. Others have given property on which to build churches. One sister, with the consent of her family, gave her inherited land to build and furnish a church. Her children even saved their daily pocket money to help raise the structure. In addition, many believers have given various kinds of cars to pastors and missionaries to help facilitate their movements. The AGC General Superintendent currently lives in a duplex donated by a Cameroonian brother. He had constructed it for his retirement, but willingly gave it to the church for the Superintendent's lodging.

In order to enhance the self-supporting vision of the church, and to increase its ability to reach out with the gospel, the missionary introduced a concept to help facilitate the national church's missionary vision. Since the Cameroonian soil is very rich, he helped the church to establish agricultural projects that promise to help the church stand on its feet.

In addition, the missionary helped the AGC to institute a missions giving program dubbed Missions Covenant Price (MCP). Through the MCP program members are challenged to give just one hundred francs per month (about $2 U.S.) to missions. In receiving this special monthly offering, members are asked to come to the altar and ask for God's blessings for the sake of God's mission (Psalm 67:7). Through these offerings the people identify themselves with the mission of God. To date, proceeds from the MCP program have been used to purchase ten hectares (about 25 acres) of land containing about 1,200 palm trees. Some of the palm trees have already began to produce a harvest. One more prosperous local church caught the vision and is already harvesting and selling its produce. Other local church pastors in the rain forest zone have led their churches into similar projects. Today the AGN church has handed the work over to the Cameroonians, and, by God's grace, the work is supporting itself and growing stronger every day.

Self-governing

Soon after the AGC was planted, a local Counseling Committee was established. This committee was made up of three local leaders and two Nigerian missionaries. This scheme helped the church to learn to govern itself and prepared it for the future. When the time came to hand over the governance of the church to the Cameroonians, some felt that they were not ready, but, to God's glory, today the AGC is moving forward under local leadership. The missionaries now serve the church as partners and advisers. Today, the relationship between the sending church and the Cameroonians is cordial. Such handovers should not be viewed as national churches obtaining their freedom from the colonial missionaries, but as friends passing the baton to other friends. Effectively fulfilling the mission of God calls for brotherly partnership.

Working with Others

Missionary work calls for partnership on various levels. The missionary must learn to work with the sending church or agency, the nationals, and with other missionary colleagues. For these relationships to work effectively, great care must be exercised by all of the concerned parties, including the missionary. He must function as, what Jim Collin calls, a "Level 5 Leader," that is, he must model servant leadership.[9] He must strive to serve, not his own purposes, but the people to whom he is called, and he must serve well whether he is appreciated or not. William E. Goff has observed that "most missions' decisions are made by the group of missionaries in a given country or area. Ministries are carried out by the individual missionary family, but they are accountable to the mission and to the mission board through the regional staff."[10] While this may be true in a Western missionary-sending context, in reality, since in Africa missions is still in the emerging stage, there are some facets of the work that will need to be worked out on the field. Some of us African missionaries are thus serving as "test-tube missionaries." This situation calls for even greater understanding and patience on both the part of the missionaries and the sending church. It is, therefore, essential that we learn well from each of our experiences and from the Spirit of God.

Relationship with the Sending Church

The missionary and the sending church work together as a missions team. The missionary receives instructions from the sending church and faithfully presents the demands of the field back to them. On its part, the sending church must carefully avoid actions and situations that contribute to missionary attrition. As AGN missionaries, whenever we have appealed to our leadership for help, our sending church has always shown their trust in us and responded positively. This has been very encouraging, and helps to keep us going.

Relationship with the Nationals

The missionary's relationship with nationals should always be based on mutual respect and concern. The missionary must never see himself as the people's superior, and neither should he attempt to impose his culture on them. Also, in his effort to present the gospel, the missionary should carefully consider the cultural context of the people.

Sometimes nationals may become suspicious of missionaries, especially when those missionaries are fellow Africans. There is often the thought that fellow Africans, due to their limited resources, may not have the financial means to satisfy the economic demands of the nationals. However, when the missionary acts with openness and integrity, suspicion is alleviated, and a good relationship develops.

Relationship with the Missionary Colleagues

Sometimes difficulty is experienced when working with other missionaries on the field. Such difficulty occurs when certain missionary colleagues hold to visions, values, and goals that differ from the shared goals of the field fellowship. This situation can be exacerbated when missionaries on the field have no written policies establishing guidelines and limits for individual behavior.

If they are to achieve maximum effectiveness, missionary colleagues working on a given field should work together closely as a team. Like any organization, a team has structure; however, unlike other organizations, a team is more relational in approach and thus requires disciplined participation of each member. Teams are made up of peers who must necessarily cooperate with one another.[11] Missionary teams must therefore maintain a highly disciplined culture to ensure unity. By doing this they make it difficult for the enemy to invade their ranks.

Africa has joined other Two-Third World continents as an emerging missions-sending force.[12] As young missions agencies, many sending churches have yet to develop adequate policies and manuals to guide their operations on the field. Therefore, African missionaries in the field ought to exercise great patience and tolerance with one another and should assume servant-leadership attitudes. They should serve one another and their host cultures as under-shepherds "not lording it over those entrusted to you, but being examples" (1 Pet. 5: 3).

MISSIONARY MOTIVATION FOR THE AFRICAN CHURCH

Do you not say, "Four months more and then the harvest"? I tell you, open your eyes and look at the fields! They are ripe for harvest. Even now the reaper draws his wages, even now he harvests the crop for eternal life, so that the sower and the reaper may be glad together. (John 4:35-36)

Allow me to now end my paper with a few thoughts based on the above saying of Jesus.

Do Not Say Four Months

The disciples of Jesus were preoccupied with other lesser matters. So, when they saw Him talking with the Samaritan woman, they were oblivious to the fact that it was harvest time. In this context, the Lord warned them of the danger of procrastination during the time of harvest. His message was then, and still is today, *"The harvest is now!"*

A number of factors reveal such procrastination in the African church as it relates to missions. Sometimes we Africans look at our failing economies, the political crises in our countries, the continuing upheavals across the continent, the endemic hunger and starvation, the HIV/AIDS pandemic, and the great ethnic diversity of the continent, and we are tempted to ignore God's clarion call for missions. We fear leaving our comfort zones and launching out into the unknown. But the fact is, the conditions in Africa may never improve. Nevertheless, the gospel of the kingdom must still be preached throughout Africa and to the ends of the earth. Africa must heed the call of the Spirit. We as God's missionary people do not depend on our national economies, we rather depend on the economy of the Lord of the Harvest, and we must trust Him to supply our every need.

Open Your Eyes

The Lord of the Harvest told his disciples to lift up their heads and open their eyes and look on the fields. Only when we do the same will we see the realities around us. Africa is ripe for harvest. Many countries and ethnic groups are yet to be unreached with the gospel. Consider, for instance, Central Africa. If you lift up your eyes and look, you will see the great challenges awaiting the church. Poverty is rife in places like Central Africa Republic, Chad, and Niger. Political upheavals ravage many places, and in places Islam has engulfed the people, and may soon enslave them as it has enslaved North Africa thus making these places very difficult to penetrate with the gospel. And yet, at the same time, God is moving by His Spirit preparing these places for a great harvest. What we do, we must do now.

Even the so-called "reached" areas of Africa are being smothered by a cheap "prosperity gospel" that causes one to wonder about the true state of biblical Christianity on the continent. These challenges demand the establishment of more missions-oriented Bible colleges across Africa along with a curriculum review of the established ones.

The AG Africa needs a new synergy to fulfill its Decade of Pentecost mandate of reaching the unreached of the continent with the gospel before Christ's soon coming. We can partner with one another, and stronger national churches aiding and strengthening the weaker ones. Weaker churches can in turn welcome the stronger one to help them to reach the areas they are, at present, unable reach themselves. As in the days of Joshua, the missionary task can be apportioned and reached for Christ. In this regards, we would do well to heed the words of William D. Taylor, "We should never struggle to do something alone, that we can do better if we cooperate with others in partnership."[13]

The Field is Ripe

While God has called the church to many tasks, our supreme task is to take the gospel of the kingdom to the ends of the earth. It is to multiply churches throughout the earth.[14] As we lift up our eyes and look, we begin to see things as God sees them. Before us we see several challenges and many unreached peoples and places. For instance, we see the challenges of globalization and urbanization. We see theological shallowness of the church and the resurgence of traditional African culture. These factors and more present a clear challenge to the church, and we cannot afford to wink at any of them. We must not, however, allow any of these things to blind us to the fact that the fields of Africa, and the nations of the world, are ripe for harvest.

It is Time to Draw Wages

Every day we see the people of Africa thronging the streets of our cities and towns in a quest to earn wages. We also earn wages in the missions enterprise. The Lord of the Harvest has promised to reward those who labor for Him. This is the time to acquire stars for our heavenly crowns, and our hundredfold reward here on earth (Mark 10:30). God is a faithful rewarder of all who do His will (Rev. 22:12).

Joy Awaits the Sower and Reaper

Jesus has promised joy for both the sower and the reaper. When the unreached are reached, the sending church and the missionary can rejoice together. We also rejoice when we see the found join us in seeking for the lost. When I look at the church in Cameroon great joy fills my heart, knowing that Cecilia and I have, by God's grace, done our part in the harvest there. During the time of harvest the farmer forgets all of his tireless labors. The joy of the harvest outweighs the suffering of the planting and growing seasons. Fulfilled mission results in a fulfilled life!

CONCLUSION

In every missions endeavor challenges abound; however, nothing can quench the unspeakable joy of fully participating in the mission of God. Our experience in Cameroon has shown us that the work is not ours but the Lord's, for it is "not by might nor by power, but by my Spirit, says the Lord Almighty" (Zech. 4:6). The work does not depend on the efforts of man but solely on the great mercies of God (Rom.9:16).

In Africa today it is normal to be involved in intra-city and local evangelism. Some even venture into local cross-cultural efforts. There is, however, an alarming trend in many of our churches. Too often pastors and church leaders clamor for large churches in the cities where personal perks and benefits abound. And, once a pastor has settled into his church in the city, he seldom thinks of those remote areas where people languish with no knowledge of Christ and His salvation. How tragic! Christ's mandate for the church it to take the gospel to "all nations" and to the "ends of the earth" (Matt. 28:19; Acts 1:8).

The time has come for the church of Africa to arise to the challenge of missions. We must awake fully to our missionary calling. We must desire above all else a personal encounter with God and intimacy with the Holy Spirit, the true owner of missions. We must aggressively develop prayer programs that will prepare us for the challenges ahead. And we must do all knowing that the one who gives himself fully to participates in missions will receive great reward, both in this life and in the life to come.

ENDNOTES

1. William E. Goff, "Missionary Call and Service" in *Missiology: An Introduction to the Foundations, History, and Strategies of World Missions,* eds. John Mark Terry, Ebbie Smith, and Justice Anderson (Nashville, Tennessee: Broadman & Holman Publshers,1998), 334.
2. Attrition is when the missionary for any reason takes his or her "hand from the plow" or "looks back." In attrition, according to William D. Taylor in *Too Valuable to Loose,* the missionary leaves the field before the mission or church thinks they should for any reason. The reasons may vary.
3. John V. York, *Mission in the Age of the Spirit* (Springfield, MO: Logion Press, 2000), 215.
4 A "Damascus road experience" is considered by the author as having such a convincing experience that gives one the certitude of his or her calling. In every circumstance the person can hold on to such experience.
5 Kenneth C. Fleming, *None Dare Say No: An Introduction to Missions* (Emmaus Correspondence Course: nd), 99.
6. Denzil R. Miller, *Empowered for Global Mission: A Missionary Look at the Book of Acts* (Springfield MO: Africa's Hope, 2005), 114.
7. C. Peter Wagner, "The Fourth Dimension of Missions Strategy" in *Perspectives on World Christian Movements,* (Pasadena, CA: William Carey Library, 1981), 547.

8. Larry Bossidy and Ram Charan, *Execution: The Discipline of Getting Things Done* (New York: Crown Business, 2002), 110.
9. According to Jim Collins in *Good to Great,* the Level 5 Leader combines personal humility and professional will. He works to accomplish the goal of the group with no regard to who gets the credit (2001, 17).
10. Goff, 345.
11. Michael Pocock, Gailyn Van Rheenen, and Douglas McConnell, *The Changing Face of World Missions: Engaging Contemporary Issues and Trends* (Grand Rapids: Baker Academic, 2007), 252.
12. Denis Lane, *Tuning God's New Instruments: A Handbook for Missions for the Two-Third World* (Singapore: World Evangelical Fellowship, 1990), I.
13. William D. Taylor, ed., *Kingdom Partnerships for Synergy in Missions* (Pasadena, CA: William Carey Library, 1994), ix.
14. Donald A. McGavran, "Today's Task, Opportunity, and Imperative" in *Perspectives on the World Christian Movement: A Reader* (Pasadena, CA: William Carey Library, 1981), 541.

Missionary Care: the African Church's Challenge in Its Missions Enterprise

MILWARD MWAMVANI

In June 2012, after a long year of dealing with a seemingly endless string of stress-ridden issues, including being accused of being a foreign spy, a missionary family was expelled from the country of their calling. Emotionally spent, they painfully moved back home. Arriving there they longed to share their experiences with their church leadership and to and chart the way forward for their missionary career. Eight months passed and not one missions official had approached them, except for a communication informing them that their financial support would be terminated in three months. No one cared to know where the family stayed or what they were doing to sustain themselves. No one sought to advise them, or to listen to what they were thinking concerning their future in missions. Even the members of the missionary family's local church had no idea why the family was home, or for how long.

Tragically, this story is not unique. This family is like far too many other African missionaries, loudly acclaimed in meetings and forums, but desperately neglected in the reality of missions implementation.

In writing this paper I make no claim to comprehensive knowledge on these issues, nor do I seek sympathy. I merely tell a personal story, a story from which possibly others can learn, and through which the African missions enterprise may be saved from catastrophic consequences. It is a story representative of various African friends across the continent who have been involved in missions and who may at present be bitter and disillusioned as to how and why they even thought they could be missionaries in the African context. I trust that my story will minister to them and to the African missionary enterprise.

BACKGROUND

The closing decade of the twentieth century saw an impressive development in global Christianity as the then non-traditional missionary-sending regions of the world became actively involved in sending out their own missionaries. Movements like the Africa Assemblies of God's "Decade of Harvest" from 1990-2000, adopted the theme, "Missions, we can do it too!" This exciting mobilization in the Africa Assemblies of God (AG) helped to awaken the African church to its mandate to proclaim the gospel, not only in their home countries, but in cross-border endeavors also.

The concurrent launching of the Eleventh Hour Institute further emphasized this noble call that had began to gain popularity in the African AG.[1] Such mobilization campaigns reflected Emil Brunner's words, "The church exists by mission as fire exists by burning."[2] Africa's bold response was an acknowledgment of this honorable responsibility. The church in Africa was at last taking its rightful place as a full participant in God's mission to redeem the nations.

However, this otherwise noble response eventually began to reveal a not-so-noble trend that threatens to stall Africa's emerging missions endeavor. Exhibiting a genuine zeal in responding to the urgent call, and, in some cases, responding to the pressure to confirm published reports that the missionary sending epicenter of Christianity had shifted to the south, crucial issues concerning the sending and sustaining of missionaries were overlooked. Aware of these issues, Stan Guthrie addressed various trends and issues affecting missions.[3] Among these trends is the issue of missionary care. In this paper I will discuss this trend in more detail, especially as it relates to the missionary enterprise of the Africa AG.

The early church sent its best into the mission field (Acts 13:1-3). The church today should do the same. In doing this, one challenge, then, is how to keep the missionaries at their best. I submit that the issue of missionary care is possibly the most neglected issue in Africa's missionary movement. This issue threatens to derail Africa's efforts at mobilizing the church for missions. In addressing this trend, I seek to highlight certain gaps in missionary care and to propose possible solutions that, I believe, will help to secure the gains that have been made in mobilizing the African church for missions.

Guthrie noted how the non-Western missions movement is better known for sending people out than keeping them on the field.[4] This observation is very disturbing, and, while it is very sad, it remains very true. He has further observed three key contributing factors of this trend: lack of training, a lack of on-field pastoral support, and a lack of finances. Other pertinent issues should be addressed concerning missionary care. For instance,

- How will the emerging church sustain its missions if the major sending agencies are unable retain their workers on the field?
- Does a missionary have any say or determination in regard to the issue of missionary care on the field?
- Who determines the missionary's care needs?
- Does the missionary at any time have the right to demand relevant care?
- Who sets the standard for missionary care?
- What channels could be used in caring for missionaries on the field and at home on furlough?
- What systems need to be developed to ensure adequate missionary care?

I trust that these and other important issues concerning missionary care will be comprehensively addressed and answered by our Africa AG churches who are mobilizing and sending out missionaries.

MISSIONARY CARE IN THE LIGHT OF BIBLICAL MANDATE AND MISSION OF GOD

The salvation of the nations has always been at the heart of God. Clearly, the theme of all Scripture centers on the *missio Dei*.[5] According to W. R. Schenk, "Mission ... has its source in the nature and purpose of God."[6] Philip M. Steyne contends that it is not possible to understand the theology of the Bible apart from God's mission in the world.[7] Commenting on the significance of biblical theology in understanding missions, Graeme Goldsworthy asserts that the rationale for a comprehensive biblical theology rests on the consistent recognition of the person and work of Jesus of Nazareth as the goal towards which the whole Old Testament moves.[8]

A biblical theological understanding of missions helps us to better grasp the theology of sending. The accomplishment of God's mission necessarily involves sending, and the Lord who sends cares for those whom He sends. This truth is made obvious from many biblical examples, including the example of Jonah (4:6). Also, when Jesus sent out His disciples, He addressed the aspect of care and provisions (cf. Matt. 10:5-16; Mark 6:7-13; Luke 9:2-6). He knew these would be a concern to those He sent out. In addition, Jesus contrasted the requirements of short-term missionaries with those of long-term ones (contrast Luke 9:2-6 with Luke 22:35-38).

Antioch's Spirit-filled community included those God would send out as apostles (Acts 13:1-4). This passage echoes the apostolic practice of Jesus who Himself sent out apostles (John 20:21). It is significant that the word "sent" appearing in verses verse 3 and 4 is translated from two Greek words. The word used in verse 3 is *apoluosan*, meaning to free fully or dismiss (cf. Matt. 14:22; Mark 8:9; Luke 8:38), while verse 4 uses *ekpempthnentes*, means to dispatch or send forth (cf. Acts 17:10). This fact implies that God the Holy Spirit sent forth Saul and Barnabas, while the church simply released them to go. This insight is critical in our understanding a sending theology, and it helps us understand that God is central to sending. Also, the way the church in Antioch received the apostles at the end of each of their return journeys reveals the church's responsibility and participation in the sending of the apostles (Acts 14:26-26; 15:30; 18:22-23). Just as Jesus debriefed His disciples on their return from ministry (Luke 10:1-20), Paul and Barnabas were debriefed by their sending church. These accounts indicate that there was some kind of ongoing link and care for the sent by the senders.

J. Herbert Kane advised that missionaries and pastors—and all others with a vital interest in the evangelization of the world—should search the Scriptures in order to come to an understanding of the biblical basis for the Christian mission.[9] Reflecting similar views, G. Burbank believes that the ministry of sending is biblical, and it is useful to study Paul's communication with the people who sent him.[10] Doing member care reflects both God's heart and kingdom values. All through the Bible, God challenged and stretched His people. He wanted them to develop into all they could be to His honor and glory.[11] Agreeing with Bruce Swanson, David Pollock noted how "Barnabas separated from a rewarding, positive, long-term relationship with Paul in order to care for a wounded disciple named John Mark. The latter ultimately recovered to become 'profitable' to Paul (Acts 15:36ff; 2 Tim. 4:11)."[12] This shows that, along with God's call of the church to mission, He requires appropriate care for those going out to fulfill the missions mandate. This care allows them to serve with the knowledge that there are others who think about them and care about the work they do.

HISTORICAL REVIEW OF MISSIONARY CARE

William Carey is often referred to as the "father of modern missions." William P. Barker described him as an "indefatigable pioneer of the modern missionary movement."[13] Carey's personal life, however, was not so glorious but was filled with tragedy. His children and wife all succumbed to the diseases and climate of India.[14] Even today observers fail to appreciate the grave challenges of pioneer missions work. Taken alone, Carey's example may not give a full picture of the gravity of the subject. A clearer picture is revealed in the light of the experiences of other pioneering missionaries of that time.

Those nineteenth-century missionaries not only faced challenges of preaching the gospel to unbelieving communities, they also faced physical, emotional, and psychological challenges. Dorothy Carey's story of mental breakdown in India is well known, and earlier, in the 1700s, David Brainerd, a successful missionary to the native Americans, suffered depression and loneliness. Adoniram Judson is another example. The death of his wife and daughter resulted in a personal mental disorder from which he, thankfully, recovered. J. Hudson Taylor also experienced depression and related difficulties, and Mary Morrison struggled with adjustment, depression, and mental breakdown. Mary Livingstone was sent back to England alone with her children only to be ignored by them and struggle with alcoholism.[15] All of these serve as early examples of how psychological issues impact the lives of missionaries.

These are disturbing stories that many would want to ignore; however, we must ask ourselves some probing questions, such as, "Why did this happen?" and "What could have been done differently?" Take, for example, the issue of Mary Livingstone. What caused the church to ignore her? Could appropriate and necessary attention have been rendered? Are missionaries such "disposables"? Clearly, even in those days, there was serious need for adequate and compassionate care for missionaries.

These examples are from Western countries. Over the years, the sending churches in those countries have recognized the need to deliberately emphasize missionary care. Unfortunately, the Two-thirds World (TTW) missions sending agencies are repeating the same mistakes. The saddening fact is that "the health of African missionaries has not yet received much attention in many quarters. Generally, there is a lack of organized, consistent, ongoing provision for healthcare"[16] Naomi Famonure cites an example of a large denominational church in Central Africa that was jolted into the practical reality of the need for missionary care when one of its proven workers returned home devastated, broken, and will possibly never return to the field.[17] She observed that many African missionaries work under austere conditions, and are often stressed by many factors, including long years of work without vacation, lack of adequate provision, family and children's issues, trauma from civil or religious wars, communal clashes, and so on.[18]

Missionary care should not, however, be mistakenly identified as only a responsibility of the sending body. To a certain extent, care depends on the missionaries themselves. There is a part played by the missionary and the part played by the sending church. Unfortunately, due to the confusion of who is responsible for which part in missionary care, many missionaries go to the field without the necessary skills, adequate field supervision, mentoring, or appropriate care. In some cases, missionaries go themselves, to unreached and difficult fields without the support of any sending church or agency. In most cases, these untrained missionaries crash woefully and return home broken. Others manage to weather the storms and stay on; however, they sometimes harm the work and, consequently, shut the door to further mission efforts among the people group they serve.[19]

Although the malaise of inadequate missionary care predominantly affects the African church, Famonure has observed that occasionally there is similar confusion among missionaries from the West. Once a well-known missionary from an established missionary-sending country set up viable work among street children on a mission field. Then, for whatever reason, she became arrogant and stopped fellowshipping with the missionary community. She even defied counsel offered by leaders who made an effort to come from the home country to the mission field to help restore her. During the process she made threats to expose all of the underground missionaries in the sensitive country. Eventually all attempts at reconciliation failed, and the missionary was escorted from the country like a criminal. This happened, nevertheless, only after causing great damage to the missionary community. This story underscores the fact that both the missionaries and sending agencies have a significant part to play in determining the quality of missionary care.

A CLOSER LOOK AT MISSIONARY CARE ISSUES

We will now identify and analyze three missionary care issues that deserve immediate attention by the African church leadership, those of finances, training, and pastoral care. Ronald L. Koteskey has identified some pertinent issues in missionary care, including friendship, encouragement, affirmation, help, fellowship, sharing, communicating, visiting, guiding, comforting, counseling and debriefing. All of these and more are facets of care given by someone who understands the special needs of missionaries;[20] however, we will address only three.

Financial Care

As mentioned above, certain writers have discussed how the church's missionary sending epicenter has shifted from the Northern Hemisphere to the Southern. As a result, the world's new typical missionary is from the Two-thirds World.[21] Although all nations of the world face economic challenges, the TTW nations, including African nations, typically have more intense financial struggles. This in turn affects the resources for missionary support.

This economic hardship affects Africa missions in two notable ways: either it slows down the missionary sending momentum, or it "radicalizes" missionaries with a philosophy of going out in faith. This radical form of mission, sometimes called faith missions, is characterized by going to the field with no clear promise of support from a sending agency. This type of missions typified much of the mission enterprise of the nineteenth century. Most Pentecostal missions, including the AG at the beginning of the twentieth century, followed this model. Finance was not the determining factor in the deployment of those early Pentecostal missionaries. For the most part, they ignored missionary organizations and simply trusted God for support and guidance. Some of them, however, had more zeal than knowledge.[22]

Presently, the TTW missions endeavor faces similar challenges. While missionary sending zeal burns in African hearts, finances limit the process. As a result, Africa has its own missionary adventurers like those just mentioned. These courageous souls boldly declare, "I don't care for a mission board to back me with pledged financial support; I just need people of like precious faith to uphold me with their prayers and fellowship." They assert that, according to Acts 13:1-4, the Lord's method of sending forth missionaries is for the Spirit to call them, and then the church to send them.[23] While such declarations may help keep the fire burning and workers going forth, it is unlikely to effectively sustain the African missionary movement in the long run.

The philosophy that drives the faith mission model is not necessarily wrong; it simply reveals the importance of more coordinated efforts from the sending church. When such coordinated efforts fail, radicalization is inevitable. It is the only option left. The twenty-first century missionary force from the developing nations is sometimes poor; however, it is almost always spiritually radical. Therefore, juxtaposed to the more affluent church of the West, the new missions force is more in touch with poverty, oppression, and the supernatural.[24]

Additionally, the conditions on the world's remaining mission fields may no longer favor the faith mission model. The world is dynamic, and though missionaries are still required to go out in faith, situations in the missionary fields are not the same as they were a half century ago. Dick Brogden addressed this issue arguing for a partnership model among missionaries from different countries in order to more effectively reach the remaining challenging areas of the world.[25]

Another fact to consider is that the African missionary is often not the first to get to a particular field. Usually there are a number of other missionaries already there when they arrive, and there is a high probability that these first-comers are from the West and that they are better off financially than the TTW missionary. Negative social behaviors result from such situations. First, if the TTW missionary is not careful, when they compare their living conditions with those of the Western missionary, they are tempted to fall into the *dambos,* (Chichewa for "quicksand") of self-pity, Second, because the TTW missionaries, especially those from Africa, do not have financial resources to share with the national church (where it exists), the locals often view them as inferior to their Western counterparts. These are real issues, and they are sometimes so traumatic that missionaries leave the field and return home.

The above realities bring to the fore the fact that, while it is possible to be successfully involved in missions without the necessary financial support, it is clearly not desirable. Zeal without knowledge leads to frustration and disappointment.

Additionally, the extended family networks characteristic of Africa place additional pressure on the African missionary. This is because, in most cases, the missionary may be the first person in their family to get the chance of good education. As a result, parents and the rest of the extended family look to them for financial support. This stressful situation is worsened by the fact that, from a non-Christian perspective, an organization that sends you to work in another country must pay you very well. At the same time, the TTW missionary may go to a country where the cost of living is higher than in their home country, and hence, they actually live far below their perceived economic standard.

Typically, extended family members do not know the actual dynamics on the mission field, and as a result, they harbor high expectations for the missionary to support them—even more so now than when the missionary was living at home. This family pressure places additional stress on the African missionary, especially when they face the reality that they do not have enough money to support their parents. This scenario is similar to that of the Chinese. Garcia Wiarda has observed that many Chinese missionaries continue to give their parents a monthly allowance while they are away. To their parents this allowance represents a token of the child's gratitude for their care and provision when they were young. In similar manner, most African parents expect this token even if they may not openly ask for it.[26]

Regrettably, lack of financial discipline and a corresponding lack transparency in financial reporting stalks Africa's missions enterprise. This want of transparency is possibly the movement's greatest challenge. All too often missions funds are ill administered. For example, churches and individuals may make and fulfill pledges towards the support of a certain missionary or missions project, and then these designated funds are used to support the home office. This causes the missionaries to go without their needed support. To make matters worse, there is sometimes no communication with the missionary to let them know what is going on. These financial issues, if not addressed and remedied threaten to do irreparable harm to the emerging African missionary enterprise.

Pastoral Care

Appropriate pastoral care constitutes a powerful element of missionary care. Nevertheless, the ability to shepherd and care for missionaries is sorely lacking in most African missions departments. I personally consider the need for the pastoral care of missionaries to outweigh even that of financial support. Good pastoral care would greatly ameliorate most of the issues arising from financial concern. For example, effective pastoral care would easily affirm and counsel the African missionary living in self-pity because he does not have as much as his Western colleague. When a TTW missionary worries over such issues for too long, hope fades; however, when a perceptive pastoral team from home regularly and compassionately communicate with this missionary, the missionary is encouraged and his or her confidence is renewed.

Loneliness and a feeling of not belonging play a major role in missionary attrition. Mission work is hard, at times extremely hard. It is true, to a large degree workers need to be able to tough it out and to "hang in there," giving proper honor to their duty and to the Lord's call. However —and this is a huge however —the majority of good, hardy workers wear out if they are not developed and cared for, not just the "weak" ones. It is not necessarily weakness that leads to the failure of missionaries; sometimes it is a lack of good pastoral care.

I would, nevertheless, hasten to add that the missionaries themselves play a vital role in the implementation of effective pastoral care. Thus, for missionary care to work effectively, the missionary and sending church must come into mutual agreement on the necessary policies, procedures and infrastructures to facilitate such care.

Pastoral care should aim at supporting the missionary physically, emotionally, and spiritually. Such care is an essential component in determining the ultimate success of the missionary. Would it too be radical to postulate that most missionaries who fall into sin do so because of lack of pastoral care? The pastoral care of missionaries should include accountability partnerships which may be set up on the field. Careful reading of even the most eulogistic missionary biographies of the past reveals the need for, and, sometimes acute absence of, pastoral care of the missionary.[27]

Such pastoral care is an ongoing need for the missionary and missionary family, and it is essential during every phase of the missionary cycle, including the pre-field and re-entry phrases. It further includes the times when the missionary returns home for furlough, fund raising, medical reviews, or whenever they move from one mission field to another. Each phase has its own financial, psychological and emotional challenges. Missionaries experience cultural shock on varying scales either when they go to the field or when they return home.[29]

Is the Two-thirds World mission, especially in the African church, ready to fine-tune its ability to offer pastoral care to its missionaries? If not, and the leaders of the sending churches remain short sighted on this issue, missions casualties and missionary attrition will continue to increase. The failure to consult on the issues, coupled with the lack of financial resources, only make the situation worse. For example, most

African AG churches do not have in place a system to care for missionaries during their time of re-entry. Issues of deployment, re-assignment, re-entry, pension, along with a myriad of other issues of missionary care, must be addressed.

Even as early as during the training and deployment process missionaries must be made aware of how they may prepare for their return home. Peter Jordan likened the returning missionary to a spaceship returning to earth.[30] For both the spaceship and the missionary there is need for continuous monitoring and re-entry preparations. This also applies to tentmaking missionaries. They, too, can be victims of the reverse culture shock if they do not receive adequate pastoral care during their re-entry phase.

One way the sending body can offer pastoral care to the missionary is through intercessory prayer. Missionaries on the field are expected to continually give from their spiritual reservoir. With the passing of time, however, missionaries become less effective in ministry if they themselves are not spiritually replenished. The sending body has a great responsibility to spiritually support the missionary. Too often, while missionaries go about praying for others, no one prays for them. There is need to set up avenues for the church at home to regularly pray for missionaries. And there is a need to continually remind them that the church is praying.

Good communication is an essential attribute of any successful organization. Observation reveals that most African senders neglect this attribute Two-way communication between the missionary and his home church and friends forms a lifeline that must never be severed. Just as a lifeline enables a diver to perform normal functions in a different environment, so communication with the home church can enable the missionary. Cut the lifeline, and the diver struggles for life and has to abandon his work. In like manner, when the home church cuts the lines of communications, the missionary struggles and is tempted to give up the fight.[31]

Successful sending churches establish clear and open channels of communication. With open channels, missionaries are able to communicate and unload their burdens, both personally and in relation to the sending body. I have even observed delegations from their home church visit Western missionaries just to encourage them. While this might be costly from an African perspective, the sometimes total neglect of the missionary is an extreme that must be avoided.

Today, with missions from various sending agencies working together on the same field, missionaries are afforded the opportunity of developing two forms of partnerships. First, the missionary can establish partnerships with colleagues from other agencies and regions. Next, other official partnerships may evolve between various sending organizations. These partnerships provide great opportunities in addressing the pastoral care of missionaries.[32]

Training

Missionary training is intrinsically linked with missionary care. Effective training provides opportunities for significant discussions on missionary care issues. Training as part of the missionary recruitment process alerts the missionary to issues they may face on the field. The Eleventh Hour Institute (EHI) held in Lilongwe, Malawi, in 1999 enlightened me to this fact. The institute also helped to orient and prepare me for my first missions assignment. My favorite topic was "Surviving and Thriving in the Hardest of Places" taught by Dick Brogden.[33] I enjoyed this topic especially because the facilitator shared practical issues of missionary life in the country that I was entering.

Training prepares the missionary for the realities they will face on the field. Conversely, as Guthrie has noted, lack of training for TTW missionaries contributes highly to missionary attrition.[34] Missionary training should be robust and dynamic, and should present different models. Training is even more essential after the missionary arrives on the field. Such refresher courses could help very much. Effective training is outcome-oriented, field-based, and forthrightly addresses financial and pastoral issues. It must also include topics suggested by practicing missionaries. Such field input is essential and if used with appropriate consideration and reflection, could greatly enhance missionary training. On the other hand, lack of adequate training helps to engender lack of missionary care.

Deploying missionaries without proper training is like engaging a carpenter without the necessary tools. While training alone does not make a missionary effective, there is, nevertheless, a direct relationship between the quality and amount of training a missionary receives and his or her long-term effectiveness on the field.[35] Famonure observes that African missions agencies, much like their Western predecessors, have not adequately grasped the need for training or for the patient, careful selection of missionary candidates.[36] In some cases, however, it is not that the sending church does not grasp the need, but, because of the urgent and pressing need for workers, and the lack of necessary resources, training is not done.[37]

RESPONSE PROPOSAL

I am convinced that the African missions enterprise must immediately address the issue of missionary care. If the trends and issues discussed above are not adequately addressed, the African missions movement will be greatly and negatively affected. Western missions, after stumbling over the same stones in their formative years—and observing the disastrous outcomes—have in the more recent past aggressively addressed the issue of missionary care. In some cases they have instituted various specialized ministries to care for their missionaries.[38] Half a century ago missions sending agencies gave no serious consideration to missionary care; however, during the last quarter century they have become interested in member care. Today many agencies have mature member care departments and conferences are held on the topic.[39] The question, then, that begs to be answered is, "Will the African church have to have its own Dorothy Careys and Mary Livingstones before it wakes up to the need to take appropriate action?" I sincerely hope that his is not the case. The church already has enough such examples graphically revealing the need for missionary care.

In addition to the increased missions awareness and preparation engendered through mobilization approaches such as the EHI, there remains a need for more regular, localized training systems that will address the specific needs of prospective African missionaries. These systems should include input from serving and returned African missionaries. Since they will inevitably address practical issues, such training ventures would benefit both serving and prospective missionaries. Therefore, in lieu of the fact that casualties continue to rise among African missionaries, I will venture to make the following six recommendations, followed by a proposal:

Pre-deployment Training

First, I recommend that national missions departments should arrange pre-deployment missions training schools to orient their missionaries. This training might not necessarily mean that the church sends out a missionary every year, but annual missions training models nevertheless are a good habit to get into as the church gears for growth that will eventually lead to deploying at least one missionary unit each year. Missions training sessions can also be organized by local congregations to sensitize and mobilize church members. I am unaware of the progress in implementing one proposed partnership model that came out of Dick Brogden's presentation at the Pentecostal Missions Consultation in Limuru, Kenya on April 28-29, 2011.[40] I believe such activity could play a productive role in raising awareness of such training model.

Training is essential and greatly helps in dealing with unresolved issues in prospective missionaries' lives, issues which often become more haunting on the mission field. Pertinent information relating to the life of a missionary on the field should, as much as possible, be made available to missionaries. It is crucial that potentially debilitating personal issues be resolved before the missionaries leave, because, in most cases, resources are not available on the field to deal with them. Inevitably, missionaries will have more stresses on the field than in their own culture with their own support system.[41] Therefore, pre-deployment training and preventive pastoral care is a crucial issue in the survival of the missionary.

Missionary Care Systems

Second, I recommend that in addition to their sending and supervisory activities, the sending agencies should consider establishing mechanisms for the pastoral care of missionaries. While different sending agencies have developed different pastoral care strategies, at present few care systems are accessible to the African missionary. There are, however, some possible ways the African church can better provide pastoral care to its missionaries. As a beginning step, national church systems and local congregations need to immediately initiate pastoral care, counseling, prayer, and follow-up mechanisms for the care of missionaries. For instance, a select group of people could be commissioned and empowered to continuously communicate with the missionary on the field. These people, chosen as the permanent representatives, would then recruit others to join them in praying for and communicating with the missionary. This flow of care should begin with the missionaries' local church body and then move to the relationship with the sending agency.[42] For every missionary there should be at least ten very committed people for support. A missionary should not leave home without a group of people who are equally as committed and excited about the mission as are he and his family.[43]

Missions committees both at the local congregation level and the national level are also a source of pastoral care and oversight to the spiritual life of the missionary.[44] The mission committee's responsibility is to follow-up those that pledge to communicate with the missionary to make sure they are doing it. Mission executives or supervisors are the closest to the missionary and, therefore, should serve as the first line of pastoral care. They should communicate personally with the missionary, not only on official issues, but also on personal issues, just to know how the missionary is doing. Missionary supervisors should source personal prayer needs that the missionary wants to let the church know about. Part of a missions committee's responsibility would be to source the necessary funds needed for missions supervisors to visit the missionaries on the field during times of special need.

Missionary Care Partnerships

Third, I suggest that the African church would do well to seek out missionary care agreements with their Western partners who have already instituted missionary care systems in various areas. Such partnerships would be of great benefit to the African missions enterprise. Whatever the form of partnerships reached, they should aim at empowering rather than debilitating the African church. In forming these missionary care agreements, issues must be openly discussed and all possible ramifications investigated. These and other questions would need to be openly discussed and answered:

- Can Africans be legitimately recruited by Western mission agencies?
- Can the African missionary have full access the care systems established by the Western mission agency?[45]

Reentry Issues

Fourth, one oft-overlooked aspect of missions is the missionary family's re-entry into their home culture. I, therefore, recommend that this process, along with the necessary pastoral care issues surrounding it, should be addressed in forums such as the Eleventh Hour Institute and included in the missionary's pre-field orientation. This issue could also be discussed in local church missions training awareness courses. In addition, there is a need for every missions leader to undergo training on how to care for returning missionaries. This sensitivity must then be passed on to congregations since every church member needs to know that returning missionaries need special handling to help them to re-adjust to their home culture.

Financial Care

Fifth, financial care for missionaries is another crucial and sensitive issued demanding attention from the African church. Even a cursory look at African missions today reveals that support towards missions is generally insufficient and inconsistent. I, therefore, recommend that the church immediately begin to explore all possible means of increasing and strengthening the financial support of missionaries. Mission executives would do well to intensify visits to stakeholder churches in order to develop a good financial base. Developing a healthy financial base would help to ease many of the finance-related missionary issues. When the missionary and missions agency are well supported, pastoral visits to missionaries, as recommended above, can become a real possibility.

Since a lack of adequate financial support is a major contributor to missionary attrition, there is an immediate and critical need for the African missionary sending church to institute means of raising adequate missionary funds. The African church faces a dilemma. Despite insufficient financial income for mission work, there remains a necessity to dramatically increase missionary funding. While the current state of missions income is pitiable and discouraging, with wisdom and through consistent sacrificial giving, the financial base will grow increasingly healthier, and eventually it will be able to send more missionaries and to better care properly for those who are sent.

Tragically, as mentioned earlier, there have been times when sending agencies have unconscionably mishandled funds given for the support of missionaries on the fields and used them in other activities, leaving the hapless missionaries to despair and suffer unnecessarily. National churches and missions departments must therefore institute and enforce strict financial policies to ensure that the missionaries always receive their promised monthly support. Therefore, rigorous accounting policies and auditing procedures are essential in the administration of all mission funds. By exploring and utilizing various means of fund raising, missions-sending agencies should develop financial safety nets for the missionary. When adequate financial support for the missionary is not forthcoming, the national church or missions sending agency should serve as the safety net and cover the missionaries support until the situation is remedied. In no case should the missionary on the field be left to suffer without the means to live and minister.

Learning from Practitioners

Sixth, it is crucial that, in the successful implementation of the above proposals, that leaders be willing to listen to and learn from the actual missionary practitioners. In far too many cases missions leaders appear to be unaware or too busy to seriously consider issues affecting missionaries. And, in extreme cases, they seem to simply be unconcerned. Many times there is excitement in talking about how many missionaries a church or country claims to have sent out; however, commensurate excitement is often missing when it comes to tending the wounds of those same missionaries when they are wounded in battle.

A PROPOSAL

I, therefore, propose that the Africa Assemblies of God Alliance through its World Missions Commission should create guidelines and systems of mutual accountability in the area of missionary care among its constituent member churches. National churches could, then, be able to see how their colleagues in ministry are faring in the area of missionary care. Such a system could institute checks and balances among member sending churches.

CONCLUSION

Excitement regarding the involvement of the African church in missions is mounting, and, despite many challenges, the church has taken bold steps to move forward in missions. In spite of great financial limitations, the African church continues to do the impossible and send missionaries to the field. Nevertheless, the lack of adequate financial support, pastoral care, and training for African missionaries threatens the continued development and prolonged involvement of this emerging missions force. This fact must spur the African church to put into place mechanisms which will enable its new missions force to grow and thrive.

Such provision for the adequate care of serving missionaries would greatly strengthen the resolve of those involved in active missionary service. It would also motivate would-be missionaries to join the missionary force, knowing that they are serving under men and women who genuinely care about their well-being. I strongly believe that the slow progress in mobilizing workers in the African setting is, at least in part, due to the uncertainties that prospective missionaries struggle with concerning how they will be cared for, concerns which have been addressed in this paper.

In conclusion, I, therefore submit that it is incumbent upon the leadership of the African church to determine that the missionaries they send into the harvest fields of the earth will never be left without a compassionate caring base. The will never be allowed to crash and burn beyond recovery because their leaders failed to set up systems to ensure their appropriate care. The success or failure of the African missions enterprise, to a large extent, will rest on how we care for our missionaries.

ENDNOTES

1. The Eleventh Hour Institute (EHI) is a non-residential, mobile missions mobilization and training school operating under the auspices of Africa's Hope ministry in Springfield, MO, USA.
2. As cited by C. Van Engen in *God's Missionary People: Rethinking the Purpose of the Local Church* (Grand Rapids, MI: Baker Book House, 1991), 27.
3. Stan Guthrie, *Mission In The Third Millennium: 21 Key Trends for the 21st Century* (Waynesboro, GA: Paternoster Press, 2000).
4. Ibid., 31.
5. John V. York, *Missions in the Age of the Spirit* (Springfield, MO: Logion Press, 2000).
6. W. R. Schenk, "Mission Strategies," in *Toward the 21st Century in Christian Mission*, J. M. Phillips and R. T. Coote, eds. (Grand Rapids, MI: Wm. B. Eerdmans, 1993), 221; 231.
7. Philip M. Steyne, *In Step With The God Of The Nations: A Biblical Theology of Missions* (Louisville, KY: Cornerstone Publishing, 1992), 303.
8. Graeme Goldsworthy, "Biblical Theology and the Shape of Paul's Mission," in *The Gospel to the Nations: Perspectives on Paul's Mission*, P. Bolt and M. Thompson, eds. (Leicester, England: Apollos, 2000), 9-10.
9. J. Herbert Kane, *Christian Missions in Biblical Perspective* (Grand Rapids, MI: Baker Book House, 1976), 16.

10. G. Burbank, "Caring for Missionaries: Before, During and After" in *New Wineskins for Global Mission*, Sharon Stockdale and Helen Camlin, eds. (Pasadena, CA: William Carey Library, 1996), 164.
11. Bruce Swanson, "A Mind Set and Department For Member Care" in *Doing Member Care Well: Perspectives and Practices from Around the World*, K. O'Donnell, ed. (Pasadena, CA: William Carey Library, 2002), 436.
12. David Pollock, "Developing A Flow of Care And Care Givers" in *Doing Member Care Well: Perspectives and Practices from Around the World*, K. O'Donnell, ed. (Pasadena, CA: William Carey Library, 2002), 31.
13. William P. Barker, *Who's Who in Church History* (Grand Rapids, MI: Baker book House, 1969), 62.
14. Ibid., 63.
15. Brent Lindquist, "Psychology and Missions: A History of Member care in Cross-Cultural Ministry" in *Missiology and the Social Sciences: Contributions, Cautions, Conclusions*, E. Rommen and G. Corwin, eds. (Pasadena, CA: William Carey Library, 1993), 76.
16. Naomi Famonure, "Member Care for African Mission Personnel" in *Doing Member Care Well: Perspectives and Practices from Around the World*, K. O'Donnell, ed. (Pasadena, CA: William Carey. Library, 2002), 104.
17. Ibid., 96.
18. Ibid., 105.
29. Ibid., 96-97.
20. Ronald L. Koteskey, *What Missionaries Ought to Know: A Handbook for Life and Service* (Wilmore, KY: 2003), 183. (E-book downloaded from http://www.missionarycare.com/ebook.htm)
21. The phrase "Two-thirds World" gets its meaning from the world of economics. Demographers use "developing" and "developed" countries to contrast the Two-thirds World and the Western World. These terms reflect the economic status of the respective world regions.
22. Harold R. Carpenter, *Mandate and Mission: The Theory and Practice of Assemblies of God Missions* (Springfield, MO: CBC Press, 1988), 92.
23. Ibid., 94-95.

24. David Shibley, *The Missions Addiction: Capturing God's Passion for the World* (Lake Mary, FL: Charisma House, 2001), 167.
25. Dick Brogden, "Planting Churches among Unreached Peoples: How Do We Partner in Actively Reaching These UPGs?" in *Globalizing Pentecostal Missions in Africa,* Denzil R. Miller and Enson Lwesya, eds. (Springfield, MO: AIA Publications, 2011), 11-36.
26. Gracia Wiarda, "Challenges and Care for Asian Missionaries," in *Doing Member Care Well: Perspectives and Practices from Around the World,* K. O'Donnell, ed., (Pasadena, CA: William Carey Library, 2002), 47-48.
27. Swanson, 437.
28. Harold W. Fife, "The Pastoral Care of Missionaries," in *Evangelical Missions Quarterly,* 7:1, Fall 1970, 19, 21.
29. Ibid., 21.
30. Peter Jordan, *Re-Entry: Making the Transition from Missions to Life at Home* (Seattle, WA: Youth With A Mission Publishing, 1992), 14-22.
31. Denis Lane, *Tuning God's New Instruments: A Handbook for Missions from the Two-thirds World* (Singapore: World Evangelical Fellowship, 1990), 95.
32. The model propagated and tried by Dick Brogden might stand to be the best model yet practically applied in the African setting.
33. Dick Brogden, "Surviving and Thriving in the Hardest of Places" in *The Eleventh Hour Institute Handbook,* Murriell McCulley, ed. (Springfield, MO: Africa's Hope, 2000), 104-120.
34. Guthrie.
35. Larry D. Pate, "Pentecostal Missions from the Two-thirds World" in *Called and Empowered: Global Mission in Pentecostal Perspective,* M. A Dempster, B.D. Klaus, and D. Peterson, eds. (Peabody, MA: Hendrickson Publishers, 1991), 256.
36. Famonure, 96.
37. James Butare and Beth Snodderly have noted this need in "Another Alternative Training for Missionaries and Other Leaders Through World Christian Foundations" in *Missions Frontiers* (July-August 2004), 19.
38. Guthrie.
39. Koteskey, 182.
40. Brogden, "Planting Churches," 11-36.

41. Burbank (1996), p. 162
42. Pollock, 25.
43. Burbank, 164.
44. Ibid., 165.
45. Yusufu. Turaki, "Evangelical Missiology from Africa: Strengths and Weaknesses," in *Global Missiology for the 21st Century: The Iguassu Dialogue*, W. D. Taylor, ed. (Grand Rapids, MI: Baker Academic, 2000), 279.

Missions Possible: The Argentine Experience and the Africa Missions Movement

BRAD WALZ

Though there has been great advancement in the missions movement of Latin America, much of it is still in the pioneer stage, that is, the "infant" stage, the stage of "talking more than doing." Among all missional agencies in Latin America, the Argentina Assemblies of God (AAGA) is the largest. Its growth, however, is not a result of a general missions growth within Latin America. It is, rather, in spite of that fact that Latin America is stuck in the phase of talking rather than doing. The AAGA National Missions Department (NMD) has sent and supports about 160 missionaries in nearly 40 countries. Annually, missions offerings total about $1.5 million.

Several countries have borrowed ideas from the AAGA-NMD, and as a result, have themselves experienced growth in their missions movements. This is especially true of the Venezuela AG. The Argentina AG sent a missionary to them to help them form their missions sending structure. The El Salvador AG also has a strong missions structure, with 90 missionaries and an annual missions income of one half million dollars.

Allow me to share some of the principles and guidelines upon which the Argentina AG missions enterprise has been built.

FOUNDATIONAL KEYS IN THE GROWTH OF MISSIONARY VISION

The Foundation: God Calling People to Go

An effective missions structure must be built on the firm foundation of trust in the call of God. When Jesus sent out the Seventy-two, He told them, "The harvest is great, the workers are few; pray to the Lord of the harvest to call forth workers into His harvest" (Luke 10:2). Thus, we begin our missions work by calling on God. We, ourselves, cannot call anyone into missions; only the Spirit of God can do that. We can, however, pray for workers. In our Argentine experience, the Holy Spirit had already been calling workers, but the church was not ready to send them. We will talk more about this later.

The Right Leader at the Right Time

Building an effective missions agency requires the right people in leadership. In 1984 God called me go to Argentina as a missionary. Much of the foundation of that call occurred while I was in Liberia during the previous year. When my wife, Rhonda, and I arrived in Argentine, it was in God's timing. Our first six years were difficult; however, we were able to lay the foundation that sustained the explosion of new missionary candidates that began in 1995.

Today, in many African countries the circumstances are ripe for powerful missions growth. In many cases, however, that growth is not taking place because the right leadership is not in place. To complicate things further, it will take between ten and fifteen years for future leaders to emerge from those missionaries who will be sent, that is, missionaries who have actual missions experience. In Latin America, it is only now that experienced missionaries are taking over the missions leadership in their countries. It is very difficult to lead something you have not experienced. Also, it is important to understand that part-time, rather than full-time, leadership will slow growth. Therefore, in the beginning a national missions work must use much wisdom and extreme care in choosing the right person with the right gifts to lead the organization.

Focusing on the "Sending Call"

One key to the growth of the AAGA-NMD is the way the missions department helped the church understand the message of Romans 10:15: "And how can they preach, unless they are sent?" If God calls people to go, but the church does not understand its call to send, there is a breakdown in the process, the work is stalled, and the church does not fulfill the Great Commission.

Breaking the Poverty Mentality

Before any church—especially a church in the Majority World—can successfully engage in missions, the "poverty mentality" enslaving the people must be broken. In Argentina it has been a generation-long battle to break the mentality of *"No se puede"* ("It can't be done"). This deception from the enemy has long been used by Satan to keep a people's focus on themselves and off the people around the world for whom Christ died.

Correct Structures

In the beginning the AAGA copied the U.S. Assemblies God World Missions model of requiring that all missionaries be ordained before being sent to the field. However, in Argentine ordination in takes about ten years, not the two to three years as in the U.S. We were therefore forced to reassess our structures and make them more flexible and more in line with the Argentine context. We sought to be more responsive to the need and to those whom God was calling. Without compromising standards, our structures must be flexible.

One reason the AG emerged in the U.S. was that existing church structures were inflexible in their stances concerning the baptism of the Holy Spirit. And yet, today we Pentecostals sometimes make the same mistake. We create inflexible structures that are unresponsive to the move of the Holy Spirit. Because of such inflexibility, some with a genuine call from God have been forced to go outside the movement in order to fulfill their missionary calling.

One way the NMD became more flexible was to create various categories of missionaries. We created a Missionary in Training program for younger people who had no previous ministerial experience. We also created a short-term missionary category of one to six months deployment in order to help people gain missions experience and explore their missionary calling and commitment. We further created a bi-vocational category, and a category for those who will serve as pastors in other countries and not depend on Argentina for financial support while, at the same time, wishing to maintain a spiritual connection with the home church.

Having several missionary categories helped us to be able to receive younger people with a call. The vast majority of these have been successful in their missionary careers. Tony Pedrozo, for example, had been a health professional before applying for missions appointment. He thus had no official ministerial experience when we approved him as a missionary in training. Now, after successful missions terms in DRC and Chad, Tony serves the NMD as Director of Missionary Personnel. Had we not changed our structure and become more flexible, he, and others like him, would have never been able to go.

Funding the Mission

For a missions agency to be successful it must maintain complete transparency in the handling of funds. Tragically, corruption and poor administration of funds have hurt many Latin American and African programs. Several times someone has had to resign because of the mishandling of missions monies. Also, national churches that have tried to use a "pool system" in soliciting missions offerings have had much greater problems in raising funds than those that seek funding for individual missionaries, even if the funds are handled through a central office. People living in countries with endemic governmental corruption are skeptical about of giving money to a central office. They have a hard time trusting "bureaucrats" to faithfully distribute the funds. They want to know that their offerings are going to the persons or programs to which they were given.

Fortunately, the AAGA has been able to impact the rest of Latin America in breaking the it-can't-be-done mentality. Just a few years ago, Latin America had very few missionaries. Today, every AG national church in Latin America except Cuba has a missions sending structure. There are more than 500 Latin American missionaries being send out and supported in 79 countries throughout the world. Cumulatively, missions receipts have now exceeded five million dollars, and last year alone increased by nearly one million dollars.

A BRIEF HISTORY OF THE GROWTH OF MISSIONS IN ARGENTINA

Allow me to share with you a brief outline of the missions history of the Argentina Assemblies of God. It is my prayer that a few years from now the Africa AG will be able to share similar stories. Officially, the Argentine missions department started in 1983; however, shortly after that it almost closed due to meager results. Then, in 1989, it was "re-born" and in 1995 the explosion of new candidates began. Finally, in 1997 the we-can't-do-it mentality was broken as many missionaries went out. In 2009 the million-dollar mark was surpassed. The history of the AAGA missions program can be divided into the following five periods:

1. The Foundational Period

The early years of the AAGA-NMD (1989-1995) were a time of foundation laying both for the structure and vision of the future missionary movement. The agenda during that period included, among other things, conducting missions events, visiting churches to promote missions, producing missions materials, forming a national missions committee, and opening a missions office. During this period our first missionaries were deployed.

2. The Period of Explosive Growth

Between 1995 and 1998 the AAGA missions movement experienced explosive growth. During these years many who had earlier been called to missions came forward and began the process of missions appointment. The missions department responded in faith and began to aggressively send out those whom God had called.

3. The First Period of Consolidation

As a result of the explosive growth of the AAGA missions work, the NMD had to do some serious catching up. Between the years 1998 and 2004 we worked hard to revise and expand our management structures and policies to reflect the new realities. During this time we were forced to face and respond to Argentina's 2002 economic collapse. This collapse resulted in a huge devaluation of the Argentine peso. However, God was faithful, and by His grace no missionary had to return home because of lack of funding!

4. The Period of Maturity

During the next period, from 2004-2009, the NMD became a "mature" missions sending agency. We began to prepare for what we felt would be the next wave of missions deployment. In doing this we added more staff and brought veteran missionaries home from the field to help us in our administrative duties. Other adjustments were made. In 2008-2009 more candidates were processed and sent out.

5. Today: Looking to the Future

Today, in our Future Potential Missionary group we are discipling more than 200 candidates called to more than 70 nations of the world. Our breaking the million dollar barrier in 2009 has been a powerful symbol in inspiring the Latin American AG missions movement. After the barrier was broken the movement experienced explosive growth in new givers in both 2010 and 2011. By God's grace, the future is bright for the AAGA missions movement.

CHALLENGES IN THE PROCESS OF BECOMING "SERIOUS SENDERS"

Any national church desiring to launch a missionary movement must become serious about not just inspiring committed "goers," but about raising up and mobilizing serious "senders." In doing this a church faces certain challenges. One challenge is channeling a move of God among lay people in a church culture of pastors. In our Argentina experience, in the beginning of the missionary movement many of those open to hearing God were lay people, *"el pueblo,"* and not the pastors and leaders. This development inevitably caused tension in the ranks, since in the past every new initiative had come from the pastors.

The pastors often had a vision of "It can't be done!" and embraced a poverty mentality. They often expressed the sentiment that the Argentine church was too poor to send missionaries. A saying used in Latin America is "The pastor can be the key, or he can be the nail." In other words, he can unlock the door or he can nail it shut.

It is difficult but essential that the missions movement of a national church reach, what Bill Taylor calls, "critical mass" in sending out missionaries (*Global Mission Handbook: A Guide for Cross-cultural Service.* Steve Hoke and Bill Taylor, eds. Downers Grove, IL: InterVarsity Press, 2009). By that he means that the movement must send out enough missionaries that the people perceive its structure to be solid. They must be confident that the movement is sound and will not disappear. According to Taylor, critical mass is reached when a church sends at least 50 workers to the field. In Argentina we believe that we reached critical mass at 30 missionaries.

If, for example, a national church has only three missionary families in the field, and one of them gets discouraged and quits, or has a unexpected emergency, health problem, or moral failure, it affects a full one third, of the entire missionary force. But if you have 30-40 missionary units in the field, the impact is not as great.

KEYS TO THE TRANSITION FROM A RECEIVING MENTALITY TO A SENDING VISION

How can a national missions department move a people from a receiving mentality to a sending mentality? In order to develop a sending vision in a national church the missions leadership can do the following:

Start!

First, we must simply *start!* In Africa the time for talking is finished; the time for doing had arrived. In the beginning, however, do not expect the masses to follow your vision. Just start with the few who will quickly embrace the missionary vision. In Argentina we started with five donors and churches; today have about 1,200. In 1989 we received only $2,000 in donations during the entire year. Now, that much comes in every four hours of an eight hour day. But first we had to start.

Good Leadership

Next, it is essential that you start with good leadership team. Find those great leaders, then empower them to do the work. Whatever you do, do not appoint someone who is not a real leader or someone who does not have a genuine passion for missions. To do so will kill the work from the beginning.

Perseverance

In addition, if the church in Africa is to transition from a receiving to a sending mentality, it must be prepared to persevere in the effort. Problems and challenges will surely come, but we must never give up. God has promised to reward our faithful commitment to His mission (Gal. 6:9).

Prayer

Committed, faithful prayer is another essential key for mounting a successful missions movement and for transitioning a church from a receiving to a sending mentality. Pray and organize prayer meetings for harvest workers. While we need to pray for many things, we cannot mount a missionary movement without two things: workers who will go and people who will send. We cannot call the workers ourselves, but God will if we will ask Him to. We must, therefore, "Ask the Lord of the harvest, therefore, to send out workers into his harvest field" (Luke 10:2). The Scriptures assure us that our tears will soften the dry soil and make it ready for the future harvest (Psalm 126:5).

KEYS IN DEVELOPING A SENDING VISION

There are several keys to developing and cultivating a sending vision in a national church. Here are some of them:

Work with the "Now"

As Africa develops its sending vision, it is important to remember that we can only work effectively in the "now" and not the in future. We must take things as they are and move in the direction they need to be. In Argentina we had to work not just the future church through Bible school training, but also with local churches and pastors. In mobilizing a church for missions our Bible school programs are very important and must not be neglected; however, an effective missions department is even more important. If you do not reach the now, the future gets discouraged. It has to work for many years under the reality of how things are in the "now." While it is important to sow seeds for the future through Bible school training, it is just as important to work in the now through missions departments.

Go Church by Church

As you develop your national sending vision, it is important that you go church by church casting the vision of mission. Start with those who are open. Soon they will begin to help you spread the message. When we began our missions program in Argentina, we went to every local church that would allow us to come and we helped them get started. Personal contact and working with local churches are key factors in the growth of a national missions movement.

Create a Promotional Network

As you seek to cast your missions vision in the church, very early in the process you should create a promotional network. This will be a network of pastors and lay people who share the missionary vision. Once you locate these people, mobilize them to help you spread the vision. In Argentina we used lay people and some key pastors who shared our burden. We made them missions coordinators and mobilized them to help sow the vision church by church in their areas of influence.

Visit the Churches

Once we had chosen our missionaries we required them to visit the churches raising their own support. Many said that it would not work, but it did. The personal contact between the missionaries and the local churches was a key factor in the growth that followed. As the missionaries were raising their own support, they were also spreading the vision of missions, and the churches caught the vision through these missionary visits. They began to identify with particular missionaries and wanted to support them. We found that this method worked much better than using a central fund into which churches gave to be distributed by those at the head office.

Utilize Events

In order to instill a missions vision into a national church it is necessary to take advantage of every national and district event. Do your best to be at every major function of the church to promote the missions vision. Leaders should give space for a missions presentation at each event.

Accurately Report Finances

If the missions enterprise is to grow and prosper in Africa, there must be absolute fidelity in handling funds and complete transparency in financial reporting. Annual reports must be accurate, clear, and thorough. In Argentina we prepare and present annual printed reports. We report even our administrative expenses so that no one can make incorrect assumptions about our use of missions funds. This transparency has resulted in great confidence among the constituency and has lead to increased giving.

Make Annual Tours

It is important that we take the message of missions to the grassroots. National missions tours can go a long way in helping to instill a sending vision in the church. Once a year in Argentina we conducted a two-week missions tour. During the tour we preach the same message throughout the country, exposing thousands of people from hundreds of churches to the national missions vision.

Work with Other Departments

The missions department must work hand-in-hand with other departments of the church. The women, the men, the youth, and others must all be encouraged to support and promote the missions vision of the church, and in turn the missions department must support the programs of the departments.

Use Statistics

In instilling a missions vision in the church it is important to gather and use statistics. Accurate statistics can be used to inspire and challenge the people. They can help to make missions a reachable goal. In Argentina we took common household products, such as tea, and showed people how a little bit of daily or weekly sacrifice on the part of many can lead to huge amounts of giving. For example, if everyone would give the value of a cup of tea just five times a month we would be able to generate three million dollars a year for missions. The same thing could be done in Africa. What if everyone would fast just one bowl of rice per month and give the money saved to missions. Millions of dollars could be raised for missions. This could help to destroy the poverty mentality and the we-can't-do-it spirit in many of our churches.

Involve Leaders

Do not make the mistake of only having a few insiders make all of the missions decisions. Build a large team by involving as many leaders as possible in your national missions committee. In Argentina, we were able to place many key leaders on our missions committee and involve them in decision making. This helped add credibility to the message and caused widespread buy in of the missions program.

Teach about Missions

Ultimately, missions is discipleship. On every level of training teach what the Bible says about missions. Train people concerning missions vision and biblical principals of giving. Just as Christians need to learn about tithing, they also need to learn about their responsibility to give in order that the gospel my go to the nations. This is a vital part of discipleship.

TEMPTATIONS TO KEEP US FROM ADVANCING

As we mobilize our churches for missions many hindrances and temptations will come, tempting us to back off or give up the fight. We cannot let such temptations stop us. We must press on until the victory is won. Such temptations include the following:

Satanic opposition

As we seek to advance the kingdom of God in the world, we must understand that we are involved in a great spiritual warfare. Our enemy, the devil, does not want missions to prosper, and he will do anything he can to limit the church's vision to its own country. We must resist him through Spirit-anointed prayer and through spiritual warfare.

Discouragement

We will at times become discouraged and be tempted to give up the fight. We must not, however, lose focus of the vision and the objective. During times of discouragement we must trust firmly in the promises of God. It is His work, and His vision, and He will bring it to pass.

Wrong Attitudes

Further, as we move forward in mission, we must guard our hearts against all wrong attitudes. It is very disheartening to see men of God reject a missions vision, and we may be tempted to become resentful and bitter. We must, however, resist such attitudes. We must, rather, seek to cultivate a positive attitude and a strong confidence in God. As we speak with a prophetic voice, calling our churches to the mission of God, we must do so out of sincere hearts. Also, during the early days, when the work is small and struggling, we must resist the temptation to feel insignificant. We must never "despise the day of small beginnings." If we will persevere, God is faithful, and He will prosper the work.

Trust in Self

We must avoid the temptation to trust in ourselves and in our own abilities and ingenuity. On the contrary, we must trust fully in the leadership and guidance of the Holy Spirit, and not in our own "creative" methods. We use ideas, but we depend on God.

It may seem that missions is an impossible task, but it is very possible! Argentina has faced and overcome many of the same challenges that Africa faces today. When we face the impossible, we must remember the words of the prophet: it is "not by might, nor by power, but by His Spirit says the Lord of hosts" (Zech. 4:6). Truly, we "can do all things through Him who gives us strength" (Phil. 4:13). Missions is not impossible—*it is possible!*

CASTING VISION FOR THE MISSION OF GOD

Let's now discuss the issue of how to cast a vision for the mission of God in a national church.

Moving from a Mission Field to a Mission Force

In 1987 a historical meeting was held in San Pablo, Brazil. It was the forerunner for what would become "COMIBAM," the Latin American Interdenominational Missions Network. In that gathering, sponsored in part by Luis Bush, the gathered leaders made a historical declaration. "From now on," they boldly declared, "Latin America is not just a mission field, but a missions force."

However, there is a saying in Spanish, *"De dicho al hecho hay un gran trecho."* This proverb declares that "between saying something to making it happen there is a great ditch." And so it has been in those 25 years since that historical pronouncement. Today, Latin America has become recognized as a missions force, yet the tragic reality is that most of the churches in these countries are still in the infant (or pioneer) stage of missions.

Through the years hundreds of God-called young people have

become discouraged and have abandoned their call because their church leaders had no missions vision. Today, in all of Latin America, there are only one or two missions agencies that have sent out 100 or more workers. One of those agencies is the Argentine AG Missions Department. In the remainder of this paper I will seek to help the African church avoid the tragic fate of the Latin American church, that is, of getting lost in the *trecho,* the great gap between saying and doing. It is easy to talk about missions; it is not as easy to do it. It is easy to say Africa has great potential—for indeed it does—but it is not so easy to turn that potential into reality.

In a sense, Africa has already spent more than a decade in the *trecho.* The church has held its Eleventh Hour Institutes and its Missions Consultations throughout the continent. I can remember back as far as 1999 when John York frequently shared his vision that Africa would transition from a missions field into a missions force. The themes discussed in this Missions Congress are not new. They have been discussed before. And hence the challenge: *it is time to get out of the trecho and move to the reality of sending.* As Dr. Lazarus Chakwera declared in 2009 in Limuru, Kenya, at a consultation on Islam, "Africa needs to stop talking about doing missions and start doing it!" And, in the words of Tony Pedrozo during the Pentecostal Missions Consultation held in Limuru, Kenya, in 2011, we need to adopt a "Nike theology" of missions for Africa. It is time to *"Just do it!"*

In order for an infant missions movement to transition from an idea into a reality, its leadership must have a clear vision from God. However, it is not enough for the leaders alone to have the vision. They must share the vision with the younger people to whom God is also speaking. Then, for the vision to become a reality will require much work, sacrifice, and commitment.

Vision Begins with Revelation

A true vision for the mission of God always begins with a revelation from God. There were two major disappointments in our missions experience in Argentina. The first was how, in the beginning, many of the leaders did not understand the missions vision. As a result the vision often came from lay people, or even the young people as they were being called into missions service. A second disappointment was how many of our larger and more otherwise visionary churches did not catch the vision for world missions. It was confusing, because some would ask, "How can God's leaders not have a vision for what is so close to the heart of God?"

Reasons for No Missions Vision

There are a number of reasons why the leaders did not have a vision for missions. While I cannot speak with authority about why many African leaders have not caught the missions vision, I can speak with some confidence about Latin America. I am sure that many of the factors present in Latin America are also present in Africa. Here are five of them:

1. Feeling satisfied that we have reached our country and not realizing that God wants us to reach the world. How can it be that Christian leaders in countries that are 10%, 20%, or 30% evangelical feel no urgency to reach out to countries with Christians numbering only in the hundreds, or even dozens? How can we be satisfied with the growth of the church in our country when Christ's commission is for us to reach the world?

2. Having a "great vision" that does not include the Great Commission. Some have a vision that involves great buildings and great numbers of people without realizing that the Great Commission is at the heart of any truly great vision. Sadly, some of the greatest visionaries in our countries have had some of the smallest world visions. A great vision cannot be limited to buildings and numbers; a great vision is focused on the Great Commission.

3. The inability to break a poverty mentality. Some Latin American and African leaders continue to think, "We cannot do missions because we do not have the resources of the West." Missions, however, does not begin with money, but with people. It was so for Jesus and His disciples. Jesus did not say that there was a shortage of resources, but a shortage of workers (Luke 10:2). The spirit of poverty is one of the greatest hindrances to the growth of missions in the Majority World. In most of our Latin American and Africa countries we are not even giving 1 to 2 cents per person per month to missions. There is no shortage of money or resources in our churches; there is a shortage of vision.

4. Not realizing that God is calling our young people to reach the nations. Some leaders fail to realize that God is calling the youth of our churches to go to the nations. In some cases leaders even discourage them from being willing to pay a price for that call. Often, in the beginning, young people and lay people quickly embrace a vision, while the pastors and leaders reject or resist it. In Argentine, many young people went to the field without the emotional and spiritual support of their leaders. Oftentimes missions surged from the grass roots instead of from the leadership.

5. Being bound by rigid policies and politics. Sometimes leaders are so bound by policies and church politics that they are unwilling to institute new more dynamic structures that better respond to the urgency of the hour. For instance, even today there are several national churches who elect their missions leaders from the national assembly floor in spite of the fact that 85% of those pastors casting their votes refuse to support missions. Tragically, we have sometimes allowed our Constitutions and By-laws to limit our missions vision. Let us not make the same errors that forced early Pentecostals to abandon their old churches and form new ones. Let us not allow our structures be more important than our responses to the Spirit. We must rather adjust our structures to respond to the move of the Holy Spirit.

Africa can learn from Latin America's mistakes, and speed up the process of their climbing out of their own *trecho*. It is time for Africa to move from talking about missions to doing missions.

Needed: A Fresh Vision from God

True missions vision comes only by divine revelation. Only the Spirit of God can cause us to understand God's great love for the nations and His desire to include them into His family. If we had understood God's call, we would have already obeyed, and, if we have understood, and yet we have not obeyed, then we stand guilty before God.

Often our preconceived ideas keep us from understanding God's call on our lives. We need His intervention to cause us to see things as He sees them. Think of Peter. He was genuinely full of the Spirit and was mightily used by God in word and deed. And yet, it took a heavenly vision to open his eyes to how God wanted to include the Gentiles into His family (Acts 10-11). God's rooftop revelation to Peter contained no new truths, for Jesus had already taught Peter about these very things. However, until then, Peter had not understood. So God intervened by using a seeking Gentile man and a heavenly vision to alter Peter's perception of His will. The next day at Cornelius' house Peter testified of his own "conversion" experience. He told Cornelius, "I now realize how true it is that God does not show favoritism, but accepts from every nation the one who fears him and does what is right" (v. 34).

Peter's revelation of God's will concerning the Gentiles was made even more profound when God astonished Peter and his Jewish companions by pouring out His Spirit "even on the Gentiles" (10:44). Peter later testified, "If God gave them the same gift he gave to us ... who was I to think that I could stand in God's way?" (11:16). As it was for Peter, so it must be with us today. Only divine revelation can open our hearts and our eyes to see God's great love for the unreached peoples and places of the world.

If the African church is ever going to move from saying to doing, it, like Peter, will need a fresh revelation from God. And it will need a deep conviction that will drive it to new priorities and a new commitment to reach the lost at any cost. We must solemnly resolve that ten years from now there will not be another consultation dealing with these same issues. It is time for Africa to finally embrace a Nike, or *"Just do it,"* theology of missions.

Securing God's Provision

In Africa there may be a shortage of vision, passion, and commitment to God's mission, but there is no shortage of resources to carry out the mission. The story of how God provided for Elijah in the midst of a widespread economic depression in Israel has strong missiological implications (1 Kings 17:11-16). In the story God led the prophet away from a place of provision to a place of dependency. He led Elijah to depend on a poor widow woman, something that was, at that time, culturally spiteful. God did this, not because He needed the help of the widow take care of Elijah, but because He wanted to use her and bless her. In the same manner, God does not need our help, and yet He wants to use and bless us. Unfortunately our fear, like the fear of the widow, often keeps us from obeying God. We, therefore, like her, must overcome our fear, and through faithful and obedient giving, secure divine provision. This story illustrates the principal that, when we depend on God, there will be no shortage of resources for sending missionaries. While God can miraculously rain down manna from heaven, He usually supplies our needs, as He did through the widow of Zarephath, through the gifts of His people. So it is with funding missions.

We've considered divine supply, now let's consider how God can use our human resources to fund His mission. Let's look at four representative examples from Africa AG national churches:

1. *National Church A* has 10,000 churches, and 2,582,000 adherents.
   - If everyone of its local churches would give only $10 per month to missions (you can convert the amounts into your local currency using the current exchange rate), in a year's time that would result in more than one million dollars being given to missions. And, if every church gave $50 per month, that would result in more than five million dollars being given to missions.
   - If every member would give only 10 cents per month (or the equivalent of about one bowl of rice), that would result in more than $3 million being given to missions in a year. And if each one gave $1 per month to missions, that would result in more than $30 million being given to missions in one year.

2. *National Church B* has 3,343 churches and 1,050,000 adherents.
   - If every local church would give only $10 per month to missions, in one year's time that would result in more than $400,000 being given to missions. If every church gave $25 per month per months to missions, that would result in more than one million dollars per year being given to missions.
   - If every member would give only 10 cents per month to missions, that would result in more than $1 million being given to missions in one year. But If every believer would give $1 per month to missions, that would result in over $12 million being given to missions in one year.
3. *National Church C* has 3,218 churches and 483,000 adherents. (Note: This is the ninth largest AAGA-related national church in Africa, which means that there are eight national churches larger.)
   - If everyone of its local church would give only $10 dollars per month to missions, that would result in $386,160 being given to missions in one year.
   - If every member would give only 10 cents per month to missions, that would result in about $579,600 being given to missions in one year.
4. *National Church D* has 2,706 churches and 1,571,000 adherents.
   - If every local church gave only $10 dollars per month to missions, that would result in $324,720 being given to missions in one year.
   - If every member would give only 10 cents per month to missions, that would result in about $1.9 million being given to missions in one year. But, if every believer would double that figure and give 20 cents per month to missions, that would result in of $3.8 million being given to missions in one year. Further, if every believer gave $1 per month, that would result in more than $18 million being given to missions in a year!

As you can see, there is no shortage of financial potential in Africa.

If the Africa AG would catch the vision for missions, and act on that vision, the potential is staggering. Today the Africa AG, conservatively speaking, has 16 million adherents meeting in 65,000 local churches across the continent. Therefore, if every local church gave just $10 per month to missions, in one year 7.8 million dollars would be given to missions. With that amount the Africa AG could send and support 650 missionaries at $1,000 per month each. Likewise, if every member gave just 10 cents per month to missions, that would result in 19.2 million dollars being given to missions in one year. With that money 1,600 missionaries could be supported at $1,000 per month each. And, if each one gave just 20 cents per month to missions, that would result in a whopping $38 million dollars being given to missions in one year!

So you see, there is no shortage of resources in Africa to send out missionaries. There is rather a shortage of vision, of passion, commitment, and action. In Latin America we have used a kilo of bread, tea, coffee, or rice to illustrate this principle. You could use similar illustrations from your African context.

In 1989, when Theodore Williams from India was preaching in Argentina, he challenged believers, "It's not what you do not have, but it's what you do with what you do have!" Far too long many in the African church have focused on what they do not have, rather than doing what they can with the abundant resources that God has given to them. Remember, just as the man in the parable of Jesus who buried his one talent was given no more, a poverty mentality begets more poverty. Not being good stewards of our God-given resources means that we will have even less to invest in the future. It is time that we begin doing what we can with what we have. We will then be amazed at how God will bless and multiply our resources so we can do even more in the future.

When African Missionaries Go

When African missionaries go to the field several positive things result. First, when they go, they reaffirm the truth that the God of Scripture is not a Western God, but the God all peoples, tongues, tribes, and nations. While it is true that many of the early missionaries were white and from the West, this must no longer be the case. During this, the time of the "Eleventh Hour Harvest," and the Africa Assemblies of God "Decade of Pentecost," how glorious it will be to have missionaries who truly reflect the ethnic diversity of the Day of Pentecost—a diversity, not of just those receiving missionaries, but of those sending missionaries to the nations (cf. Acts 2:5-12).

Second, when African missionaries go, we are reminded that it is "not by might, nor by power, but by My Spirit" that God accomplishes His purposes in the earth (cf. Zech. 4:6). Through African missionaries we will once again discover that missions is not built on the powerful economies of powerful nations of the world, but on a missionally-focused, Spirit-empowered church.

Third, when Africa's missionaries go forth it multiplies the spiritual army needed to reach the least-reached peoples of the world. It is impossible for any one segment of the church to penetrate all of these yet-to-be-reached nations and people groups of the world. We must finish the task together.

Fourth, when African missionaries go to the nations, it multiplies the prayer power and prayer focus of the church. This is because those who have a immediate contact with the unreached peoples and places of the world can best pray for them. We naturally pray more intensely for those peoples upon whom we have a direct impact, and with whom we have a closer relationship.

Fifth, when African missionaries go out, economic blessings are unleashed on those sending them to the nations. These blessings come directly upon the sending church and indirectly on the country in which the church resides. Argentine evangelist, Carlos Annacondia, once declared, "Argentina will never become an economically blessed nation until it first becomes a missionary nation." The same is true for any country in Africa. God's blesses those churches and nations who serve Him and His mission.

CONCLUSION

In fulfilling its missionary destiny the African church is engaged in great spiritual warfare. Using the illustration of a general leading his armies, we can imagine our archenemy, the devil. He knows that he has already lost many countries of Africa. In these countries the church is strong and growing stronger every day. The devil must, therefore, reluctantly concede that the kingdom of Christ has gained the victory in these countries. Now, his obsession is to limit the damage as best he can. What he fears most, however, is a church with missionary vision, that is, a church which threatens to boldly advance into new territories with the message of Christ. Therefore, in Africa the devil's top priority is to thwart the missions vision of the church—even if that means distracting leaders with the fascination of even more growth in their own countries. As long as their focus is limited to their own national or ethnic boundaries, he is satisfied. If the advance of the church is confined to the areas he has already conceded, it is a manageable concession. An African church with a vision for the unreached nations of the world is what Satan fears most!

May we open our spiritual eyes and receive a revelation for missions as never before. May we come to profoundly understand that we are involved in a great spiritual warfare, and on some grounds the enemy has been gaining the edge. Churches which should by now have hundreds of workers serving around the world, have a mere handful. Let us not be blind to the spiritual aspect of this battle. Satan does not want the African church to have a vision for missions.

Will our vision be like Peter's or will it be like Paul's? Will we be satisfied with the growth of the church only among our "Jews" and in our "Jerusalems" and "Judeas"? Will we continue to ignore the "Samaritans" and "Gentiles" in our own countries and around the world? Or, will we hear the call of God to go in the power of the Spirit to the ends of the earth proclaiming the gospel of Christ? (Acts 1:8). Will we allow the African church to continue to be stymied, or will we receive a powerful new revelation from God, and will we respond with a new commitment that will result in the greatest missionary advance in the two thousand-year history of the African church, a faith-filled response that will resound in the history of the worldwide church? The answer, my African friends, is up to us.

Resource Mobilization for Africa's Mission: Lessons Learned from Argentina

TONY PEDROZO

At the heart missions is the church, and at the heart of the church is the work of the Holy Spirit. As the "Continuer" of the work of Christ on the earth, the Holy Spirit gave birth to the church and continues to develop and empower it for effective witness. The question we ask today is, "To what job does the Spirit call the church in Africa in the coming years?" We further ask, "How are we to understand God's mission for the church?" and "What new challenges will the Lord put into our hands?"

This paper will address three issues concerning the work of the church in missions. First, it will address the nature and role of the church as it relates to missions. Next, it will discuss the assets and attitudes required for a church to effectively engage in the missionary task. Finally, it will discuss the issue of financing the work of missions. My desire is that these insights will serve the church in Africa to mobilize for effective missions outreach to the continent and to the nations of the world.

THE CHURCH: GOD'S CHOSEN AGENT IN MISSIONS

When we speak of the church in mission we speak primarily of the local church, for it is in the local church that the church worldwide finds its basis for existence. The worldwide church—or for that matter, any national church—is nothing more than an immense family of local churches. Within this great family of churches it is essential that each be open to all. As a member of the family, each local church must be prepared to minister to the needs of the others, and each must be prepared to share its material and spiritual goods with the others.

Since missions is the grand propose for which Christ established the church, it is expected that the church remain in a state of mission at all times. The arena of mission is the world, and each local church bears its part of responsibility in reaching the world with the gospel. The local congregation should therefore be regarded as the primary agent of missions both in its own country and in all of the entire world.

The church has been commissioned by Christ to share the message of the gospel. It is God's kingdom community representing Him to a dying world. It fulfills its responsibility through the universal priesthood of all believers and by sending missionaries to the nations (1 Peter 2:9; Matt. 28:18-20).

The task of missions thus belongs to the church as a whole and to each local church individually. As a result, God calls every church in every place composed of any and every *ethne* to fully participate in His mission. This includes the church of Africa with all of its ethnic, regional, and cultural diversity.

In the book of Acts the Antiochian church played an important role in the early advancement of missions. It can serve as a grand example of how a truly missional church should look and function today. The church of Antioch was a church that

- crossed social barriers (Acts 11:19-20).
- restored broken lives (Acts 11:21-24).
- elicited for the participation of others (Acts 11:25-26).
- ministered to people's physical and spiritual needs (Acts 11:27-30).
- had a shared leadership formed in a pastoral team (Acts 13:1).
- resolved doctrinal conflicts (Acts 15).
- was willing to extend the boundaries of the kingdom of God to the ends of the earth (Acts 13:2-3).

Moved by the Spirit, the church Antioch embraced its responsibility and became a glowing example of how any church can participate in world evangelization. Under the directions of the Holy Spirit we are challenged to emulate that model.

As servants of the Almighty God we understand that when we engage in missions, we are privileged to share in the mission of our missionary God. We are not simply working on a personal project, we are, under the leadership of the Spirit, serving the *missio Dei*. Our mission, then, is to share His mission. We listen, we discover, and we obey the voice of the Spirit sending us as His servants, sometimes to sow, sometimes to water the soil, and sometimes to reap what has already been sown and watered with tears. The fulfillment of this mission will demand high sacrifice from each of us for many years. It may even require the shedding of blood. This is the model laid down by Jesus and the early church. It is the model we are called to follow.

WHAT IS NEEDED TO RUN A MISSIONS PROGRAM

Jesus taught that one must carefully count the cost before becoming His disciple (Luke 14:28-33). As the African church mobilizes to do missions, it must realistically count the cost of running an effective missions program. Involvement in missions will require huge investments of both money and people, and while both are essential, people are the greatest resource for missions. We can do missions without money, but we can do missions without people.

God has a harvest plan for our days, and it is He who has called, and will continue to call, workers to participate in His harvest. He often calls young people; however, He calls whoever is open to respond to His voice. Jesus exhorted His disciples to pray. "The harvest is plentiful," He said, "but the workers are few. Ask the Lord of the harvest, therefore, to send out workers into his harvest field" (Luke 10:2). God calls laborers in answer to the prayers of His missionary people.

And yet, even though the call is divine, it requires a human response. If, however, no one answers the call, it can be frustrated. People often respond inadequately because they fail to understand the call. Here are some common misunderstandings concerning God's call to missions:

1. Confusing a burden with a calling. Some confuse a burden for the lost with a missionary call. While a call to be a missionary involves a burden for the lost, the two are not necessarily the same. While God wants everyone to have a burden for the lost people of the world, the call to go as a missionary involves much more.

2. Wrong timing. Some are mistaken as to the form and timing of the call. In their enthusiasm for the work, these people hasten to the field without ever receiving a genuine call from God. Others have a genuine call, however, in their zeal they run ahead of God's timing.

3. Unrealistic expectations. Some have unrealistic expectations about the call to missions. These people have a romantic view of missions. They long to travel to exotic and interesting places to work for God. However, when they arrive and face the hard realities of missions, they give up the work and return home.

4. Inadequate preparation. Some believe that the call of God is all they need, and therefore, proper preparation and training are not required. While the call of God is the first step in the preparation of the missionary, it is not the last. The next step is to acquire good training. Missions is a long-term commitment and requires proper spiritual, academic, and practical preparation. It also often involves language training.

5. Misunderstandings about divine provision. Some wrongly assume that a missionary calling automatically ensures divine provision. As a result they run to the field without an adequate support base. This is a formula for disaster.

Our churches cannot continue to ignore the fact that they must understand their call to missions. They must freely send their best servants to the lost of the world. God has called and commissioned His church, including the church of Africa, to spread His passion for missions to all. We cannot, however, be naive about the realities of sending missionaries to the nations. It will require a firm commitment to build the necessary financial and spiritual infrastructures in order to support and sustain the work.

Tony Pedrozo

Missionary Qualifications

We should not feel pressured to quickly run into missions unprepared simply because others are doing it or because we have a burden to go. While we know that God is calling us to go, we must seek understanding about how to properly establish and run an effective missions-sending organization. If God has called us, He will help us to acquire the knowledge and skills necessary to get the job done. In his book, *Tuning God's New Instruments: A Handbook for Missions from the Two-thirds World,* Denis Lane identifies ten basic requirements for missionary candidates:

1. A sense of vocation and walk with God. A candidate missionary must have a deep sense of vocational calling and an abiding walk with God. Paul testified that "God ... set me apart from my mother's womb and called me by his grace" (Gal. 1:15). While God has called all to participate in His mission to take the good news to all people, this general call to share Christ with others is not to be confused with a calling to vocational missionary service. It will be this clear sense of calling, and one's deep relationship with God, that will sustain him or her on the mission field, even in the midst of trying circumstances.

2. Spiritual maturity. Spiritual maturity is another necessary character trait of an effective cross-cultural missionary. This spiritual maturity is evidenced by the fruit of the Spirit and integrity of life and action. On the field the missionary's character will be tested in many ways. During these times of testing great gifts will be no substitute for a close walk with God.

3. A willingness to be a servant. Our Lord Jesus Christ Himself "did not come to be served but to serve, and to give his life as a ransom for many" (Mark 10:45). And so must it be with the missionary. Arrogance is the opposite of a servant heart, and a self-serving attitude has short circuited many missionary careers. Like Jesus, the effective missionary must be willing to wrap himself or herself in a towel and wash the feet of those to whom they have been called.

4. Self-discipline. Lane identifies self-discipline as another essential missionary quality. Often, the missionary in the field has no boss to hold him accountable. Therefore, he will be able to do whatever he pleases whenever he pleases. It his responsibility to organize himself and to be disciplined in the management of his time and tasks.

5. Evangelistic concern. A mission field needs gifted people of all kinds; however, the main goal of every missionary must be to present Christ to the spiritually lost. Every ministry must include an evangelistic component. While not every missionary is called to be an evangelist, all must have a burden for lost souls and exemplify a life of soul winning.

6. Something to share with others. The missionary not only shares the gospel with the lost, he or she must also have innate talents and skills to share with the host culture and the receiving church. The church needs to be made aware of the gifts of the missionary in order that they may utilize him or her to the fullest in their mission to reach their own people and others with the gospel.

7. Experience of life and ministry. It is also important for the missionary to have quality life experiences to carry with him or her to the field. These life experiences can include both ministerial experience and everyday life experiences, including experience in the secular workforce. All such experiences help the missionary to face the myriad of challenges on the field. Personally, I am grateful to God and to my parents who encouraged me to go to medical school and taught me how to relate to people other than brothers and sisters in Christ. Before becoming a missionary, I worked in one of the busiest hospitals of my city where I lived. There I acquired experience and had many opportunities to share the gospel with others. These experiences helped prepare me for my missionary ministry in Africa.

8. Emotional stability. Another quality required in the life of a missionary is the emotional stability. He or she must be able to deal sensibly with challenging situations and make mature decisions. The missionary must also be adept at forming healthy relationships with others. He must be comfortable with his own cultural identity and respectful of the cultural identity of others. Further, the missionary's work will require that he have the mental stability needed to cope with the numerous cultural challenges he will face on the field, and he must have the ability to help his family with the same. His life must be free of controlling habits and harmful attitudes such as pride, insecurity, bitterness, jealousy, and hard feelings.

9. Medical fitness. Medical fitness is another requirement for effective missionary ministry. The cross-cultural worker will inevitably experience heightened levels of stress and fatigue as he or she ministers in their new environment. Coping with these new stresses will require a fit body. Good health will also allow the missionary to face the added demands of increased travel, new routines and schedules, and adjustment to the new climate and dietary challenges. The cumulative physical stress of these and other demands can derail the physically unfit missionary. The wise missionary will respect his or her body as the temple of the Holy Spirit, and will care for it as such.

10. Language motivation. Effective missionary work usually requires learning a new language. If one does not have the necessary motivation to master a new language, their missionary ministry will be greatly curtailed, and may even be terminated. Language acquisition requires, commitment, determination, and persistence. Prayerful reliance on the "Helper," the Holy Spirit, is an essential asset in learning a new language.

Examining New Missions Candidates

When selecting missionaries to send to the nations, mission leaders need to ask a number of pertinent questions. For instance,

- *Has the candidate made any significant contribution to the local church where he or she has been ministering?* If the candidate has not demonstrated an ability to inaugurate some new ministry or expand and enhance some existing program in their own culture and in their own local church, he or she will likely be unable to do the same overseas. Perseverance and capability is an important quality in the life of the prospective missionary.
- *Has the candidate initiated any new ministry or project?* If he has not demonstrated any initiative to tackle some new project in his own culture, how can he be expected to found a church in an alien culture? He will not likely acquire that skill simply because he has suddenly landed on the mission field.

- *Will the candidate be able to work in a multinational team?* The missionary will not only have to minister in a new culture, he or she will very likely have to work in a multinational, multi-cultural missionary team in their field of service. Team players, and not "lone rangers," make a great contribution on the field.
- *Does the candidate have any experience in serving with people of another culture?* On the field the missionary will work with people who think differently from him or her. If the person has had such experience before going to the field, their chance of success will be enhanced.
- *Will the missionary candidate listen to counsel?* A missionary on the field must first listen before he talks. He must be willing to listen to the advice of both his missionary colleagues and the nationals he is serving and seeking to reach for Christ. He must at all times show patience in learning about his new culture. Along with powerful preaching, effective missionary service involves patient listening.
- *Is the candidate a person others will want to follow?* Is he or she respected by people in their own culture? Is he a leader, and do people look to him because he has something of value to offer? Is the candidate a leader in his or her own family? If one cannot lead their own family, how can they lead others? (cf. 1 Tim. 3:5)
- *Is the candidate able to communicate effectively?* An effective missionary is able to express his or her thoughts and ideas in a clearly and understandable way.

Every missions-sending agency must have a well-conceived set of criteria for accepting and orienting new missionary candidates. As drops of water come together to form a great river, the missionaries and missionary leaders of a national church come together to form a national missionary movement. When the drops are pure, the river is pure. When the leaders and missionaries chosen by a national church are spiritual and competent, the agency will be the same. Therefore, we cannot ignore these basic building blocks of an emerging missions agency.

Tony Pedrozo

MISSIONS FINANCING

Funding is needed carry out the mission of God. If a missions movement is to thrive, it must give serious attention to how it raises and handles missions funds. As church members contribute to missions they will grow in their commitment to the cause of world evangelization. People contribute to what they believe in; therefore, to a large extent, the priorities of a church are expressed by their annual budget.

Principles in Finances for Missions

If a national or local church seeks to inspire its members to give generously to missions, they should consider the following:

- *Personalization.* Each member of the church must be made to feel that he or she can personally participate in world evangelization through their prayers and financial contributions.
- *Personal involvement.* Every man, woman, and child in the church should be encouraged to participate in the church's financial support of missions.
- *Missions awareness.* Every person who contributes financially to the missions program of the church should be kept informed about where their contributions have gone and how they are being used. People will give more generously and consistently if they know the missionary or missions program they are supporting. They want to know where the missionary works and the nature and effectiveness of their work on the field.
- *Opportunities.* Every local missions committee should seek to create an ongoing awareness of the opportunities for everyone to participate in missions through prayer and sacrificial giving.
- *Top Priority.* If we really believe that the evangelization of the nations is the "the supreme task of the church," then our financial involvement in missions should reflect that belief. Therefore, in budgeting the church's resources, and in the lives and actions of

its members, missions and missions giving must remain a top priority.

Ways of Contributing Financially

There are a number of ways that a local church and its members may participate financially in supporting the work of missions. Here are three of those ways:

- *Budget allocation.* Allocating a certain percentage of the church's budget to missions will ensure consistency in the church's financial commitment to missions. Such an allocation provides an opportunity for leaders to demonstrate the church's firm commitment to world evangelization. This kind of giving is institutional rather than personal. The people must also be taught to give personally to missions.
- *Special missions offerings.* Special offerings for the needs of missionaries and missions programs provide an opportunity for the members to personalize their financial involvement. Such offerings are normally designated to a special project or a special need in the life of a missionary or in missions field. One down side of this kind of offering is that, if it is the only way a church supports missions, it leads to inconsistency and an incomplete concept of how missions is to be supported.
- *The faith promise.* Faith promise giving is an excellent way for a church to support missions. It is giving based on confidence in God's ongoing provision. When instituted properly into a church's missions program, it becomes a natural and normal way for people to give to missions, and it provides an opportunity for people of all ages to become directly involved in world evangelization. Faith promise giving also helps to produces a financial growth in the church. As believers exercise the faith and trust God to supply the means to fulfill their faith promises, their faith is built up and they grow spiritually. Let's now examine faith promise giving in more detail.

Tony Pedrozo

FAITH PROMISE GIVING

A faith promise is a faith agreement between a believer and God. The believer commits to a monthly contribution to the missions program of the local church as God's supplies the need. Such faith promise giving is based on biblical principles.

Biblical Principles of Faith Promise Giving

In writing to the believers in Corinth Paul addressed the issue of an offering the church was raising for needy Christians. In doing this he laid down certain biblical principles of giving (2 Cor. 8-9). These principles can be applied to raising funds for missionary work. Here are a few of the principles he presented:

- *It was not part of the tithe.* This was an offering to a special need and was not to be considered as part of their regular tithe.
- *It was voluntary.* "For I testify that they gave as much as they were able, and even beyond their ability. Entirely on their own, they urgently pleaded with us for the privilege of sharing in this service to the saints" (8:3-4).
- *It was an early engagement.* They made their commitment to give about a year in advance of the offering: "So I thought it necessary to urge the brothers to visit you in advance and finish the arrangements for the generous gift you had promised. Then it will be ready as a generous gift, not as one grudgingly given" (9:5).
- *It was a faith act.* There giving was not dependent on their own ability but on God's provision: "For I testify that they gave as much as they were able, and even beyond their ability" (8:3).
- *It involved sacrifice, love, and generosity:* "And they did not do as we expected, but they gave themselves first to the Lord and then to us in keeping with God's will" (8:5).

As we look at the spiritual darkness of the world, the need seems to be greater than our capacity to address it, but we know that, in God's strength, we can rise to the challenge. These principles found in scripture can be applied in our desire to respond to the tremendous spiritual need of the world.

Fulfilling the Faith Promise

Once a member makes a faith promise, he can then depend on God to help him fulfill his commitment. Sometimes God will supply the need miraculously, sometimes the believer will need to seek creative ways to raise the funds. Here are some ways that God can use to provide the faith promise offering through the believer:

- *Through faithful stewardship.* When we trust God, He enables us to better manage our resources and to raise the funds needed to fulfill our faith promise.
- *Employment opportunities.* God may supply a second job so a believer can use some of his free time to raise additional income. This additional income can be used to fulfill his or her faith promise.
- *An unexpected blessing.* Once we make our faith promise, God may give us an unexpected gift or a raise in salary. When such blessings come, we must be faithful to use this increase to fulfill our faith promise to missions.
- *A miracle.* As mentioned above, sometimes God will simply give us an outright financial miracle.

God is very creative in the ways He will supply our need in order that we might fulfill our missionary faith promises. Our job is to trust Him and be faithful in allocating His provision to fulfill the promise we made to Him and His mission.

Implementing the Faith Promise Plan

How then may the pastor and the leadership of a church implement the faith promise giving plan into the missions program of the church? To begin with, a faith promise plan is not meant to replace other methods of missions giving in the church, it is rather meant to add to and supplement these means. Some pastors become nervous when they think about implementing this kind of giving into their churches. They wrongly think that it will be necessary to forget all of the previous methods they have been using. But this is not true. If a church has been using a traditional way of raising funds for missions, it should retain that method. However, it can add a faith promise plan to help to raise even more funds for missions.

Even in churches with already large missions budgets the leadership is often surprised to discover how many people will get involved through a faith promise plan. The important question is not "How much is my church presently giving to missions?" but "What is our true potential for missions giving? How much, with God's help, can we actually give?"

The best time to receive faith promises from the people is at the end of the church's annual missions conference. The people's hearts have been touched by the themes of the workshops, by the preaching, and by Holy Spirit Himself. The leadership must be wise, however, in setting the financial goals for the church's missions giving. The goals should be high enough to challenge the people, but not so high that the people will see them as impossible and refuse to participate. Advance cautiously, but advance surely and faithfully. God is faithful and He will fulfill His promises.

Once the faith promises have been gathered, use them as a basis for planning the distribution of funds among the missionaries and projects you have chosen. Generally, in churches involved in world missions, about 85% of the funds come through faith promise giving and the remaining 15% comes through special offerings.

Once you have received the faith promises, you must then work to keep the flame of mission burning in the people's hearts. Constantly present the needs of missions to your people, and each month remind them of their faith promise commitments. Whenever you collect tithes and offerings in the church service, remind the members of their missions commitments. Pray often for your missionaries, and as you do, remind the people of their financial commitments to those missionaries on the field.

To Give or Not to Give, That Is the Question

Every church and believer must decide for themselves whether they want to be faithful and participate in God's mission to redeem the nations. When a church does not contribute to missions, it, in effect opposes the preaching of the gospel to every person in the world, and it closes the channel of God's blessings to the congregation. Speaking of the missionary offerings the church had sent to him, Paul wrote, "Not that I am looking for a gift, but I am looking for what may be credited to your account.... And my God will meet all your needs according to his glorious riches in Christ Jesus" (Phil. 4:, 17, 19). Giving to missions brings the provision of God.

When a church contributes to missions it helps to advance the gospel to the ends of the earth, and it becomes financially blessed as it reaps what it sows. Paul reminded the Corinthians, "Whoever sows sparingly will also reap sparingly, and whoever sows generously will also reap generously" (2 Cor. 9:6). Generous giving to missions results in generous reciprocal financial blessing to the giver. Both the church and the members who give will be blessed.

CONCLUSION

The priorities of the church are revealed in their annual budget. The church that gives to missions demonstrates that reaching the lost at home and around the world is important to them. In conclusion, we would do well to remember the promise of God through the ancient Hebrew prophet: *"Test me in this," says the Lord Almighty, "and see if I will not throw open the floodgates of heaven and pour out so much blessing that there will not be room enough to store it. I will prevent pests from devouring your crops, and the vines in your fields will not drop their fruit before it is ripe," says the Lord Almighty. "Then all the nations will call you blessed, for yours will be a delightful land," says the Lord Almighty. (Malachi 3:10-12).*

Apostolic Ambition: By Way of Reminder: Missiological Reflections from Romans 15:14-29

JOHN L. EASTER

MISSION THEOLOGY IN ROMANS

Most biblical scholars would agree that in his epistle to the Romans the apostle Paul offers the clearest and most complete explanation of the gospel in the New Testament. It should, therefore, not surprise us that the book also provides rich insight to Paul's theology of mission. It was, in fact, out of the context of mission that Paul developed the theology he presents in Romans. In addition to Paul's epistles, Luke's account of Paul's missionary ministry in Acts augments our understanding of God's mission at work, and highlights the dynamic relationships between missionary teams and communities of faith. Paul's teaching on mission in Romans, however, extends beyond Luke's historical approach and provides a rich theological account of his missionary ministry. In addition, the message of Romans has application far beyond Paul's first-century audience. It reaches beyond the years and speaks persuasively to issues in our contemporary world.

Thus, in all of Paul's writings Romans 15 stands out as his most significant thematic passage concerning his own mission. In this well-developed and coherent presentation, Paul provides his readers a lens through which they may interpret and apply the lessons emerging from the text. In addition, the passage affords a special glimpse into the restless, pioneer spirit of Paul and his fixed ambition to preach Christ in the remote western regions of the empire. The climax of this chapter is found in verses 14-33, which provides rich insights into Paul's own view of the unfinished task of world-wide evangelization as it coincides with that of the Roman church.

Writing with Apostolic Intent

Several factors contributed to Paul's motivation for writing the Christians in Rome. In chapter 1 he expressed his long-held desire to visit the Romans so that he might impart unto them "some spiritual gift" in order to strengthen their faith. He also wanted to enjoy a time of mutual encouragement and to reap a harvest of souls from among them (1:11-13). Paul further wrote to encourage the Romans in the vibrant faith that had sustained them in the midst of hostility and great suffering. In doing this he presents an apologetic of Christian doctrine and of pastoral care to them. Paul also wrote to voice his deep concern for Jewish and Gentile unity as these two groups sought to fulfill God's divine plan together (cf., 3:27-31; 9-11; 12:1-15:13). In addition, before making his way to Rome, Paul wanted to request prayer for a prior trip to Jerusalem in which he would carry an offering from the Gentile churches to the impoverished believers there. He was concerned about possible conflict that might arise with unbelievers in Judea (15:22-33).[1] Finally, Paul wrote for another, more weighty reason, one that carried great importance in his mind. This concern of Paul's materializes in Romans 15.

Paul was eager to continue his work as the "apostle to the Gentiles" until their number was full (11:13-14; 25-26). His heart was now set on ranging westward into Spain (15:24). A mission base in the capital city of the Roman world would provide a strategic base from which his apostolic band could penetrate these new frontiers. Also, a partnership with the congregations of Rome would aid him and his missionary team to advance into Spain (vv. 24, 28). Rome would thus become for Paul another regional missions center, much like the ones he has established in other cities such as Antioch, Philippi, Thessalonica, Corinth, and Ephesus. Paul thus wrote to invite the Roman believers to support his new missionary venture. Paul understood that a partnership of this kind would require a relationship of mutual trust and dependency. To help build this relationship he sought to lay a foundational theology of mission on which it would stand.

Unlike many of the churches to whom Paul wrote, he could make no claim to have fathered the first congregations in Rome. Nevertheless, through mutual contacts an indirect relationship had emerged with the church. A number of Paul's missionary colleagues had migrated to Rome and had become active believers in the house churches there. He had worked with some of these people on his missionary journeys, and in this apostolic context a passion for frontier missions ministry must have become a shared value. In concluding his epistle, Paul lists 29 specific people in Rome whom he personally admires and reveres as his spiritual brothers, sisters, and mothers. He considered them all to be his co-workers in gospel ministry (16:1-16). These men and women who shared Paul's apostolic DNA would have no doubt exercised a certain level of missionary influence in the Roman church.

Defining Apostolic Ministry

In Romans 15:14-33 Paul revisits and expands upon themes he first introduced in 1:8-15, themes concerning the scope and purpose of his ministry.[2] In doing this he unveils his plans to turn from his missionary endeavors in the east and venture into the unreached Mediterranean west.[3] He also makes his appeal to the Roman believers for support, calling on them to underwrite his planned pioneer missionary initiative into Iberia. As the letter climaxes, Paul cites four key features which define his missionary apostolate: *apostolic consciousness, apostolic ambition, apostolic hope,* and *apostolic partnership.* Let's now look at each of these elements:

APOSTOLIC CONSCIOUSNESS

Paul begins his explanation of his ministry by expressing confidence in the Roman believers:

I myself am satisfied about you, my brothers, that you yourselves are full of goodness, filled with all knowledge and able to instruct one another (v. 14, ESV).

He commends the believers in this emerging church for their spiritual vitality, maturing faith, and sound Christian practice. His words are reminiscent of an earlier commendation, where he had applauded them noting that their faith was being "proclaimed in all the world" (1:8). Nevertheless, while Paul is sincere and affectionate in his recognition of their Christian maturity, his diplomatic words also suggest certain deficiencies in their understanding of the Christian faith: *"But on some points,"* he states, *"I have written to you very boldly by way of reminder, because of the grace given me by God "* (v. 15).

Triumphalism and the Unfinished Task

This straightforward admonishment arises out of Paul's desire to see the Roman believers fully embrace their role in God's universal mission. He wants them to think beyond their own provincial setting, and in doing so, to envision a platform of greater influence and effectiveness. As did Peter, Paul seeks to inspire these believers to action by stirring up their sincere minds "by way of reminder" (2 Pet. 3:1, cf. 1:12). Positioning himself very much in the role of an Old Testament prophet, Paul reminds God's missionary people of their original message and calling.[4] Thus, on the one hand, Paul commends the Romans for their faith, knowledge, and witness; on the other, he provokes them to greater awareness and action.

Inherent in Paul's apostolic consciousness is a warning for the Roman believers to guard against the temptation of triumphalism in their local context. Such self-centered thinking could potentially hinder the church from fully engaging the unfinished task. An unhealthy fascination on their past successes could result in loss of focused direction, which would in turn prevent the gospel from arriving in time for those who have not yet heard (Rom. 10:14-15; 15:21).

Paul's Priestly Calling

Apostolic consciousness calls the church, and us as its emissaries, to not only be mindful of the urgent need to proclaim Christ to all nations, but to be aware of our priestly role in God's mission. Paul was very aware that his individual role was only part of what God was doing in world, and yet, his role was always in the forefront of his thinking. He viewed himself as *"a minister of Christ Jesus to the Gentiles in the priestly service of the gospel of God, so that the offering of the Gentiles may be acceptable, sanctified by the Holy Spirit"* (vv. 15b-16). With these carefully chosen words Paul reveals how he viewed himself as standing in historic continuity with the Old Testament priestly role of serving both Israel and the nations (e.g., Ex. 29:33ff).

What kind of priestly service did Paul offer? In the context of his apostolic calling, his priestly service finds expression in offering up the Gentiles as living sacrifices to God. Figuratively speaking—and with all the significance that such imagery employs—Paul viewed his Gentile converts as sacrifices of thanksgiving to God, with which He was well pleased. Paul's apostolic ministry thus exemplified the prophecy of Isaiah which declared that the diaspora Jews—of whom Paul was one—would proclaim God's glory in distant lands and bring His people back "from all the nations as an offering to the Lord" (Isa. 66:20).[5] It is the same for us today as we call the unreached tribes of Africa to Christ and offer them up to God as offerings of thanksgiving and as sacrifices of His living purpose.

Paul however refused to boast in his missionary service. He rather gloried in Christ Jesus concerning his Gentile mission. The exercise of his priestly ministry was thus conditioned by both his dependence on the Spirit's power and by his glory in Jesus Christ who had called him: *"For I will not venture to speak of anything except what Christ has accomplished through me to bring the Gentiles to obedience—by word and deed, by the power of signs and wonders, by the power of the Spirit of God ...*" (vv. 15b-19a). In this way Paul perceived himself as a vessel through whom Christ worked to achieve His mission. His apostolate was characterized by both word and works, all being accomplished through the supernatural empowerment of the Holy Spirit. As a consequence, Paul's methods involved both "truth encounter" and "power encounter." In order to bring unregenerate men and women to conversion he joined the powerful message of the gospel with mighty demonstrations of the Holy Spirit's power.

APOSTOLIC AMBITION

Paul's divine call to proclaim Christ among those who had not yet heard profoundly shaped his personal self-image and firmly established his life's purpose. He further saw himself as one commissioned and sent out by the church (cf. Acts 13:1-4a). Paul thus describes his *apostolic ambition:* by his own testimony his singular purpose in life was

> ... *to bring the Gentiles to obedience—by word and deed, by the power of signs and wonders, by the power of the Spirit of God—so that from Jerusalem and all the way around to Illyricum I have fulfilled the ministry of the gospel of Christ; and thus I make it my ambition to preach the gospel, not where Christ has already been named, lest I build on someone else's foundation ...* (vv. 18-20)

Proclaiming Christ to the Unreached

How then should we understand Paul's ambition, this overwhelming desire of his to fulfill Christ's purpose for his life? Unlike many whose ambitions are driven by self interest, Paul's was grounded in the holy. It was forged in the authority of Christ and His calling. It was sustained by his confidence in the gospel and ignited by the effectual working of the Holy Spirit in his life. In addition, the apostle was deeply moved by the immeasurable need of humankind for salvation. As a result, he was intensely driven by a compulsion to proclaim Christ, plant the church, and make disciples among those who had no access to the gospel.

In this passage Paul stresses the proclamational nature of his ministry, which functioned primarily through the use of words (15:18).[6] Admittedly, he clearly testifies to the importance of good deeds, the necessity of the Spirit's power, and the beneficial role of signs, wonders, and miracles. We are not, however, to understand these qualities as supplanting the primacy of proclamation. They are rather to be understood as empowering the process and providing opportunities for more effective verbal witness. Only through preaching can Christ's name be exalted among the nations and the good news of salvation proclaimed in previously unreached areas.

Additionally, while the platforms of humanitarian care and social action are an integral part of the church's mission to the world, and must necessarily flow from the love and generosity of God's people, the proclamation of Jesus among those who have never heard of Him must remain paramount. Our words thus give meaning and clarity to the gospel message. The proclamational nature of the apostolic mission further carries with it an eschatological urgency to ensure that all hear before the imminent return of Christ.

The Obedience of Faith

Apostolic ambition, however, must never be viewed as an end in itself. The nature and purpose of Paul's calling was informed and driven by the primary objective of the kingdom mandate *"to bring about the obedience of faith for the sake of Christ's name among all the nations"* (Rom. 1:5; 15:18; 16:26). With this goal in mind, Paul and his missionary bands fulfilled their calling as apostolic emissaries sent out by the church to the nations (cf., Acts 13:1-4; Gal. 1:11-2:10). They were constantly guided by the intention of forming spiritually and ethically transformed disciples (Matt. 28:19; Isa. 2:3).[7] In order to bring about this full obedience of faith, Paul *"fully preached the gospel of Christ"* (v. 19, NASB).[8]

This kind of determined fidelity to the gospel, however, brings with it a certain level of apostolic anxiety.[9] Paul expressed this anxiety to the church in Corinth: *"And, apart from other things,"* he told them, *"there is the daily pressure on me of my anxiety for all the churches"* (2 Cor. 11:28). His concern for the spiritual health of believers and churches thus consumed his thinking and helped to shape his apostolic *modus operandi*. The formation of faith communities living out the gospel in the Spirit's power was for Paul the culmination of the apostolic mandate. His words to the Thessalonians believers reveal this facet of Paul's concern for the church: *"For what is our hope or joy or crown of boasting before our Lord Jesus at his coming? Is it not you? For you are our glory and joy"* (1 Thess. 2:19). Paul expressed similar sentiments to the believers in Corinth: *"Are not you my workmanship in the Lord? If to others I am not an apostle, at least I am to you, for you are the seal of my apostleship in the Lord"* (1 Cor. 9:1-2). Although Paul never lost sight of the need for personal salvation, obedience unto faith involves more individual experience, it involves followers of Jesus bound together into local communities of faith who are active participants in God's universal mission to take the gospel to the nations.

Collective Calling and Accountability

In calling the Romans to apostolic consciousness, Paul affirms that both local church and missionary teams must share mutual responsibility for the mission. Their understood mutual calling must give rise to a collective consciousness of ministry. Thus to effectively fulfill their God-ordained mandate to reach all nations with the gospel, both the church and the missionary team must claim ownership of the mission. And each must submit themselves to one another—and to God—in mutual accountability in fulfilling their respective roles in the mission. For Paul, it was not enough that apostolic bands independently enter new regions detached from the local church. Apostolic bands should be organically connected to the church(es) who send them out.

From Jerusalem to Illyricum to Spain

Apostolic ambition engenders "missions on the move." Paul

summarizes the geographical extent his missionary journeys: *"... from Jerusalem and all the way to Illyricum I have fulfilled the ministry of the gospel of Christ"* (v. 19). In this remarkable statement Paul unveils the vast geographical expanse of his missionary travels—all of which occurred over a period of just twenty years. The statement further reveals the level of commitment and the extent to which Paul and his companions would go to preach the gospel in "the regions beyond" (2 Cor. 10:16, NASB). Thus, Paul's missionary band was always pressing forward, always looking for a harvest in the unreached regions.

Paul's rehearsal of his past pioneer ministry may have been motivated, at least in part, by hopes for support from the Roman church. He hoped that this report would help to generate enthusiasm in their hearts motivating them to support this westward advance into Spain. Thus, while apostolic ambition of necessity holds special meaning for a pioneer missionary team, it must be shared and understood by the sending body as well.

As we in the Africa Assemblies of God move forward together in mission, it will be critical that we ask and answer for ourselves certain probing questions: How should this apostolic ambition find expression within the Pentecostal church in Africa today? How should it shape our commitment to the unfinished task of reaching the unreached peoples of Africa and beyond? How will we finance this ambition? What structures will be necessary to carry it out? What strategic partnerships will we need to form? As missional leaders in the twenty-first century African church, will we measure ourselves by what we have already accomplished, or will we measure ourselves by our commitment to the unfinished task? Answering and applying these and other pertinent questions will better prepare us for task ahead.

APOSTOLIC HOPE

Ambition without hope is dead. Therefore, to make sure his readers do not miss the connection between the two, Paul immediately follows his statement of ambition with a declaration of hope. He does this by quoting from the Hebrew prophet Isaiah: *"Those who have never been told of him will see, and those who have never heard will understand"* (v. 21; cf. Isa. 52:15). It was often Paul's custom to quote from Old Testament Scripture in his writing and preaching. While his view of mission was inevitably informed by his involvement in frontier ministry, his theology of mission and his missionary practice was shaped chiefly by Scripture.

Old and New Testament Priorities

Paul's apostolic hope was undergirded by his understanding of the "big picture" of God's redemptive plan for the nations. This fact is indicated by his frequent appeals to the writings of the OT prophets. In these promises he finds hope that the Gentile nations will indeed be included in God's redemptive plan. And for Paul, hope was amply confirmed by the Spirit's work that he has personally observed among the Gentiles (cf. Acts 15:12; 28:31). In citing Isaiah, Paul affirms that the Gentiles will indeed "see," "hear," and "understand." Even today, as we move out to reach the unreached tribes of Africa and beyond, we too can be assured that they will see, hear, understand, and receive. This assurance gives us great hope that God will indeed give us a harvest among those we are seeking to reach. While many will reject the message, some will receive and heartily embrace it. The critical question that remains is will we, buoyed by this apostolic hope, provide an effective gospel witness to these lost peoples?

Thus for Paul, this realization that his own calling, and that of the Roman Christians, was "inextricably linked with the mysterious outworking of God's redemptive purpose" resulted in apostolic hope for both Israel and the Gentiles.[10] Now, as the end of the age rapidly approaches, we are gripped as never before by an "eschatological urgency," understanding that the pace of the mission is accelerating. Nevertheless, in all that we do the mission priority of Christ's exaltation among all peoples remains unwavering.

Confidence in the Gospel

For Paul apostolic hope also sprang out of his supreme confidence in the gospel (cf. Rom. 1:16) and from his experience with the Spirit (cf. Acts 9:17-18; 13:9ff). Many times he had personally observed the Spirit's effectual power as the gospel was lived out and boldly proclaimed by committed disciples in a hostile world. Today, we too can place complete confidence in the power of the gospel and in the Spirit who empowers the messengers and then applies the message to the hearts of those who hear. Were it not for this confidence in the gospel—this apostolic hope—the immense scope and daunting nature of the task would overwhelm us. As we contemplate the depth of human depravity, the opposition of demonic powers, and the difficulty in communicating the gospel to peoples of different worldviews, cultures, and languages, we are tempted to become discouraged and give up task. When we hear that more than 16,000 distinct people groups inhabit the earth today, and when we contemplate the fact that there remains over 6,500 people groups, representing nearly 3.5 billion people, who do not have an adequate witness of the gospel, we are tempted to throw up our hands in resignation.

Nevertheless, in all of this we are sustained in the work by apostolic hope. Such a hope reminds us that the success of the mission ultimately rests, not in human ingenuity, but in God's power and in His sovereign plan for the nations. Paul had an unwavering confidence in the unchanging power of the gospel—no matter the context, people, or times (Rom. 1:16): Christ *will* build his church in the East and in the West (cf. Matt. 16:18; 1 Cor. 3:5-7). He understood that the task of world evangelization would only be accomplished in *"word and deed, by the power of signs and wonders, and by the power of the Spirit of God"* (Rom. 15:18-19). In like manner, as we venture to the worlds of Islam, Hinduism, Buddhism, and humanistic secularism we, like Paul, must look with great hope to the Lord of the Harvest. We can take hope from Paul's final apostolic affirmation in Acts: *"Therefore, let it be known to you that this salvation of God has been sent to the Gentiles; they will listen."* (28:28).

APOSTOLIC PARTNERSHIPS

Paul now turns his attention to one of his key reasons for writing to the Roman church, that is, to address the issue of *apostolic partnerships*. For fifteen chapters he has presented a detailed, coherent description of the gospel he preached. This description has provided Paul with a theological platform from which he can now present his partnership plan to the Roman believers. Included in Paul's description of the gospel was a strong appeal for a sending theology. In this appeal Paul asks four rhetorical questions meant to provoke reflection concerning the need for dynamic apostolic partnerships:

> *How then will they call on him in whom they have not believed? And how are they to believe in him of whom they have never heard? And how are they to hear without someone preaching? And how are they to preach unless they are sent? As it is written, "How beautiful are the feet of those who preach the good news!"* (Rom. 10:14-15)

Paul thus reveals how the Roman believers should understand their role in missions. Beyond local evangelism initiatives and care for their members, something else is expected of this (and every) community of faith. According to Paul, they should join the Holy Spirit in sending preachers to those who have never heard the good news of Christ (cf. Acts 13:1-4). Therefore, in the closing paragraphs of his letter, Paul invites the Roman church to join him in taking the gospel to Spain by serving as senders:

> *This is the reason why I have so often been hindered from coming to you. But now, since I no longer have any room for work in these regions, and since I have longed for many years to come to you, I hope to see you in passing as I go to Spain, and to be helped on my journey there by you, once I have enjoyed your company for a while.* (15:22-24)

Like the Roman churches, every local body of believers today should also see themselves as participants in reaching the unreached for Christ by serving as both goers and senders to the unreached peoples and places of the world.

Partnering Together to Reach Spain

Amazingly, Paul informed his fellow believers in Rome that he had fulfilled his ministry in the East. The reason he gives for doing this is quite intriguing. He tells them, *"I no longer have any room for work in these regions"* (v. 23). To be properly understood this statement must be read in view of his previous statement that *"I make it my ambition to preach the gospel, not where Christ has already been named, lest I build on someone else's foundation"* (v. 20). Paul had no room to work in the East because of the way he had prioritized his ministry focus. (Or should we say, the way Christ had prioritized his ministry focus for him: Acts 9:15; 22:21; 26:16-18). God had called Paul to work exclusively among those who had never had the opportunity to hear the gospel of Christ.

As a result of Paul's apostolic work—and the work of others following in his example—the influence of Christianity now flowed from the major cities of eastern Mediterranean region into the surrounding provinces, thus enabling local believers to engage in effective near-neighbor evangelism. Now, feeling as though his church-planting ministry in the East (spanning from Jerusalem in the east to as far west as modern-day Albania) was now drawing to a close, Paul boldly announced his intention to shift this attention to the farthest western frontiers of the empire (15:19). What makes this scenario even more remarkable is that none of the churches in the vast eastern geographical region could have been more than 25 years old.

As we contemplate this missionary strategy of Paul, we can learn a valuable lesson. Unlike most modern missionary strategies, Paul never sought to establish a permanent mission base in any place he planted a church. Neither did he call on the churches in Jerusalem or Antioch to send reinforcements to settle down and help strengthen and sustain the work for a lifetime. Instead, Paul's strategy was to constantly press forward into the frontiers. Now, in writing to the Romans, he has his eyes steadfastly fixed on Spain in the far west (15:24).

So when Paul said that he had "fulfilled" his ministry in the East, he did not mean that God had completed His mission in that geographical region, nor was he saying that there was no work left for others to do there. He was rather saying that, based on his own apostolic calling his work in the region had been completed. In doing this he was also establishing a more general template for all believers to participate in pioneer missionary service.

Paul nevertheless believed that all followers of Christ share responsibility in reaching the unreached nations with the gospel. By way of Rome he intended to continue his focus on new frontiers in Spain. He thus appealed to the Christians in Rome to partner with him his anticipated mission. In this way he and his apostolic band would be assisted in this new missionary initiative. Together, with the aid of the Romans, they would evangelize Spain. They would thus accomplish the task as an on-the-ground cross-cultural frontier missionary team supported by the prayers, finances, and potential personnel from the churches in Roman.

Partnership in Reaching, Training, and Mobilizing

Scripture indicates that Paul's apostolic methodology included the continued training of church leaders resulting in the multiplication of Spirit-empowered missional indigenous churches. These churches would themselves be mobilized to engage in the apostolic function of sending out their own missionaries and church planters (Acts 11:25-26; 19:1-10). As previously stated, Paul testified that God had called him to bring the Gentile nations to the "obedience of faith" (1:5; cf. 15:18). This goal demanded that nations not only be *reached,* they must also be *discipled.* While Paul declared his work "complete" in already-evangelized areas and pressed on into unreached areas, he understood that the fulfillment of this goal required a continued commitment to the training and mobilization of workers, if not by his own hands, then by the hands of fellow missionaries.[11]

Done properly, discipleship training will never undermine the pioneer work of the church. It will rather strengthen and enlarge the sending base for greater engagement in frontier missions. Paul often sent mission workers back as teachers and mobilizers to develop local leadership and nurture the churches (e.g., Acts 19:22; 1 Cor. 3:4-6; 4:6, 17; 2 Cor. 12:18;

Phil. 2:19; 1 Thess. 3:6). This apostolic practice not only produced numerical and spiritual growth, it also ensured the transferal of the apostolic nature to these younger churches. In return, these emerging churches faithfully responded to the Spirit's call and began themselves to participate in the apostolic mission (cf. Rom. 15-16; 2 Cor. 1-13; 1 Thess. 1). And so the work multiplied.

Paul understood that, as these newly-planted churches grew in numbers, faith, and godly zeal, he would indirectly participate in their success, and the result would have an even greater harvest. He shared this hope with the believers in Corinth:

> Our hope is that as your faith increases, our area of influence among you may be greatly enlarged, so that we may preach the gospel in lands beyond you, without boasting of work already done in another's area of influence" (2 Cor. 10:15-16).

In the same way, we in Africa must strategically work hand in hand to plant the church among all nations, including the unreached tribes of Africa. African must partner with African, African must partner with American, and both must partner with others who may choose to join the mission. Since Christ's commission applies equally to both the African and American churches, everything we do to strengthen either will only multiply our ability to finish the task of the Great Commission.

In calling the Roman church to apostolic consciousness, Paul contended that both the local church and missionary team share responsibility in reaching the unreached for Christ. For this to occur a collective consciousness must be at work in the community of faith. This collective consciousness will serve to guide the church's missional trajectory and to guard the community from missional drift. Yet, a collective missional consciousness, in and of itself, is not enough. At some point concrete action must occur. National churches and missions organizations, working in close partnership, must inaugurate specific measures to launch a focused thrust to reach the unreached peoples of Africa and beyond. Spirit-engendered plans must be developed, systems must be established, and workable mechanisms must be put into place to mobilize the church for missions. Once this occurs, missions teams can be recruited, trained and sent into the eleventh hour harvest.

CONCLUDING THOUGHTS

The force of Romans 15 is enhanced by the personal way in which Paul opens up concerning his own ministry and about his admiration for the Roman believers. Compelled by an ambition to make Christ known among the nations, he appeals to the Romans to embrace, live, and spread the gospel. The task of world evangelization demands many things, and among them is our commitment as a church body to move beyond awareness and prayer to meaningful mobilization that results in the sending of missionaries into the unreached peoples of Africa and beyond.

In conclusion, nine significant implications emerge from our investigation of Paul's missionary discourse in Romans 15:14-29:

1. The task of world evangelization requires committed cross-cultural missionaries. While local churches can, and must, engage in meaningful evangelism, trained cross-cultural missionary teams are required to cross significant geographical, linguistic, and cultural barriers into areas where the average congregant cannot go.
2. Sending missionaries into the harvest demands that effective mechanisms and systems be put into place in order to financially and morally maintain a mission sending program.
3. To effectively sustain their missions programs, local churches must possess a keen apostolic consciousness that compels them to participate in the *missio Dei* through sending, praying, giving, and other resourcing.
4. Like Paul, every church and sending agency must maintain a Christological focus in all that it does. Ultimately the motive of all missions activity must be to exalt Christ's name among the nations.

5. The proclamation of the gospel requires the use of words. If Christ is to be truly exalted among the nations, His name must be clearly and boldly proclaimed.
6. The task of reaching the unreached can only be accomplished in the power of the Holy Spirit.
7. The primary goal of world mission is to bring about the obedience of faith among the nations for the sake of Christ's name.
8. As we seek to penetrate new areas with the gospel, making disciples should remain a central focus of our mission strategy.
9. A truly biblical missionary enterprise is a partnership between communities of faith and missionary teams. Strategic missionary engagement must, therefore, strive to cultivate strong relationships between the missionary team, the supporting base, and the receiving community.

ENDNOTES

1. See the following scriptural references associated in part with this offering and its significance to Gentile-Jewish solidarity, sacrificial love, and mutual care: Acts 20:4; 21:17ff; 1 Corinthians 16:1; and 2 Corinthians 8-9.
2. J. Ross Wagner, *Heralds of the Good News: Isaiah and Paul in Concert in the Letter to the Romans* (Boston: Brill Academic Publishers, 2003), 329.
3. Paul's reference to the Greek offering for the poverty-stricken Jerusalem church takes on added meaning in light of his decision to turn his attention to the West and the Western church. As Wagner suggests, Paul's accompanying the delegation of believers from the East to personally present this offering provides him with a symbolic way of bringing closure to his ministry in the Eastern regions in order to advance the church in the West (329).
4. In part, Paul's self-perception as an apostle finds meaning in the historical continuity between his role and that of the OT prophets. This

claim can be observed by comparing passages like Galatians 1:15-16, Isaiah 49:1, and Jeremiah 1:5.
5. John R. W. Stott, *The Message of Romans* (Downers Grove, IL: InterVarsity Press, 1994), 379.
6. O'Brian points out that, in verse, 19 Paul's use of ευαγγέλιον (*euangelion*) shares the same dynamic connotation as the act of proclamation or the work of evangelism (compare the parallel use of the cognate verb *euangelizomai* in verse 20). P. T. O'Brian, *Gospel and Mission in the Writing of Paul: An Exegetical and Theological Analysis* (Grand Rapids, MI: Baker Books, 1995), 38-39.
7. For a scholarly examination of Paul's mission in view of moral and ethical implications, see Michael Barram, *Mission and Moral Reflection in Paul* (New York: Peter Lang, 2006).
8. Literally translated as "fulfilled the gospel" (πεπληρωκέναι τὸ ευαγγέλιον). Paul does not mean that to "fully proclaim the gospel" (NIV) is to preach in every township and village between the geographical points of Jerusalem to Illyricum. It rather means that he faithfully preached the apostolic message in influential cities along the way, while equipping local believers to evangelize their own neighborhoods and surrounding territories. See, Everett F. Harrison, "Romans," In *The Expositors Bible Commentary,"* ed. Frank E. Gaebelein., vol. 10 (Grand Rapids, MI: Zondervan Publishing Company, 1976), 156-157.
9. Donald Senior and Carroll Stuhlmueller, *The Biblical Foundations for Mission* (New York: Orbis Books, 1983), 184.
10. Wagner, 336.
11. Paul's willingness to release his closest companions (such as Timothy, Titus, or Epaphroditus) to continue relating to previously established churches shows the importance he placed on relationship and continued partnership in mission as fellow workers in kingdom work. Paul's view of Apollos in relation to the Corinthian church provides insight into his view about partnership (cf. 1 Cor. 1:12; 3:4-6, 22; 4:6; esp. 16:12).

Appendix 1
AFRICA ASSEMBLIES OF GOD
DECADE OF PENTECOST (2010-2020)
CONTINENTAL GOALS

Continental Beginning Statistics
(January 1, 2010 Statistics:)

- Churches and Preaching Points: 47,985 + 17,237   = 65,222
- Members and Adherents: 6,988,872 + 8,971,905   = 15,960,777
- Credentialed and Lay Ministers: 22,735 + 27,583   = 50,318
- Baptized in the Holy Spirit: = 3,008,739 (19%)
- Bible and Extension School Students   7,509 + 4,624   = 12,133

Continental Goals

- Ten million new believers baptized in the Holy Spirit and mobilized as Spirit-empowered witnesses.
- Millions of new believers coming to Christ and added to the churches.
- Tens of thousands of new churches planted.
- Tens of thousands of new witnesses, pastors, and missionaries trained.
- 100,000 Spirit-filled intercessors mobilized.
- Hundreds of African missionaries recruited, deployed, and supported.
- The remaining unreached peoples of sub-Sahara Africa engaged with the gospel.
- The five countries of North Africa penetrated.

Appendix 2
NATIONAL CHURCH DECADE OF PENTECOST GOALS SUMMARY (2010-2020) [1]
February 2014

Notes:
1. The chart below includes only those national churches who have sent a report to the Acts in Africa office as of February 1, 2014.
2. Totals include only churches listed in chart who state specific goals. They do not include those who make only general predictions.
3. Because of space restrictions, the chart does not include the training and prayer goals which several churches included in their Decade of Pentecost commitment statements.

National Church Reporting	New Church-es Plant-ed by 2020	Spirit baptisms by 2020	New Members & Adherents by 2020	New Ministers by 2020	Missionaries deployed by 2020	Unreached People Groups Goals
West Africa Assemblies of God Alliance						
Benin AG	294 by 2012				27 by 2012	
Burkina Faso AG	1,600 new churches	1,090,000 (80% of new converts, 70% of long-time members)	800,000 new members (Win 10% of BF to Christ)	2400	88 DOP evangelists	Engage the 70± unreached people groups in Burkina Faso
Cote d'Ivoire AG	600 new churches in 2 years	80%			20 new missionaries to Africa, Europe, and the USA	
Liberia AG	800 new churches	95%	500,000 won to Christ		50 home missionaries & 2 foreign missionaries	Engage 9 unreached people groups in Liberia
Mali AG	34 new churches in 4 years	"Increase the number of Spirit-baptized believers"				"Penetrate as many 'closed areas' with the gospel as possible"
West Africa AG Alliance Totals	3,328 new church-es	70%-100% baptized in the Holy Spirit	13,000,000 new members	2,400 new minsters	160 missionaries	Engage 79 unreached people groups

223

National Church Reporting	New Churches Planted by 2020	Spirit baptisms by 2020	New Members & Adherents by 2020	New Ministers by 2020	Missionaries deployed by 2020	Unreached People Groups Goals
Central Africa Assemblies of God Alliance							
Cameroon AG	300 in 10 years	100%	21,000 new believers	450 new ministers	225 more cross-cultural missionaries inside Cameroon; 5 international missionaries	20 missionaries to the unreached people groups of Cameroon.
Cameroon Full Gospel Mission	2000 by 2020	At least 85%	Grow to 1,200,000 members and adherents			"Target all current unreached people groups in Cameroon with 60 miss. for ea. people group"
Congo Republic AG	400 (50 per year from 2012-2020)	100% of leaders. 90% of members	45,000 new members.		Deploy 2 couples	
DR Congo AG (Kisangani)	2400 new churches by 2020	100% of members			Deploy 3 external missionaries. Establish missions department.	
DR Congo AG (Kinshasa)	"Plant churches throughout Congo and the world"	"Greatest outpouring in the church's history"			"Send missionaries to the unreached"	
Gabon AG	100 new churches	100%	10,000 new members		Deploy 20 cross-cultural missionaries	
Nigeria AG	10,000 new churches by 2020	100% of church members	Bring 3 million people to faith in Christ (including water and Spirit baptism)		500 new cross-cultural missionaries. (Including 1 in every country in Africa)	Plant many churches among unreached people groups

National Church Reporting	New Church-es Plant-ed by 2020	Spirit baptisms by 2020	New Members & Adherents by 2020	New Ministers by 2020	Missionaries deployed by 2020	Unreached People Groups Goals
Central Africa AG Alliance Goals	15,200 new church-es	85%-100% baptized in the Holy Spirit	4,276,000 new members	450 new ministers	Send 752 missionaries	Reach 80 unreached people groups
East Africa Assemblies of God Alliance						
Burundi AG	150 new churches	75%		200 new ministers		
Kenya AG	4000 new churches	100%		4000 new ministers	6 foreign missionaries	Reach 10 UPG's in Kenya. "Intentionally increase cross-cultural church planting among the least-reached"
Tanzania AG	10,000 new churches by 2018	2 million baptized in the Holy Spirit by 2018	2 million bew members by 2018		10 new fully-supported international missionaries & 50 church-planting missionaries	
East Africa AG Alliance Goals	14150	75-100%	2 million by 2018	4200	16 foreign 50 home	Reach 10 UPGs
Southern Africa Assemblies of God Alliance						
Botswana AG	100 new churches by 2020	100% baptized in the Holy Spirit	183,546 adherents by 2020	100 new ministers	13 new missionaries (10 inside & 3 outside)	
Lesotho AG	Add 500 new churches to the present 77	80% baptized in the Holy Spirit	Add 25,000 new members to present 11,000	500 new ministers	1 missionary unit	
Malawi AG	Grow from 2000 to 5000 organized churches	100% baptized in the Holy Spirit	Grow to 2 million adherents		50 foreign cross-cultural missionaries	

National Church Reporting	New Churches Planted by 2020	Spirit baptisms by 2020	New Members & Adherents by 2020	New Ministers by 2020	Missionaries deployed by 2020	Unreached People Groups Goals
South Africa IAG	1,000 new churches by 2020	100% of members baptized in the Holy Spirit	Grow to 100,000 new born again members		30 new fully-supported missionaries	
Zambia, AG	450 new churches (including 74 *strategic churches*					
Zambia, PAOGZ	Plant 500 new "Spirit-empowered missionary churches"	Minimum of 80% baptized in the Holy Spirit	Grow to 1.7 million members		Send and support 20 cross-cultural missionary units to unreached people.	10 units to unreached inside Zambia. 10 units outside.
Zambia, Grace Ministries	Plant 150 new "missions-oriented, Spirit-filled churches"	100% baptized in the Holy Spirit	Win 200,000 to Christ. Grow from 15,000 to 42,000 members.	200 new church planters		
Zimbabwe, General Council AG	Plant 1000 new churches by 2022	Emphasize HS baptism that leads to evangelism and church planting.	Grow to 87,5000 Spirit-filled members.	Grow from 82 to 1,000 credentialed ministers	1 foreign unit by 2016. 2 more units by 2022.	
Southern Africa AG Alliance Goals	6700 new churches	80%-110% baptized in the Holy Spirit	3,102,546 new members	1,718 new ministers	115 by 2020 117 by 2022	10
Africa Assemblies of God Alliance Continental Goals						
Total (23 Reports)	39,378[1]	70%-100%	9391546	8768	1,097 by 2020 1099 by 2022	179 UPG's (+ The U PG's of Cameroon)

226

Appendix 3
Declaration of Commitment to
The Worldwide "Decade of Harvest" Through
Africa Harvest 2000

IN RESPONSE to the command of Jesus in John 4:35 to lift up our eyes and look on the fields which are ripe for harvest, and

RECOGNIZING that this Holy Spirit is leading us into a season of harvest across Africa and around the world, and

HAVING HEARD the clear voice of the Holy Spirit this week speaking to us as leaders, to be men and women of fervent prayer, total commitment and enlarged vision,

We, the delegates to the All Africa Leadership Conference on the Assemblies of God, unanimously adopt this DECLARATION OF COMMITMENT to the worldwide DECADE OF HARVEST through AFRICA HARVEST 2000.

WE HEREBY dedicate and consecrate ourselves:

To join our hearts and hands in spiritual unity in pursuit of the aggressive initiative of Africa Harvest 2000,

- To pray with the humility of 2 Chronicles 7:14 for a continent-wide revival accompanied by a resurgence of Pentecostal power, preaching and the full spectrum of the Spirit's work in the Church,
- To work and pray until we witness the total evangelization of Africa, and
- To persevere in leading new converts into full spiritual maturity in accordance with Jesus' command of Matthew 28:19 to disciple all nations.

WE CALL FOR every national church to initiate concerted prayer and intercession specifically for the objectives of Africa Harvest 2000.

WE CALL FOR every national church to manifest renewed and enlarged missionary vision to send forth laborers claiming the nations for Jesus Christ.

Appendix 3: Declaration of Commitment to the Worldwide "Decade of Harvest"

WE DECLARE a continent-wide spiritual offensive against the rulers and forces of darkness as mentioned in Ephesians 6:12, knowing that we are more than conquerors through Him who loves us (Romans 8:37).

WE BELIEVE GOD for 15,000,000 new Believers in Africa by 2000.

WE BELIEVE GOD for 30,000 churches by the year 2000.

WE BELIEVE GOD for 30,000 pastors by the year 2000.

WE BELIEVE GOD to do far and above what we can presently imagine as we faithfully gather the harvest.
In pursuit of the above initiatives:

- The Word of God shall be our guide and our plan of action.
- Uncompromised, unaltered biblical truth shall be our only message.
- The Spirit of God shall be our enablement and our power.
- The blood of Jesus Christ assures our ultimate triumph.

Adopted this 13th day of January 1989
All Africa Leadership Conference of the Assemblies of God
Lilongwe, Malawi
January 9-13, 1989

Appendix 4
Declaration of Commitment – "Decade of Harvest"
"Harvest Africa – 2000"
February 22-26, 1988 – Harare, Zimbabwe

BELIEVING in the Great Commission which sends us into all the world and to every creature, Believing that today is the season of harvest across Africa, and BELIEVING that the declaration by the Executive Presbytery that the 1990's be a DECADE OF HARVEST is, indeed, an initiative of the Holy Spirit designed for this hour, the missionary leadership of the Assemblies of God in Africa makes the following DECLARATION of COMMITMENT to the DECADE OF HARVEST …

WE CONSECRATE OURSELVES to fervent prayer, fasting and Pentecostal preaching in 1988-1989 in pursuit of a Holy Spirit outpouring across Africa as a prelude to the DECADE OF HARVEST. Such a re-emphasis upon the work of the Holy Spirit in our own lives as missionaries, coupled with the fullness of the Spirit's ministry in the Body of Christ, will inevitably produce the power we need to evangelize, (Acts 1:8)

WE CONSECRATE OURSELVES to the bold intent of reaching every person in Africa with an adequate gospel witness by the year 2000. Implicit in our commitment to this task is the necessity of mobilizing every available resource; radio, television, literature, computer technology, specialized ministries, and all other sources with a valid contribution to offer. We shall join hands across Africa with our national churches, our sister missions of shared doctrine, and all, who in faith, share this vision.

WE CONSECRATE OURSELVES to strengthening the hands of the burgeoning indigenous missionary endeavors coming to life in the church across Africa.

WE REAFFIRM OUR COMMITMENT to the establishing of strong local churches and to the training and equipping of those whom God will call into the harvest. We will therefore enlarge and enhance our Bible training program and facilities to provide for adequate ministerial and lay leadership for the DECADE OF HARVEST and beyond.

Appendix 4: Declaration of Commitment to "Africa Harvest 2000"

WE CONSECRATE OURSELVES to pray for and work towards the following goals in the last twelve years of this century:

- The implantation of indigenous Assemblies of God churches in as many countries, cities, towns, villages, tribes, people groups and sub-groups as possible by the year 2000.

- Maintaining, at least, the current doubling every five years of the number of believers which will see the current total of 1,400,000 become approximately 9,000,000 by the year 2000.

- Seeing, at least, 50 percent of all Assemblies of God believers and adherents baptized in the Holy Spirit and maintaining a Spirit-filled life.

- The raising up of a special arm of missionaries from many nations, equipped by the Holy Spirit for ministry to:

    1. Youth and children (1988: 46% of Africa's population under 15 years).
    2. Urban areas (both among the common people and people of rank).
    3. Women and girls.
    4. The vast Muslim population (150,000,000 strong).

- Seeing, at least, 33 percent increase every five years in the number of students in Assemblies of God Bible Schools preparing as evangelist, leaders, children's workers and ministers of every type (approximately 7000 by the year 2000).

- Increasing the number of pastors to at least, 12,000 by the year 2000.

- Increasing the number of local church to, at least, 22000 by the year 2000.

WE CONSECRATE OURSELVES to intercessory prayer to the Harvest Master that He will call forward needed laborers sufficient for the task both in Africa and around the world.

Contributors

Mitre Djikouti
President of the Togo Assemblies of God; Chairman of the Africa Assemblies of God Alliance.

John L. Easter
U.S. Assemblies of God missionary to Africa; Executive Director of Africa's Hope; Vice-Chancellor of Pan-Africa Theological Seminary.

Arto Hämäläinen
Chairman of the Pentecostal European Mission; Chairman of the World Missions Commission of the Pentecostal World Fellowship.

Enson Mbilikile Lwesya
Senior Pastor, International Christian Assembly, Lilongwe, Malawi; Deputy Vice-Chancellor of the Malawi Assemblies of God University; Director of the AAGA World Missions Commission.

Denzil R. Miller
U.S. Assemblies of God missionary; Director of the Acts in Africa Initiative.

Milward Mwamvani
Malawi Assemblies of God missionary.

Anthony E. Ogba
Director of Missions for the Assemblies of God Nigeria.

Paul M. Oganya
Nigeria Assemblies of God missionary to Cameroon.

Tony Pedrozo
Executive member of the Argentina Assemblies of God Missions Department; Area Supervisor for Africa and Asia.

Brad Walz
U.S. Assemblies of God missionary; President of the Argentina Assemblies of God Missions Department; Chairman of the World Assemblies of God Fellowship Missions Commission.

Other Decade of Pentecost Publications

*Globalizing Pentecostal Missions in Africa:
The Emerging Missionary Movement
in the Africa Assemblies of God*
(Available in English and French)

*Proclaiming Pentecost: 100 Sermons on the
Power of the Holy Spirit*
(Available in English, French, Portuguese, Spanish, and Swahili)

These and other books are available from
AIA Publications
ActsinAfrica@agmd.org

©2014 AIA Publications
580D West Central Street
Springfield, MO 65803
E-mail: ActsinAfrica@agmd.org

www.ingramcontent.com/pod-product-compliance
Lightning Source LLC
Chambersburg PA
CBHW061638040426
42446CB00010B/1471